The Pentecost Project

The Pentecost Project

B844p

THIERRY BRETON

Translated by Mark Howson

Henry Holt and Company / New York

Published in the United States by Henry Holt and Company, Inc.,
521 Fifth Avenue, New York, New York 10175.
Published in Canada by Fitzhenry & Whiteside Limited,
195 Allstate Parkway, Markham, Ontario L3R 4T8.
Originally published in France under the title *Vatican III*.

Library of Congress Cataloging-in-Publication Data
Breton, Thierry.
The Pentecost project.
Translation of: Vatican III.
I. Title.
PQ2662.R4832V313 1987 843′.914 86-33730
ISBN 0-8050-0380-0

First American Edition

Designed by Lank Graphics
Printed in the United States of America
1 2 3 4 5 6 7 8 9 10

ISBN 0-8050-0380-0

Acknowledgments

The preparation of *The Pentecost Project* was largely a team effort, and I was particularly fortunate in being surrounded by an exceptional team of colleagues and collaborators. Thanks are especially due to Robert and Laurent Laffont for their confidence, friendship, and sage counsel. Thanks also to everyone at Laffont publishers for their creative and editorial support.

Many thanks to everyone in Tokyo (ICOT), Geneva (ITU), Rome (the Vatican), Paris, Washington, and Malta who supplied essential background data for this book and preferred not to be acknowledged by name.

Special thanks to Pascale Magni and Naïma for their constant support. Thanks most of all to Valérie Baroin, without whom this book would never have seen the light of day.

—T.B.

The translator would like to thank Cary Ryan, for everything.

The Pentecost Project

On October 4, 1987, at 10:38 P.M., a bulletin from Agence France-Press informed the world that flight AF-270 had broken off radio contact. The Air France 747 had left Paris en route to Tokyo, with a stopover at Sheremetyevo Airport outside Moscow. After a routine refueling stop, it had taken off again at 6:26 local time; the crew had nothing out of the ordinary to report. At the time that AF-270's last transmission was interrupted, the plane was still well within Soviet airspace, and dawn was about to break over the high plateau of central Siberia.

A few minutes later, a second AFP bulletin revealed that AF-270 was carrying one distinguished passenger: Mr. James Wilcox, U.S. special envoy to the Vatican, the first official U.S. representative at the Holy See since Ambassador William A. Wilson had been forced to resign in disgrace over two years earlier. Most European TV stations decided to interrupt their broadcasts to pass this information on to their viewers. The past summer had seen an unusually high number of disastrous airplane crashes, but the tragedy of Korean Air Lines flight 007 was still fresh in everyone's minds. Here again, the ingredients of a tragedy of similar proportions seemed to be present: a civilian aircraft with several hundred passengers aboard, lost or strayed somewhere within the vast Soviet territory, coupled with Soviet Air Defense's well-known propensity to shoot first and issue denials later.

By 11:15 P.M. a crowd of journalists had gathered outside the Hôtel de Matignon, the official residence of the French prime minister, to await the arrival of the president of Air France; the interior and transport ministers had arrived a couple of minutes earlier. The crisis-management team was already in position, and, it was announced, "The chief of state will be kept constantly informed of developments." This was purely a formality, however, since thus far there had been no developments. The aircraft had simply disappeared somewhere along its authorized flight path, which would have taken it a little to the north of Irkutsk on the shores of Lake Baikal. The Soviet ambassador in Paris had also made himself unavailable for comment.

According to the terms of the conventions of July 30, 1985, air control at Petropavlovsk was expected to keep track of the whereabouts, and thus guarantee the safety, of all international flights in Soviet airspace. They regretted being unable to supply any additional information. At 11:27 P.M., the French government responded with a brief communiqué: "The tragedy of Flight 007 will not be repeated." It was clear that this was to be interpreted not so much as a pious hope or a prediction but as an ultimatum. At 11:34 the Soviets announced that they now had evidence that AF-270 had indeed departed from its prescribed flight path, in flagrant disregard of the conventions of July 30, 1985, and that failure to allow itself "to be escorted back to the security corridor by Soviet Air Defense forces would be punished by the strictest measures."

It was as a result of this curious sequence of events that the public first learned of the existence of Father Nicholas Resaccio, a Jesuit priest and a specialist in computer science—*informatics* as the Europeans prefer to call it—who, like the Jesuits of old, had been chosen by the Holy Father to execute a political mission of the greatest delicacy, a mission whose immense strategic importance was only to be revealed over the course of the next few months. In keeping with the tenor of the times, this was not a plan for the conquest of a kingdom or the conversion of a continent but for the most ambitious computer-assisted satellite communications relay that had ever been attempted. This was the day, October 4, 1987, on which Project Arcade was launched into the world.

Part 1

1

In the air over Siberia
October 4, 1987
3:45 A.M. *(local time)*

Nicholas Resaccio had obligingly yielded his window seat to James Wilcox, the American envoy, though the latter, wrapped up in a voluminous tartan blanket, could see nothing but occasional vague reflections against a field of impenetrable blackness. Their conversation was interrupted by the arrival of the pilot, Captain Jean-Pierre d'Orbat.

"Excuse me, Mr. Wilcox," said d'Orbat with a smile, "I was told you wished to speak to me."

"That's right, Captain. I just wanted to know how much longer we're going to be flying over this godforsaken country."

D'Orbat sighed and looked at his watch. "According to our latest fix, it should be about three hours and twenty minutes. It's now eight forty-five, Greenwich mean, so we should be arriving in Tokyo in another six hours."

Nicholas glanced at his own watch, still set on Moscow time—11:45. The American's fat chronometer showed it to be two hours earlier; he hadn't bothered to reset it since they had left Paris. D'Orbat glanced around at the empty red reclining chairs in the cabin; there were only eight or nine first-class passengers, surprisingly few for the run from Paris to Tokyo.

"Even if I can't see a damn thing outside," announced Wilcox abruptly, "I'm going to keep both eyes wide open as long as we're in Soviet airspace. How about you, Padre?"

Nicholas turned to face his traveling companion. They had exchanged pleasantries at various official functions in Rome, but this was the first opportunity they had had for a serious, unofficial encounter. So far, there had been sporadic bursts of conversation over the course of the long, tiring flight; the conversation was technical, somewhat impersonal. Nicholas felt that rather than talking with a colleague or a casual traveling companion, he was being debriefed by a senior American official, perhaps, as some had suggested, a CIA official. Unlike his unfortunate precedessor, the American special envoy to the Vatican had successfully managed to keep the exact nature and purpose of his political mission a secret from the world at large.

His predecessor, Ambassador William Wilson, had been an enthusiastic amateur diplomat of the kind that Republican administrations seemed to produce in great numbers—a wealthy California oilman and rancher, reputedly a close personal friend of President Reagan, also, somewhat contrary to type, a prominent Catholic layman. In the fall of 1985, Wilson had suddenly announced his decision to retire from public life after it was revealed that he had flown to Tripoli on two or three occasions in a corporate jet provided by an Italian oil company in order to hold talks with Colonel Qaddafi—apparently, as it turned out, without the knowledge or approval of his nominal superiors in the U.S. State Department. In any case, the talks could not have been described as an unqualified success: not many months later, Qaddafi's private encampment in Tripoli was bombed by American warplanes.

After a hiatus of many months, Wilson had been replaced by a "special envoy," James Wilcox, a career foreign-service officer who did not hold the rank of ambassador. Affable, if hapless, amateurism seemed to have given way to tight-lipped professionalism; the U.S. State Department seemed determined not to make the same mistake twice. Little was known of Wilcox's previous exploits, except for a long list of postings in the sort of places habitually described as "volatile" or "strife-torn." He was said by those who professed to some fluency in transatlantic political jargon to be a specialist in "damage control."

In light of the spectacular indiscretions of his predecessor, James Wilcox had proved thus far to be a major disappointment to both the Italian press and the rumor mills of the Vatican. And now it appeared that he and Nicholas were to be colleagues, or, in any event, that Wilcox was to play an as yet undefined advisory or supervisory role in the project of which Nicholas had been chosen to direct the technical side. It was all still rather mysterious.

"Speaking as a scientist," said Nicholas, "I'll accept the evidence of that impressive-looking scientific instrument"—he gestured at the American's watch—"that tells me that we're still in Paris. Or the captain's watch—much more reliable-looking than my own—that tells me that we're in Greenwich, a most agreeable suburb in London."

Wilcox nodded a little wearily, as if to say that he conceded the point but had been hoping for a reply that was a little less *jesuitical.* "If you say so, Padre—or should I be calling you *dottore* or *professore*?"

"It's true that we're very fond of titles where I come from," said Nicholas, "but I prefer *padre.* It's the one I had to work the hardest for."

Wilcox glanced up at the pilot with what seemed to be a slightly malicious glint in his eye. "Padre Resaccio was just telling me about something that might interest you, Captain. It seems that by the end of the century airline pilots could be entirely replaced by on-board computers supported by a relay of navigational satellites locked into a geosynchronous orbit over a fixed point on the earth that tells the computer everything it wants to know between takeoff and landing."

"Theoretically possible, I agree," said d'Orbat, perhaps a little complacently, "but computers have been known to break down from time to time, and when you also consider that the next generation of commercial airliners may be taking off with over a thousand passengers on board, then you might still want to have a couple of trained human beings on board, just to fly the plane until the repairman comes."

"And in any case," said Nicholas, who felt professionally obliged to break up an argument that was, initially at least, of his own making, "because all geostationary satellites have to run around on the same track—a track that's exactly in the plane of the equator and some thirty-six thousand kilometers above the surface of the earth—that means in ten years' time we'll only have room up there for a limited number of absolutely essential applications."

"Now, wait a minute, Padre!" Wilcox produced a tiny calculator, about the size and thickness of a playing card, from beneath the folds of his tartan blanket. "You've got a circle with a radius of thirty-six K, plus another six K to get to the center of the earth, that's forty-two K, which gives you a circumference of"—suspenseful pause while he clicked a few tiny buttons—"somewhere around two hundred sixty-five thousand kilometers, which is close enough to"—a few more staccato clicks of the keys—"a hundred sixty-five thousand miles. Now, a few minutes ago you said that one of these satellites is no bigger than a car and that we've already got three hundred of them, civil and military, up there right now, which, if laid out bumper to bumper, would account for maybe *one* of those kilometers altogether. So it seems to me, Padre, that we've got quite a ways to go before we have to start worrying about a traffic problem."

"In that sense, yes," replied Nicholas, "but the sort of traffic we're really concerned with here is electronic rather than vehicular. Two satellites transmitting television signals on neighboring frequencies should be at least seven or eight thousand miles apart if their transmissions are to be received distinctly on earth. That means there are only about twenty slots available for every frequency—for every station—along the entire orbital pathway. There are about a hundred and sixty sovereign nations in the world, and the available orbital slots and the right to transmit across certain frequencies have been parcelled out at several international conventions, more or less according to their needs and current technical capabilities.

"France was assigned an orbital slot directly over the Gulf of Guinea and the right to transmit across five different frequencies. Germany was assigned the same slot but totally different frequencies, to prevent them from accidentally jamming one another's transmissions. The Soviet Union has five satellite slots, and the United States has six, five over the Pacific and the sixth over Brazil."

Wilcox contemplated the midget keyboard of his calculator and pondered these observations for a moment before glancing over at his seatmate. The *padre-professore-dottore* was very well spoken of in the corridors of the Vatican, or at least in certain corridors. He recalled what one influential prelate had said of young Father Nicholas: "Too seductive to make a good priest, too intelligent to get rid of, too troublesome to keep, or, to sum it all up in a single word, a Jesuit."

His smooth-cheeked, slightly aquiline profile was boyish-handsome enough for a political candidate. His conversation had certainly confirmed that he was well informed to the point of actual pedantry, and there was something about the stubborn set of his jaw and his bristly, close-cropped head that suggested the possibility of trouble somewhere down the line. Whether he was capable of handling the enormous responsibility with which the Holy Father had entrusted him—in which intelligence, stubbornness, and perhaps a certain measure of seductiveness would undoubtedly come into play—was another matter. . . .

Wilcox stifled a yawn; a sudden wave of fatigue swept over him, and he felt strongly tempted to relax his vow of a few minutes earlier and close both eyes with a considerable expanse of Soviet territory left to traverse.

Captain d'Orbat had evidently taken this as his cue to break off what promised to be a fairly lengthy discussion. "If you'll forgive me, gentlemen, I think that after that pretty speech I just made a few moments ago, it would really not be very fair of me to stay back here and let the computers do all the work. . . ." And at that moment, they heard the buzz of the ship's internal telephone, and one of the cabin stewards motioned to d'Orbat that he was wanted on the bridge. D'Orbat nodded and smiled and strode off toward the companionway at the head of the cabin.

"Can I help you adjust your seat, Mr. Wilcox?" asked Nicholas.

"No, thanks, Padre. To the eyes of youth, I may seem well stricken in years, but I can generally manage. Anyway, if you'll indulge me for another minute or two, I think it's time for you and me to talk a little shop." Briskly, and somewhat to Nicholas's astonishment, Wilcox produced a slim attaché case, hitherto concealed beneath the folds of his tartan blanket, and from it a manila folder, from the folder, a map. Nicholas immediately recognized the crest in the upper right-hand corner—a shield emblazoned with a sunburst and surmounted by an eagle's head, the emblem of the Central Intelligence Agency.

"We've been discussing these satellites and some of what you might call their more *frivolous* applications—flying airplanes, live television feeds of soccer games and assassinations, and so on. Here we have something a little bit more substantial for them to take credit for—the birth of a new continent, the Islamic continent. Finally, after a period of gestation of no less than thirteen hundred years, a new superpower has been born into the world. I probably don't have to tell you the names of the attending physicians, Padre . . . three advanced industrial nations that probably should have known better. It was the French Ariane rocket that inserted the Arab telecommunications satellite into geostationary orbit, for a modest fee of one hundred and thirty-four million dollars. It was our own space shuttle, of blessed memory, that launched the second of these two satellites three months later, and it was the Japanese NEC corporation that provided the electronics and computer equipment for tracking these satellites from the ground."

Nicholas glanced at the map, as if expecting some confirmation of

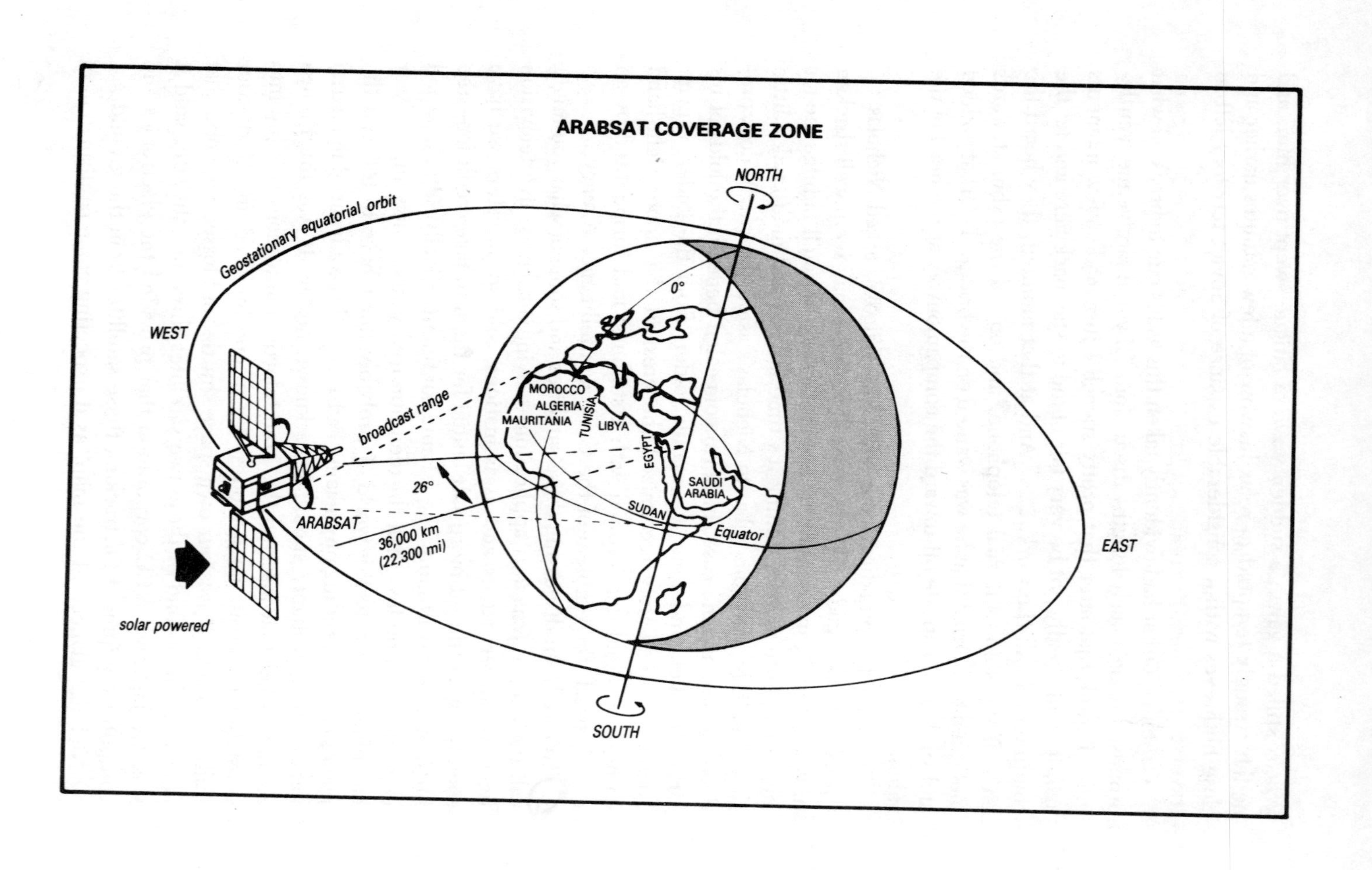
ARABSAT COVERAGE ZONE
NORTH
SOUTH
WEST
EAST
Geostationary equatorial orbit
broadcast range
26°
ARABSAT
36,000 km
(22,300 mi)
solar powered
0°
MOROCCO
ALGERIA
MAURITANIA
TUNISIA
LIBYA
EGYPT
SAUDI
ARABIA
SUDAN
Equator

these rather dramatic remarks. Instead, it simply showed, as expected, that the conical beam emanating from the satellite intersected with the surface of the earth in an elliptical broadcast zone that corresponded almost exactly with the boundaries of the Arab world, from Mauritania to Muscat.

"But frankly," said Nicholas, "I don't see anything so alarming about that. After all, it's exactly what we hope to be able to do ourselves. And if, as in this case, a group of nations share a common culture and language in addition to a common religion, then why shouldn't they be allowed to watch the same television programs as well? At best, that seems like progress, and it's certainly no worse than a steady diet of World Cup matches and televised assassinations."

"I wouldn't be any too sure of that, Padre," said Wilcox. "What this map doesn't show us is that the twenty-two member states of the Arab League—from the Libyans on the left to the Saudis and the Gulfis on the right and of course not excluding the PLO—have agreed to suppress their political differences in order to affirm what are already the strongest of the bonds that unite them: Islam and the Koran. Now, you seem to have done your homework, Padre, and frankly I don't see how you can overlook the purely political implications of Arabsat, an Islamic satellite.

"Now, we know," Wilcox went on before Nicholas had time to formulate a reply, "that *Islam* means 'submission,' to Allah and his prophets—and I think you'll agree that the Islamic world has had more than its share of prophets in recent years. Imagine the kind of weapon this could be in the hands of one of those fanatics, able to mobilize a population of two hundred million people, all attentive to the cry of the muezzin from the minaret—a minaret, I might add, that's equipped with a satellite dish aimed straight up at Arabsat."

"It strikes me, Mr. Wilcox," said Nicholas, "that you seem to know a great deal more about this than you were willing to let on a few minutes ago. And what about the Vatican satellite slot, after all—still unoccupied, admittedly, but potentially just as great a threat, perhaps, to world peace and stability."

"Right up there over the tip of Brazil, isn't it, Padre?" Wilcox was practically grinning at him now. "But we have no problem with that one—as I hope to convince you as soon as we get to Tokyo. Absolutely no problem at all, since obviously we regard the Vatican as a sovereign state, a friendly sovereign state, and hardly a threat to world peace."

When d'Orbat stepped onto the bridge, the first thing he noticed was the astounding array of warning lights flashing on the instrument panel, including three particularly ominous ones on the console of the INS—the internal navigation system—a device that consisted basically of a gyroscope and an on-board computer that was programmed by the pilot and could track the ship's position without the help of an external radio fix. Claude Rigout, the copilot, had switched the helm back to manual while Paul Chenut, the navigator, riffled frantically through the stack of looseleaf binders that constituted the documentation for the ship's three on-board computers.

"What's going on?" asked d'Orbat. "Computer trouble?"

"Among other things," said Rigout. "The radio's also completely dead."

D'Orbat replaced him at the helm and rapidly took stock of the situation, which appeared to be serious but not quite hopeless. The INS (which kept track of the plane's pitch and direction), radar, and autopilot were all inexplicably, impossibly, refusing to function; the VHF channels were filled with a sibilant static that rendered the radio equally useless. "Well, gentlemen, it looks like tonight we return to the heroic age of aviation," d'Orbat announced. "I only wish we were in a little bit nicer neighborhood if we're going to be giving an exhibition of night flying without instruments." This was of course what made the situation critical rather than merely worrisome and anomalous; the fate of KE-007 four years earlier had demonstrated that a relatively trivial defect in the on-board navigational systems could have disastrous results when combined with Soviet firepower and paranoia.

"We're going to have to get this business taken care of before we drift too far off course," said d'Orbat. "I'll try to keep us on the correct heading. Claude, I want you to reestablish radio contact, either on the VHF or the HF, and do something about the damn interference. Paul, I want you to start running the diagnostics to try and find out what the trouble is." Chenut was seated at the navigator's station between pilot and copilot, and this operation, which he had already carried out, was simply a matter of punching a button for each of the three computers.

"Jean-Pierre, this really can't be happening," the navigator replied a moment or two later. "The machines aren't responding at all." Then, with the air of someone about to utter a monstrous obscenity, he added, "There's nothing left in memory either, not even our initial coordinates for this flight." Without relinquishing the helm, d'Orbat leaned over to examine the INS console; as soon as he switched the computer into navigation mode, instead of the ship's correct flight coordinates, elapsed flight time, estimated arrival time, et cetera, an imbecile array of zeros began to file across the screen. As Chenut had done before, he punched up the diagnostic programs on the ship's computers, with something of the fatalistic air of someone pushing an elevator button for the tenth or eleventh time.

"This is insane," he said softly, feeling that the word hardly did justice to the situation.

"That's right," said Rigout. "All three machines seem to be suffering from the delusion that we're back on the ground somewhere, in a parking lot maybe, instead of blundering around at an altitude of twenty-nine thousand feet. And of course it's impossible to reinitialize the navigational programs once we're airborne."

At any rate, said d'Orbat to himself, *it's only going to be little worse than driving from Paris to Marseilles blindfolded—since around these parts, getting lost and blundering off the route seems to be a capital offense.* He thought back to the little exchange he'd had with Wilcox about computer-controlled jetliners. Of the three on-board computers, only one was really necessary to keep track of the ship's position, the other two were backups, and odds were perhaps a billion to one that all three would go out at once. *Luckily there were still humans aboard to keep the situation from getting serious*, he thought sardonically as he punched the diagnostic buttons for the fifth or sixth time, not because he expected anything to come of it, but because he couldn't think of anything else to do.

He wiped the sweat from his forehead and looked over at Rigout. "How much longer till sunrise?"

"Sunrise at eleven fifty-eight P.M. GMT, which gives us another two hours of total blackout." They were going to have to confine their wanderings to a corridor that was only twelve miles wide, stretched out like a thin silken thread across a rugged and inhospitable terrain over a million square miles in area. When the sun rose, they could at least make an attempt to calculate their position by dead reckoning, but until then all they could do was keep on flying through the frozen night.

Paris, 11:25 P.M.

"What time is it out there in Tokyo?" Father Michel d'Anglebert said into the phone, a little more loudly than necessary. Father d'Anglebert, the Jesuit provincial in France, was talking to his opposite number in Japan.

A two-second pause ensued, then the voice of Father Giuseppe Pitta came through with remarkable clarity. "Seven twenty-five, in the morning." A television set, the volume turned down, was muttering away in one corner; on the screen, a commentator flicked a pointer across an outline map of Siberia to indicate, courtesy of Tass, the last known position of AF-270, which had already drifted almost eighty miles out of its authorized flight path.

"How long has it been since we last saw each other?"

"At least seven years, since before I came out here."

"I have some news for you. The Russians are threatening to shoot down the plane that's carrying Father Resaccio and Wilcox, the American envoy."

"Do you think they will?"

"I don't know. We've been told that since that ugly Korean business the military is no longer allowed to intervene in such matters without consulting the civil authorities. But listen now, what I wanted to tell you is that Father Resaccio is bringing two highly confidential documents to Tokyo, one of them his own instructions, the other addressed to you. If these documents go astray, Project Arcade will have to be postponed for the time being, and of course any arrangements you might have already made with the Japanese in anticipation of Father Resaccio's arrival will have to be canceled."

"And by 'go astray' you mean if they're destroyed, or intercepted?"

"Certainly the Russians can't have much use for the burnt-out carcass of another Boeing," replied Father d'Anglebert.

By the time d'Anglebert had replaced the receiver, the commentator on the television had been replaced by a glittering field of electronic sleet. "Only pray to God that the Russians have the same ideas about these things as you do," he muttered to himself as he stumped off to bed.

Irkutsk, 5:15 A.M. (local time)

For Captain Valery Grigoriev, director of the air control center at the Irkutsk airport, the sixteen hours since the colonel's arrival had been an almost continuous series of snubs and irritations. Now he was feeling something much closer to relief, if not actual happiness. Relief because somebody was about to have a full-blown international incident land in his lap, with considerable impact, and it was probably going to be the colonel rather than him; happiness because the colonel's was not a personality that inspired a great deal of sympathy. The captain was accustomed to obeying orders without considering the source too closely, but that sort of stiff-backed, bitchy arrogance was a little bit hard to take from someone who, if not technically a foreigner, was far from being a real Russian.

The colonel—surname Akhmedov, first name and patronymic Nadjimaddin Akhmedovich—was one of the Aliev's protégés, and Aliev—Gaydar Ali Ali-Zadeh to give him his rightful name—was a full member of the Politburo now, also grand master of the mystic order of the KGB. Both Aliev and Akhmedov came from the same little village in Azerbaijan, just this side of the Iranian border, one of those places where you couldn't throw a stick over your shoulder without hitting a mullah or an ayatollah. Grigoriev generally regarded this sort of thing as incontrovertible evidence that the Great Russian race was on its last legs; after he'd had a couple of drinks, he was given to making pronouncements like "One of these days, we'll be taking orders from the Turks and Arabs, and then we might as well kiss it good-bye." There was no danger of letting loose with something like that in front of Colonel Akhmedov, because the colonel didn't drink. He didn't come right out and say, "Excuse it please, I happen to be a Shiite." He just didn't drink.

The telex announcing his arrival had spoken of an "unscheduled inspection tour of leading air-traffic control facilities on Union territory," and the colonel had turned up looking like those very words had been chiseled on his forehead. There could be little doubt that the colonel knew what he was up to in Irkutsk; Grigoriev was thrilled by the coincidence, or whatever it happened to be. As for the colonel, he did not give the impression of a man who had been overtaken by the rapid pace of events.

A couple of weeks after the KE-007 disaster, Air Marshal Ustinov had gone down in flames, figuratively speaking, perhaps because he had grown overfond of repeating the story that it had taken five hours before the two fighter pilots could be sobered up enough to give a coherent account of what had happened. Now it was time to see whether Aliev—who was undoubtedly the one pulling the strings—would be able to benefit from the marshal's unfortunate experience and whether the KGB would handle one of these touchy situations any better than Air Defense Commmand. In any case, it was a glorious day for the Great Russian race.

Just a few feet away in the control tower, Akhmedov was seated at the microphone, repeating his orders in a cold, quiet voice: "Pilots are absolutely forbidden to cross the visual field of the intruder without explicit authorization. Prepare for takeoff in three minutes."

In the air over Siberia, 5:45 A.M.

The three men on the bridge had not exchanged a word for at least half an hour. Copilot Rigout, in the right-hand seat, was flipping through a sheaf of navigational charts, making a rapid reconnaissance of the more prominent surface features that were displayed on chart 14H.L, covering central Siberia, which would probably be their best hope for determining their present position now that they were finally about to break though cloud cover. They had already flown right through the control sectors around Kirensk and Vitim without identifying themselves to the tower, as international protocol decreed, and they had not even been able to hear the protestations of the air controllers at either of those facilities. In the passenger section everything was perfectly calm; most of the passengers were still asleep. But the flight crew had been asked to station themselves by the windows and maintain a discreet watch for the approach of Soviet aircraft.

D'Orbat was still following their last compass bearing and darting frequent glances out through the canopy in search of some celestial sign that would confirm they were still on course. Suddenly, they passed through a small patch of turbulence and they were out of the clouds. A pinkish-gray streak along the horizon, far off to the left, was all they could see of the sunrise thus far. D'Orbat gave an anguished cry.

"My God, we're flying south! The sun's coming up to the east of us, but we should be flying straight into the sun. And the damn compass says we're heading due east!"

"We've been on a false heading for two hours now, flying east-southeast," said Rigout, "which means we could have drifted as much as a thousand kilometers off course." He held up the chart of Siberia. "We're probably down here somewhere, getting on toward Lake Baikal—heading straight for the Chinese border as a matter of fact."

D'Orbat immediately made a course correction of 70°, which caused the aircraft to sheer off abruptly to the left. "It's a miracle the Popovs haven't caught up with us yet then. Now that the sun's up, I'm not going to take any more chances, if you'll forgive the expression, of them mistaking us for some sort of spy plane. Claude, switch on all the lights. As soon as we're back on some sort of course, I'd better have a word with the passengers."

Wilcox awoke with a start; the plane had given a violent lurch, and for a moment he thought they must be about to begin their final approach into Tokyo. "What's going on? We can't be there already, can we? It's still dark."

Nicholas was awake, reading.

"It's only, let's see . . . it's a little before six, is that right?"

"Even if we've passed through another one of those mysterious time barriers," Nicholas said smiling, "we can still look forward to another three hours in the air."

Perhaps to make up for the note of tension that had crept into their earlier conversation when the talk had touched on politics, the American diplomat, now quite genial, seemed to be making an effort to draw him out. "So, Padre," he began abruptly, "you think there's room for a computer specialist among those old stones of the Vatican?"

"Room for a great many, I hope. It's only fairly recently in our history that there's been any hostility at all between the Church and the sciences. I like to think back to the days when men like Albertus Magnus and Thomas Aquinas were not only the greatest scholars but the greatest scientists of their day, when even the greatest freethinkers and heretics were clerics like Abelard and Roger Bacon." In invoking the Church's glorious intellectual legacy, Nicholas had instinctively switched from English to Italian, a language in which James Wilcox, even at this early hour, was reasonably proficient.

"But of course in those days," Nicholas went on, "the Church had a virtual monopoly not only on learning and literacy but also on the most efficient means of storing and retrieving information, which is to say the copying and distribution of manuscripts on vellum. The Church was also the first to appreciate the significance of Herr Gutenberg's invention but not, needless to say, the only one—"

"And you regret that, Padre?"

"It's a little too late for regrets about that, I'm afraid, and I hope there won't be any need to regret the fact that we've been a little slow to catch up with some of the things that are going on at the present time."

"Like computers, for instance?"

"Absolutely. Today a single mainframe computer represents a greater capacity for information storage and retrieval than all the medieval abbeys and cathedral schools put together. And the abbeys, as we know, were lonely, isolated places, whereas our computers will be able to communicate with one another whenever they need to."

"But don't you get the feeling," said Wilcox, lapsing back into English at the very first hint of controversy, "that the Church might simply have lost the knack for that sort of thing? In the old days, somebody like Aquinas could know all there was to know because science and philosophy and religion were all pretty much the same thing—and 'all there was to know' meant a shelf or two of Aristotle and the Church Fathers and the rest of it."

"And then along came Galileo and the great divorce. . . ."

"Maybe divorce was inevitable, Padre. Maybe there is a fundamental conflict between science and revealed truth. . . . What about the idea of *artificial intelligence*, for example? Doesn't that sound a little presumptuous? Like maybe we might be infringing on the prerogatives of the Almighty, just a little? Or for that matter, what if one of these supercomputers gets a little above itself and turns into—"

"A pagan oracle? A Silicon Calf?"

Wilcox was amused by this. "A substitute for God perhaps?"

"Perhaps," said Nicholas, "we should see if they're capable of taking over from the airline pilots before we start worrying about the Lord God of Hosts. You'll forgive me for saying so, Mr. Wilcox, but only someone who knows very little about computers could entertain such fantastic notions of what they're capable of."

"You believe their capabilities are limited, then?"

"I believe their capabilities are finite, certainly," said Nicholas, "as are those of the human brains that designed and built and operate them and those of the physical materials they're made of."

"And you're willing to take the risk," said Wilcox, "that by taking too much of an interest in such things, the Church might be helping to turn men's minds even further away from God?"

"I also believe," said Nicholas, "that the search for knowledge can only bring us closer to God. . . . We've spoken of Gutenberg and Galileo. If the Church had disdained to make use of Gutenberg's invention, then we'd all be pagans or Protestants today. On the other hand, by forcing Galileo to recant, the Inquisition came very close to undoing the effects of sixteen centuries of struggle and sacrifice." He smiled a little sheepishly. "Though I admit the Jesuits had a hand in that as well."

"The Church simply wasn't ready for Galileo," said Wilcox, "which actually brings me to my next question. I've recently had the pleasure of meeting quite a few of your colleagues in the Curia. Can you honestly tell me that the Church is going to be ready for Resaccio?"

"The Church has been changing for quite some time now," said Nicholas, "and it's just a matter of time before the Curia catches up to it. In 1953, you know, there were only two African bishops—bishops who'd actually been born in Africa, I mean—and now there are something like three hundred. By the end of this century, half of the world's Catholics will be Latin Americans. This is where our reinforcements are going to come from. These are countries where the Church is still regarded as a powerful force for social change, and the priests of my generation have finally come to the conclusion that technological change, like social change, is not necessarily incompatible with the message of the Gospels."

"You may be on the right track there, Padre. Certainly I'd rest a little easier if I thought those South American priests were tapping away at their terminals instead of running through the jungles with their AK-47s. However, I wonder if that's really—" There was a soft rustle of static from the public address system, and the American fell silent.

"Ladies and gentlemen, mesdames and messieurs, this is your captain speaking. I'm sorry to have to tell you that we've been experiencing some difficulties with our on-board navigational system; this problem should not prevent us from landing safely when we've reached our destination. For the moment, however, don't be alarmed if you see Soviet military aircraft flying alongside us. The Soviet authorities are aware of our situation, and it may be necessary for them to assist us in returning to our original flight path. I ask you to remain calm. I'm also going to ask those passengers with window seats to open your blinds and notify one of the cabin personnel if you catch sight of any aircraft. I'll naturally keep you informed of any developments."

A few moments later there was a chorus of excited cries from the economy-class passengers; Wilcox already had his face pressed against the chilly perspex of his porthole.

"Look!" He flattened himself against his seat so that Nicholas could look outside. A sleek, silvery fighter plane was hovering right beside them, incredibly close; when the pilot turned his head toward them, Nicholas was certain that, from behind his buglike black goggles, he could see their faces. The American watched for a moment longer, then slammed down the window blind with a snort.

"Well, Padre, maybe that's some people's idea of what a guardian angel looks like, but I can tell you right now that it certainly isn't mine."

Before Nicholas had time to reply there was another chorus of excited voices in the rear cabin; Nicholas could see that people were clustered around the portholes on the left side of the aisle. A second Soviet fighter had apparently pulled up beside them. "A forced landing!" someone shouted. "They're going to force us down!" After that, in spite of the valiant efforts of the cabin crew to restore some semblance of order, there was total chaos until d'Orbat's voice on the loudspeaker, intoning the same soothing, carefully worded message for perhaps a dozen times, finally lured the last of the passengers back to their seats.

Colonel Akhmedov was watching the radar screen. A single elongated blip, some distance outside the ruled-off grid that indicated the normal landing corridor, was approaching the shore line of Lake Baikal. It was accompanied by three smaller points of light. When they had all reached a point that was somewhere near the center of that vast, bottomless lake, Akhmedov pressed the red button on the stem of the microphone and spoke a single word. "Now."

On the bridge of the 747, d'Orbat saw that the two MiGs had detached themselves from his wing tips and were picking up speed, as if to bar the way in front of him. He suddenly felt perfectly calm and unafraid, since, at long last, he knew what was going to happen. He reached over and pressed a button on the console; beneath it was a little printed tag that read FASTEN SEAT BELTS.

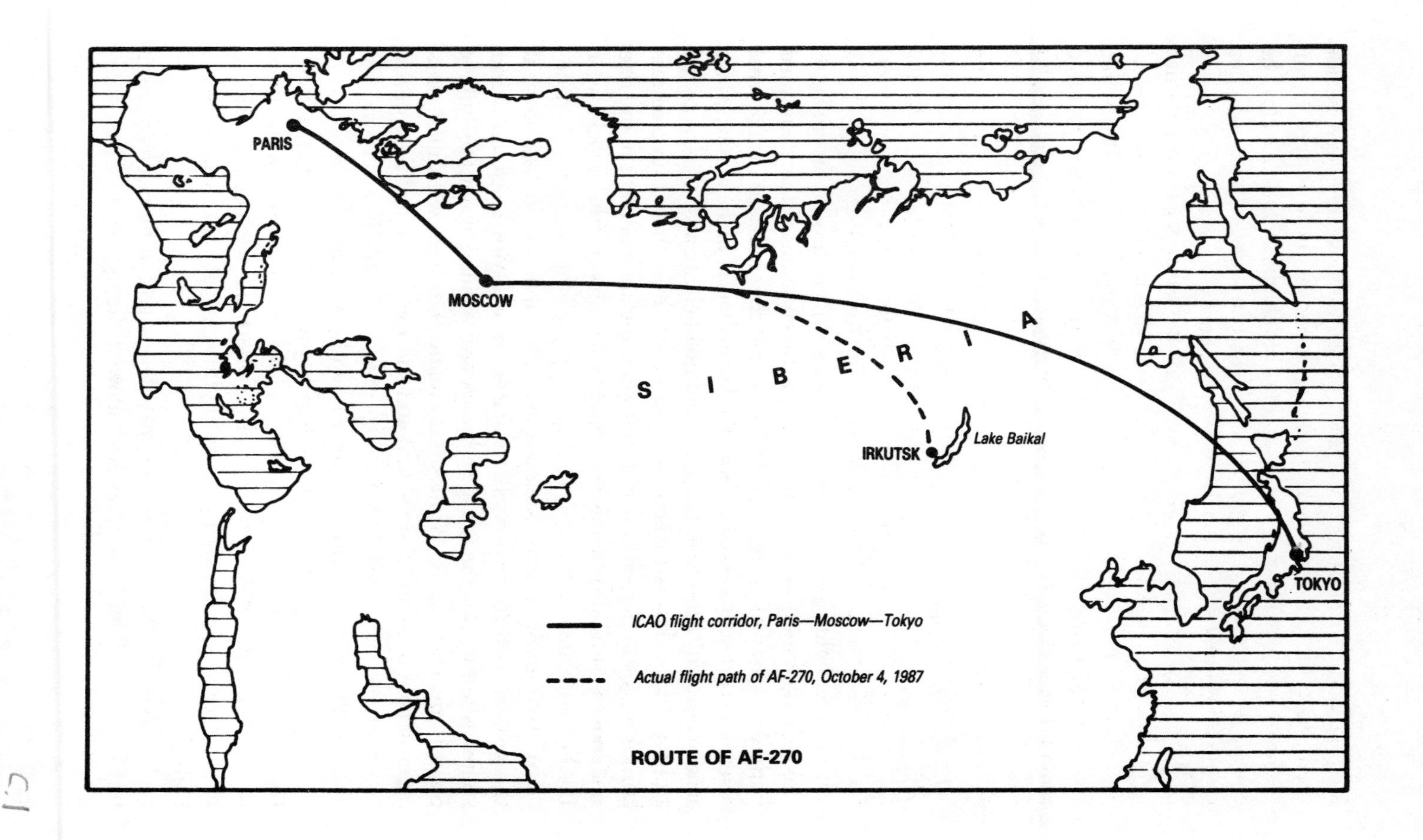
PARIS
MOSCOW
S I B E R I A
IRKUTSK
Lake Baikal
TOKYO
ICAO flight corridor, Paris—Moscow—Tokyo
Actual flight path of AF-270, October 4, 1987
ROUTE OF AF-270

2

Abbey of Faremoutiers
October 4
10:10 P.M.

All the real light in her cell seemed to be shut up inside the globe on the ceiling; the chair and the table in the middle of the floor were bathed in a kind of murky half-darkness, and the walls and the cot were already far away in the silent, bare, and stony world of the abbey, which made them both common property and no one's. It was irksome to her to have all her books tucked away on the built-in shelves in a distant corner of this underwater world, behind a curtain made out of the thin material that was also used for the mattress covers and the smocks worn by the postulants.

While Wendy Keenes hovered over the table and looked down at the *go-ban* with its grid of tiny squares strewn with black and white stones, she felt like she must be breaking the rules, if not the Rule of Saint Benedict himself. While she was here, her head was full of strategies of conquest and destruction, and she sometimes had the impression that she had unleashed the dogs of war—if only in a very modest and imaginary way—amid the drowsy and contemplative precincts of the abbey. Worse than that, she felt as though she had kept something back for herself; she had stolen time and space and was devouring them in secret in her cell—all this in a place where she was not supposed to have secrets or indeed to *possess* anything at all, not even her own body.

In any case, the white stones had clearly gotten themselves into a terrible mess. Somehow, they had allowed themselves to fritter away their energies in futile skirmishes and pursuits, and had finally been sent reeling back in defeat while the black stones had closed off every avenue of escape and piled up an appalling tally of captures and *ataris*. The stones on the board formed a complicated archipelago of contentious little islands. Unconsciously, she must have done everything in her power to make sure that black would win, an outcome that, at the present moment, could not have displeased her more. She always wanted the loser to win; it was in her nature. To be the defender of the helpless and the oppressed—the problem was that she always allowed the situation to develop a little bit past the point where she could possibly redress the balance.

Black had accumulated an impressive little string of victories by now, and she would undoubtedly end up having to impose a two-stone handicap. In the battle of Wendy against Wendy, she was predestined to come out the loser every time. She picked up a white stone on the board that was encircled by a menacing black reef. That stone, to all intents and purposes, was dead because it had been "deprived of its liberties"; it would have to be removed from the board. On the go board, a "liberty" was nothing more than a means of escape. Perhaps she identified so strongly with white because her sympathies were color-coded to match her current circumstances. Here she was, after all, in her scratchy little white smock with a stern black-robed guardian poised at every crossroads of her life, threatening—all metaphor aside now—to deprive her of her precious liberties.

She raised her eyes from the board. Beyond the window sash, there was an iron grillwork and another little pattern of squares and intersections, and beyond that a world of darkness. The white stone felt hot against the palm of her hand; she tossed it into the bowl with the others and walked over to the window. She was not allowed to have a mirror in her cell, of course, but now she could see her reflection in the window, superimposed against the grill and the dim outlines of the shrubbery in the garden. It was the phantom image of a crop-haired, freckle-faced young woman in an ill-fitting smock, a parish-bulletin, travel-poster caricature of an Irish novice.

At Oxford and in London the idea of a red-haired, freckle-faced Irish girl had seemed like such a preposterous cliché, such a howling *tautology*, that she had dyed her long luxuriant curls. However, a postulant in a religious house was not allowed the vanity of long luxuriant curls of any color, and, in any case, something had happened since then—

the terrible event that had brought her to this place—that had made her quite indifferent to such things. And then, even during her short-lived blond period, there had not been much that she could do about the freckles.

She tugged at the corners of her eyes with her index fingers to give herself what she hoped was an approximation of the slit-eyed, hooded expression of a true master of go. It was a difficult, complicated—or rather, an anarchically simple—game, but she felt certain that she was making progress without really being sure that she had reached the first *dan*, comparable to the lowest rating levels in competitive chess. As in the convent considerable effort and experience were required before one even had the right to call oneself a novice. She believed that one of those wrinkled, wise old men would simply take one look at her and tell her that she would never master the game, just as Reverend Mother had examined her with a connoisseur's eye at the end of their first interview and said, "My poor child, you will never make a good nun."

When pressed for particulars, the old nun had murmured something French and meaningless about "flaring nostrils" and a "sultry mouth." When she thought of this Wendy took a step back from the window and stared closely at her reflection to see if these undesirable features might have disappeared after a couple of months of convent life. They had not, and when Reverend Mother had said this to her, there had been not just pity, as the words surely indicated, but something like respect and admiration in her voice. In her eyes, to be the bride of Christ was the noblest of destinies, but she seemed to be implying also that Wendy should prepare herself for a vocation that would bring her much closer if not to Christ Himself, at least to some of the more eminent among his servants. Had she guessed at the real reason that had brought Wendy to Faremoutiers?

A bell struck the half hour. It was ten thirty, and her presence was required in the chapel. When she returned, she had a sudden flash of inspiration. She had thought of the perfect play for the white stone that she had maliciously allowed to get into such difficulties; she retrieved it, or one very like it, from the bowl and put it into play. Inspiration was succeeded almost instantly by the realization that this new combination was even more disastrous than the first; she was playing for black once more. She allowed herself a brief moment of triumph as she surveyed the complicated borders of her conquered realm, the attractive little pile of fresh enemy corpses in the bowl, before she reached out her hands and swept both armies into a chaotic muddle in the center of the board.

It was almost time to go. She had a constricted feeling in her chest; she felt excited, impatient, and afraid at the same time. So far she had always been able to escape, though it was not that easy for her, from both a practical and a psychological standpoint, to leave the abbey. The atmosphere of intense ardor mingled with extreme passivity was something she found almost oppressive while she was surrounded by it, but the bonds that she had formed with this place seemed to have grown stronger with every day. One night it had occurred to her that if she wanted that much to leave she would have to saw through the bars on the window. Wasn't that the proper way to escape from a cell?

She removed the cross from her breast and dropped it onto her cot, then sat down to take off her sandals. To work in the garden—which was all she was supposed to see of the world outside—she had a cream-colored wool cloak with a hood, like a coat for a shepherd or a sailor; she put it on, then stood for several minutes with her head pressed against the thin panel of the door, but all she could hear was the sound of the blood rushing through her veins. As usual the noises inside her head were louder than all the other sounds in this little world. She opened the door and shuddered involuntarily as her bare feet touched the cold stones. There was an icy draft in the corridor that allowed her to find her way in total darkness, that seemed, like a fearful guide or confederate, to be urging her to hurry toward the door. She was hunched over and on tiptoe, like a pantomime of villainous stealth, her sandals clutched to her chest.

Suddenly, the abbey was far behind her, its soft gray eaves and edges merging with the darker outlines of the trees. She was taking long strides along the shoulders at the edge of the highway; she wouldn't go back now for anything in the world. The car was parked by a big tree, its interior lights on, like a cozy little house at the edge of the road. The door on the passenger side opened, and Wendy scrambled into the seat. A hand with long, thin fingers—"musician's fingers," she called them—reached out for her; the lights flicked off, the motor revved, and Michael's hand closed around the cap of her shoulder in a tight grip.

He drove fast, spurred on by his barely controllable impatience. The treetops whisked past the moon and the clouds. Speckled slabs of concrete appeared and disappeared in the beams of the headlights. The car heeled over at the curves, and Wendy's shoulder was pressed against Michael's; she could feel his body trembling slightly. At first he had hardly seemed to acknowledge her presence; it was as if she were a prize that he had slung over his saddle and was carrying off to his bandit lair. Then he drew closer to her, squeezed her arm, her knee, stroked the fabric of her dress. "I'm just afraid," he had once explained to her, "that one day it's not really going to be you."

Between the abbey and the cottage—an old forester's cottage where Michael had been living for the last few months—stretched a long corridor of night, a neutral zone where time and everything else—words and actions—were suspended. He asked her brusque, fragmentary questions, and she replied, but their minds were both distracted, unfocused by a passion they had not been able to express, at least not yet. It always took a while for them to catch up to the elusive private selves that they were not permitted to acknowledge during the long, laborious days that separated their brief reunions.

They had first met at Oxford, and even then, surrounded by those notoriously dreamy spires and sedate Gothic quadrangles, there had been something distinctly urgent about their love for each other. They had done their graduate work in different cities; Michael had gone down to London for his medical training, Wendy had stayed on at Oxford. They had seen each other often; once he had even come back to Belfast with her to visit her family. Her memories of that epic voyage were vivid enough but jumbled and disconnected—long, uncomfortable hours spent on trains and ferryboats; trying to entertain Michael in her mother's steamy, chaotic kitchen with—another Irish cliché—a gaggle of noisy kids underfoot; the city with its battered streets, innumerable shabby churches, and riotous Republican pubs. About the pubs, she remembered that Michael had acquired an impressive store of anti-British ballads and always rose to join in the solemn singing of the Republican anthem at closing time.

Then for two years another, more drastic separation, essential as far as Wendy was concerned but inexplicable to Michael, and thus far unexplained. This was Wendy's secret from him—and almost from herself as well, since she could seldom bring herself to think of it. She knew that for him it was as if a piece had been torn out of his life for no apparent reason. He had never said this explicitly to her, but that did not prevent her from feeling that she was always under interrogation.

The tires squealed and the brush at the side of the road was pelted with gravel. The car had turned onto a dirt road between two white gateposts. Michael seemed, literally, to be breathing easier now that they were protected from the outside world by a palisade of tree trunks, a barrier almost as formidable as the walls of Faremoutiers. That, too, had been something of a shock for Michael, to discover that, like the star-crossed hero of a particularly sadistic medieval romance, he had found and lost her at the same instant, that this fiery Irish Amazon who used to make the Oxford quads resound with her Republican harangues had ended up as neither a member of Parliament nor an internee in Long Kesh jail but a voluntary inmate of a Benedictine abbey.

Perhaps wisely, Michael had not tried to understand. Of everything she had said to him, the only words that had really had any impact on him were these: "I'll take care of everything. If you come and see me, I'll take care of everything." On the strength of this not very promising offer, he had entirely rearranged his life in order to be able to present himself for the occasional moonlit tryst at Faremoutiers. He was able to scrape up an appointment as a research fellow in neuropathology at the University of Compiègne; the rector was an old acquaintance of Michael's mentor at Oxford and had been delighted to find such a promising candidate for the post.

Michael's male forebears constituted a kind of medical dynasty on Malta; the last four or five generations had all received their undergraduate training at Oxford. Michael had allowed himself a modest departure from family tradition by going in for neurology, of the experimental rather than the clinical sort. At present, he was interested in generating computer simulations—as opposed to "conceptual models"—of the neurological processes that take place in the brain; thus far, the rector of Compiègne had been more than cooperative in supplying him with research facilities and the aeons and millennia of computer time that such a project required.

"How much longer do you expect to stay in that place?" he asked her suddenly, without knowing whether the question was prompted by apprehension or desire. He wanted nothing more than to pry her out of that wretched cell, but once she was free, there was no telling where she might disappear. Wendy seemed to have the talent of appearing and disappearing at will, like an imp from a bottle, or an angel.

"I don't know" was the answer.

The little track they had been following through the forest was muddy and badly rutted; the Peugeot 205 was giving them a rude shaking-up, but Michael refused to slow down. The house, among other things, was awaiting them at the end of the track; a lantern shone from the porch. Michael stopped the car, seized Wendy in his arms, and held her tight. "Saved!" she murmured in a fluttery, rescued-princess sort of voice before she returned his embrace and kissed him violently. Now that they had arrived at their refuge, time could return to its normal, gentle, night rhythm while the trees swayed quietly in the wind.

Once inside the cottage, Michael went to turn over the logs on the hearth. The fire flared up on the grate, displaying the gnarled silhouettes of a few pieces of old country furniture standing guard over the corners of the room. Wendy took off her cape and tossed it onto an overstuffed armchair crouched by the fire, its rows of little brass buttons glowing brilliantly in the firelight. The fragrance of the trees and of the cool night air still lingered on her skin and in her hair; she stepped toward the hearth, where Michael was busy with the poker. The fire was blazing now, showering sparks and cinders onto the stones around the hearth, and the room filled with shuddering orange light.

Wendy spread her arms wide and shrugged out of her scratchy smock, tossing it carelessly over her head. Stark naked, her hair ruffled, her cheeks reddened by the heat of the flames, she stepped over to the goatskins that had been scorched a kind of reddish-brown by their many years of service in front of the hearth, stretched out full length, her toes almost touching the fire screen, and let the flickering waves of heat wash over her legs and belly. Michael stood and watched her; it took them both a little while to readjust to the idea of pleasure, and he knew that for her, as for a diver in decompression, these few moments were essential.

As he began to get undressed his eyes still wandered over her body, which seemed at once fluid and solid, light as the sky and vigorous as the ground, the body that continued to haunt every place on earth when she was no longer there. In the glow of the firelight, her soft white skin was like amber, and the curve of her belly was adorned with a little thicket the color of autumn. He knelt down beside her.

"There was a telephone call earlier," he said, with extreme reluctance. "For you. Somebody called Abdul. He said he'd call back around one o'clock in the morning."

"All right."

That was her only comment. But when he bent over to look into her eyes, Michael thought he could see another kind of excitement from the one he was hoping to find there.

"Yes," she said, in response to a different question altogether.

Michael's skin and hair, even the pupils of his eyes, had been darkened by the bright blue skies of the Mediterranean. His features, she liked to imagine, had been cut from the same hard rock as the cliffs of Malta—home of a race, as she often reminded herself, most admired for its stubbornness and tenacity. She loved the gentle strength of his long, muscular limbs, which seemed to be attached at the joints by invisible metal wires. All the violence of the many hours of waiting and all their many nights of unappeased desire had overtaken them a few moments later. When the fire on the hearth had burned down to ashes, they were finally pulled apart by the cold, and raced upstairs to the little bedroom.

Wendy stood by the window for a moment to watch the jagged ridge of the treetops against the clear night sky, like the bold scissor strokes in a Matisse cutout. Michael came up behind her and laced his arms around her, then thrust one leg between hers and gently pressed her bare breasts against the chilly windowpane. A moment later they were in bed, burrowing under the heavy quilt. Each time they had come together in front of the fire had left them feeling sated, overwhelmed, but they were astonished, and not entirely displeased, by how quickly and insistently their bodies were reawakened by desire. They both had strong presentiments of a moment, perhaps not very far in the future, when they would be separated in more than a momentary way.

When she heard the telephone ring downstairs, Wendy sat up with a start, her heart pounding. It had been like that for her ever since that December night when the call from her brother Brian's friends had awakened her and changed the course of her life forever. She pressed her palms down gently on Michael's chest, telling him not to move, that the matter was in her hands. Her skin glowing with sweat, she hurried across to the door, closed it firmly behind her, and clattered down the stairs in the half-darkness. The telephone was on the floor of the living room, near the armchair where she had left her cape. Impatiently, she fumbled for the receiver.

"*J'écoute.*"

"Wendy? Wendy Keenes?" The voice was not Abdul's; it was someone else.

"Yes, of course."

"Are you all alone, Wendy?"

"Yes, of course I am. What is it, for God's sake?"

"Our little Wendy is all alone. All right, listen very carefully. This has been a great night for us. The first stage of our operation was carried out over two hours ago. It all went according to plan. Our friends in Irkutsk have done their work well. So has our engineer from Tehran. You'll be stepping onstage for your little turn on November tenth. That leaves you just over a month for rehearsal, okay?"

"November tenth?" Wendy repeated. Then, after a short silence, she added, "I'll be ready."

There was a short bark of laughter at the other end of the line.

"What's so funny?" she asked.

"I'm so sorry I got you out of bed, Sister Wendy." The voice laughed again, quite unpleasantly, and Wendy hung up. Revolutions were supposed to be made, she thought to herself, by poets and madmen, not by idiots and stupid chauvinist bastards.

She walked back over to the staircase and sat down on the second step. The sound of Michael's footsteps in the hall upstairs was very quiet, but not so quiet that she couldn't hear them, as she heard the little squeak of the bedroom door when he pulled it shut. She sat still for another moment, then went up the stairs. Michael was stretched out on top of the quilt with a cigarette in his hand.

"You should have an extension installed up here," she said, "and save yourself the trouble of getting out of bed."

"I don't choose to discuss it," he replied. "That's the last refuge of a scoundrel who gets caught in the act, you know, not to choose to discuss it. That way there can be no awkward questions, and you save yourself the trouble of denying everything."

"What would you like to know?"

"Did you have lovers?" he asked, in a much less bantering tone. "While you were away, I mean. During those two years?"

"Of course I did—and, as you can see, they're still calling me."

Michael regretted having spoken. He hated it when she deliberately coarsened herself like that. Her cheeks were flushed, the single wrinkle that stretched across her forehead and only appeared when she was very upset or angry was now clearly visible, and her eyes, normally so soft and clear, looked as if they could strike sparks from rock. He waited for her to say something like, Well, I'm off, then. See you in two more years.

"I think I'd rather answer one of your other questions now," she said instead. "About how long I'll be staying at the abbey. I should be leaving in a couple of weeks—God willing, of course."

"On November tenth, in fact?"

"Three hours is all we have left this time," she replied. "You note that I said this time. But if you keep on like this there won't be any next time."

Irkutsk
October 5
8:30 A.M.

The last hour of the flight was not one that Captain d'Orbat would have been eager to relive, but at least it had been clear from the outset that no irreparable harm would come to his 747 and its passengers as long as he proved cooperative. As soon as the two MiGs had got themselves in position at each of his wing tips, they had waggled their wings back and forth and flashed their landing lights at irregular intervals—a recognized ICAO signal that meant, when addressed by a military to a civilian aircraft, "Follow me and prepare for landing." He had waggled his own wings in reply, a fairly cumbersome gesture when executed by a 747, to make it clear that he had understood.

A few minutes later, they had brought him to the runway where he was expected to land; it was built on top of a sort of causeway that projected for some distance—in the manner of the notorious Soviet airstrip on Grenada—into the remarkably clear water of the lake. By the onshore end of the runway there was a control tower, which looked to be still under construction, and a couple of squat concrete buildings. The surrounding shore was littered with power shovels and bulldozers, septic tanks and lengths of sewer pipes lined up inside a grid of untidy ditches, and a row of corrugated hangars painted forest green. D'Orbat counted five fighters on the ground, one of them in an advanced state of dissection. The two MiGs hovering at his wing tips swooped off into the clouds, to indicate that he was at liberty to make a brief reconnaissance of the landing strip at low altitude. The Boeing normally required a five-thousand-meter runway to make a reasonably safe landing. After a second pass over the air base, d'Orbat touched down gently as close as he dared to the offshore end of the causeway; the plane finally came to rest at the very end of the landing strip, with its nose almost touching the pylon of an enormous crane.

Sirens wailed, and a swarm of booted, fur-hatted soldiers in long green uniform coats, assault rifles at the ready, piled out of the canvas-topped trucks that were parked at the edge of the runway and deployed themselves around the forward section of the plane. A half-track lumbered out from amid the rubble of the construction site, leaving a wide, muddy spoor behind it. A light drizzle was falling, and the ground, d'Orbat noted irrelevantly, was still unfrozen on the shores of Lake Baikal. A light tank was standing guard beneath the long balance beam of the crane, and two fire trucks and an ambulance were parked just beyond the military cordon. The cordon parted to make room for a bulky staff car with little pennants fluttering on the front bumpers; it passed close enough to d'Orbat in his cockpit that the stiff-backed silhouette of what was presumably a high-ranking officer in a peaked cap was visible in the backseat.

A metal gangway was rolled up to the forward hatch of the 747, and the Russian officer stepped out of the car and climbed the stairs with a slow, deliberate tread. D'Orbat got up to meet him in the companionway directly behind the bridge. The officer saluted negligently with one gloved hand, then removed his glove and his wire-framed glasses in order to wipe the raindrops from their thick, squarish lenses. He appeared to be a Turk or a Kazakh or something of the sort, with a broad moon face, a flat, possibly broken nose, and jowly wrinkles bulging out of the stiff collar of his uniform coat.

"Permission to come aboard, Captain," he said in very passable French, his eyes wandering around the interior of the plane without looking directly at d'Orbat. "I am Colonel Akhmedov, and you, I believe, are Captain d'Orbat. Here is the procedure, Captain. I want you to instruct your passengers to get up from their seats and to leave the plane in a normal and orderly manner, taking articles of clothing with them but leaving all hand luggage behind. We have reason to suspect that there is a terrorist aboard this plane, Captain, so I don't have to tell you why this last point is of particular importance."

D'Orbat simply nodded, and Akhmedov jerked his chin up sharply in the direction of the bridge. "Then I'll leave you to it." Akhmedov turned and disappeared through the hatchway, and a few moments later a squad of soldiers came trotting up the gangway and down the aisles of the passenger cabins to station themselves, not entirely unobtrusively, in various corners of the plane. Meanwhile d'Orbat was relaying the colonel's instructions to his passengers over the public-address system.

"Ladies and gentlemen, the Soviet authorities have asked us to exit from the plane in a calm and orderly fashion. Passengers are requested for security reasons to leave all hand luggage aboard the plane."

The passengers rose from their seats and started down the aisle in little groups when the soldiers, like ushers in a crowded theater, gave them the signal to proceed. There were no shrieks or shouts, hardly any conversation at all; most of them were still only half-awake and somewhat bemused by what had happened. They realized, or suspected at any rate, that they had just escaped from some terrible danger, but no one aboard knew whether their current circumstances constituted any real improvement.

They obeyed mechanically when the Soviet soldiers gave their pantomime instructions. The soldiers were far from brutal or even discourteous, but their manner bespoke a firmness of purpose that was not conducive to protest or controversy. The soldiers were surprisingly young-looking, many of them with Asiatic features, which prompted one woman to advance the hypothesis that they must have come down in Mongolia by accident, until her husband told her to shut up. Right behind her, an elderly Japanese gentleman, who apparently understood neither French nor English, was engaged in a grim, silent struggle for the possession of his traveling bag with a burly, Tartar-faced Siberian.

The evacuation had started at the rear of the aft cabin. As soon as the plane had landed, Nicholas had gotten up to retrieve his attaché case from the overhead baggage compartment and slid it underneath the seat in front of them, by the window, then asked the American envoy to change seats with him. A few minutes later, he was beginning to suspect that in doing so he may only have attracted attention to himself. "Do you think they're going to search us?" he murmured to Wilcox in what he hoped was a normal, conversational tone. "I'm traveling on a diplomatic passport."

"In a civilized country, I'd say of course that that was out of the question. Here, I can hardly offer the same assurance."

"In that case, Mr. Wilcox, I'm going to bend down and fiddle with my shoelace. Would you be so good as to lean forward and turn a little to one side to make sure they don't see what I'm up to?"

"You'd better be quick about it, Padre."

Nicholas bent over and inserted a tiny key into the lock of his attaché case, opened it up very carefully, and reached one hand inside. The two envelopes he was looking for were almost on top, underneath a scarf that was folded in quarters, and a battered old shaving kit. Nicholas had no difficulty in removing both envelopes without making a sound.

"Nye dvigayte! Shto vy derzhayte tam v rukye?" The soldier shoved Wilcox aside, rather roughly, and flattened Nicholas against the back of his seat. The cover of the attaché case fell shut with an audible click, but a little triangle of manila paper was left protruding from beneath the thin metal strip along the edge. Nicholas reached down to push the envelope back inside the case. The soldier looked on disapprovingly, then grabbed him roughly by the shoulder as he was about to insert the key into the lock.

"Zakrivat nyelzya! Davaite kluch, batyushka. . . ." The soldier rubbed his fingers together impatiently, to indicate that Nicholas should hand over the key immediately. Meanwhile, Wilcox had gotten his breath again and had begun to bluster. While the soldier held his rough canvas glove under Nicholas's nose, palm upward, Nicholas found it difficult to focus on what he was saying. He caught a few disjointed phrases: "accredited papal diplomat," "clear violation of international law," "take this up with your superior officer," before deciding that he had no choice but to comply.

"Vykhodite-zhe!" said the soldier, and then, with a supreme bilingual effort, "Go out now!" A moment later, Nicholas and Wilcox were walking down the gangway.

While all this was going on, a thick fog had come in off the lake and settled over the airstrip. The top of the control tower could no longer be seen, and a fine freezing rain was falling, almost imperceptibly, though most of the passengers were drenched to the skin within a couple of minutes. They moved slowly in double file across the landing strip toward a low and inhospitable-looking cinder-block building, still raw and new-looking but old enough to have been mottled and discolored by the last winter's snows. A small green sedan, a Lada, followed slowly in their wake.

The cordon of soldiers came to attention with a great clatter of heels on concrete, and the head of a column came to a halt beside the metal door of the blockhouse. Even after several minutes had elapsed, the door gave no sign of opening, and Captain d'Orbat's passengers had no choice but to stand and, quite literally, cool their heels in the freezing wind and rain. The day's work was just beginning on the construction site a couple of hundred yards away, and the shorebirds were skimming out over the waters of the lake like hazardously overloaded seaplanes.

Then the Lada started to move forward again, very slowly, and the passengers, their leg muscles already stiff and complaining in the cold, were led around to the back of the blockhouse, where they were confronted with the wholly new vista of a vast unfinished hangar, its raw timberwork still peeping through in places and the doorway sealed off, except for a narrow aperture, with two substantial sheets of opaque and rigid plastic that looked like gray paraffin.

They remained here for several minutes, with an offshore breeze mingling the freezing gusts of rain, stinging grit, and wisps of fog and brandishing them energetically at eye level. The sun was a faint, dirty-yellowish glow somewhere beyond the murky aerial regions above the lake. Permission to take shelter inside the hangar was finally granted, and the passengers squeezed gingerly through the narrow space between the sheets of plastic.

Inside, there was a uniformed figure seated behind a large wooden packing crate, in lieu of a desk or counter. As the passengers entered the hangar, they were instructed to produce their passports and approach this personage, one by one, for "document control"; this involved, in almost every case, a relentlessly protracted parody of the usual passport inspection; entry and exit visa stamps were minutely scrutinized by this officer, to make sure that the decadent cosmopolite who appeared to be standing before him was not, in reality, still back in Hamburg or New York.

Finally, after staring fixedly at the photograph for several seconds, then glancing rapidly back and forth between passport and passenger—possibly with the expectation that the latter, incapable of withstanding the rigors of his criminal imposture any longer, would break down and confess—he would hand back the passport with an inscrutable blue stare.

The passengers were then herded on a little farther, where they stood for a few more minutes in a large clump on the uneven floor, amid conical piles of gravel, stacks of lumber and moist craters of sand and concrete. After a few minutes a cheerful clatter heralded the arrival of an old man in gray coveralls pushing a handcart laden with five chrome-plated samovars and an array of teacups. He filled a cup half full of a thin but steaming beverage and held it up, with an appealing glance, to the assembled company. When a couple of bolder passengers stepped forward to get their tea, he asked each of them in turn, with an almost impenetrable accent, "*Parizh?*"

When one of the passengers finally admitted to having just come from there—Paris—he shook his head mournfully and said, "*Parizh. Jamais Parizh . . . Trop vieux.*" He did not attempt any kind of conversational gambit with the Japanese passengers, but when he saw the little cross embroidered in the lapel of Nicholas's jacket, he smiled and, after a furtive glance assured him that the "passport control" officer was not looking in his direction, rapidily crossed himself with three fingers and from right to left in the Eastern Orthodox manner.

Colonel Akhmedov was the only one aboard the plane. He called off the search of the cabins that Captain Grigoriev's men had already begun and ordered the captain back to supervise the inspection of the luggage bays. It was clear that Grigoriev deeply resented being deprived of this opportunity to swagger about the interior of his captured prize, but the colonel was not especially concerned at the moment with soothing the captain's feelings. He walked briskly over to the seat that Nicholas had occupied in the first-class cabin, knelt down to retrieve the attaché case, then laid it flat on the adjoining seat. He inserted the key the soldier had given him in the lock, but it was not even locked; he flicked up the metal catches, opened the lid, and discovered the two envelopes protruding from beneath the folds of a scarf.

Both were closed with wax seals stamped with the papal arms. The colonel removed an airsickness bag from the little pouch at the back of the seat and enlarged the opening. He broke the seals very carefully, slid the fragments of wax into the bag, then spread the contents of the envelopes on top of the attaché case. He unbuttoned his coat, removed a small Japanese-made camera, and took two photographs of each of the sheets.

Next, he picked up his own briefcase, which he had set down in the aisle beside him, and removed a small collection of envelopes of various colors and sizes. Holding them up to the cabin window, he finally selected two that seemed to match, put the documents inside them, then produced a butane lighter, a stick of sealing wax, and a stubby cylinder of metal from the pockets of his uniform coat. He sealed the flap of each envelope with a blob of wax, then pressed the cylinder lightly against the wax, leaving an impression that was to all appearances identical to the original seal.

He stared at his handiwork for a moment and his features relaxed into a thin little smile before he closed the attaché and put it back under the seat. He dusted off the seat with the back of his hand and tossed the tiny key as far as he could down the center aisle. A few minutes later he was back on the runway with Grigoriev.

All the luggage had been removed from the plane's cargo bays and spread out on the slick concrete surface of the runway. Grigoriev, still smarting from the accumulated snubs and slurs, as he imagined them, of his all-night vigil with Akhmedov, was apparently determined to carry out his part of the operation with maniacal zeal. All the locks that resisted had been forced; all the luggage that was packed too tightly to be examined conveniently was spilled out onto the wet runway. Grigoriev's men were busily rummaging through these moist little hummocks of clothes and miscellaneous personal effects, carefully palpating the linings of suitcases, riffling through the pages of books and magazines.

Occasionally one of them would bring a particularly scandalous-looking specimen over to Grigoriev, who would simply wave him away with an impatient scowl. Whatever this was really all about, it seemed unlikely that this plane had deliberately wandered over a thousand kilometers off course for the purpose of smuggling subversive literature into a third-rate military airfield in Irkutsk. And while Grigoriev suspected that Akhmedov was fully capable of subjecting a whole planeload of harmless foreigners to this sort of humiliation and terror for no other reason than simple sadism and meanness, there was clearly a bit more to it than that. When Corporal Usupov had come up to them with some sort of rigmarole about a "Roman priest" and a briefcase and a key, Akhmedov had taken the key out of the corporal's dirty paw and gone about his business, after kicking them both off the plane, of course, without another word.

Grigoriev glanced over at his men, who seemed to be enjoying themselves a bit more than the circumstances called for. Although the idea of plunder and pillage, however tempting, was clearly ruled out by the presence of a representative of the state security organs, they had gone into a sort of consumerist feeding frenzy, gathering excitedly to exclaim over every exotic treasure that was turned up by the search—a portable computer, a portable compact-disk player, cassette players, the sleekest of quartz-powered alarm clocks and cordless electric razors, the minutest of calculators, and, the greatest wonder of all, a salesman's sample case full of the latest Japanese hand-held video games. Grigoriev was just about to call them back to order when one of the men gave a sharp exclamation. From the man's expression, Grigoriev knew immediately that he had just found the plum in the plum cake.

The prize was a large fiberboard suitcase, its exterior scuffed and battered and thoroughly unprepossessing; the inside of the lid was heavily padded, and the bottom was filled with three black metal cases equipped with knobs and dials and other protuberances and connected by a tangle of insulated wiring. The soldier who had come upon this prize looked up at Grigoriev. "*Elektronika,*" he announced solemnly. In the next moment Akhmedov was standing beside them; he reached down and tore off the baggage check from the handle of the suitcase and passed it over to Grigoriev. "I want this man brought to me," he said curtly, then turned and stalked off.

In the hangar the passengers were stamping their feet to ward off the cold. The tea had left an acrid trail from throat to stomach, but the precious warmth had dissipated long before. The arrival of Captain Grigoriev, accompanied by two soldiers and a civilian with a bullhorn, promised at least an interesting new development, though the possibility of release from their incomprehensible confinement had begun to seem very remote. Captain d'Orbat advanced a few steps to meet them, but the announcement made by the interpreter with the bullhorn concerned only one of the passengers—one Mohammed Khomsi—who was asked to come forward "to assist with further verification of identity."

Mohammed Khomsi turned out to be a tall, elegantly dressed, ascetic-looking gentleman of Middle Eastern appearance. He stepped forward without the slightest hesitation, but when he was within a few feet of Grigoriev and his escort, the two soldiers seized him and pinioned his arms as roughly as if he had been making a desperate attempt to escape. At this, there was a rustle of protest from the crowd, which quickly subsided as the passengers sank back into a kind of reptilian torpor in the chilly air of the hangar. The man with the tea wagon had added a few liters of boiling water to his samovar to produce a brew that, as Nicholas noted with approval, was almost entirely tasteless, with only the slightest hint of bitterness, and extremely refreshing.

The passengers spent another hour shivering and stamping before the interpreter with the bullhorn returned, this time without military escort, and asked d'Orbat to accompany him. The pilot seemed willing, almost eager, to comply, which the others found highly encouraging, even though d'Orbat—as he had reminded them several times during the past several hours—really had no clearer idea about what to expect than anybody else did.

The captain was brought to a bare little room which, apart from a desk and a couple of chairs, contained just three Soviet interrogators and Mohammed Khomsi. The interrogators were Colonel Akhmedov, Captain Grigoriev, and Grigoriev's orderly, a Second Lieutenant Bronski, who, until a few minutes earlier, had been struggling to keep a stenographic record of Khomsi's voluminous confession. Far from attempting to exonerate himself, Khomsi had immediately launched into a grandiloquent tirade, claiming full credit for the act of electronic piracy and sabotage that had thrown the aircraft off course. Khomsi was traveling on an Iranian passport, and Grigoriev had no difficulty in classifying this particular subspecies—a dangerous fanatic, a modern-day assassin, one of the terrorist zealots that the ayatollah's regime was turning out by the hundreds. This was the first time the Soviet Union had become directly involved with any of these medieval throwbacks—except in Afghanistan, of course—but it was clearly the sort of thing that was bound to happen eventually.

Mohammed Khomsi also turned out to be a native of Tabriz, the capital of the Iranian province of Azerbaijan, just a dozen or so miles from the Soviet frontier. He spoke a kind of hideous pidgin Russian that put the stress on the wrong syllables, disdained to conjugate verbs, and bit off the endings of most other words, but in other respects, Grigoriev was forced to admit, he had a certain imbecile eloquence and had little difficulty making himself understood. The only other person—or rather, Being—he had implicated in his confession was Allah; Allah had put him up to it—and Grigoriev noted that Akhmedov glared at him with particular ferocity whenever he invoked the holy name.

More specifically, Allah had instructed Khomsi and his unnamed confederates—who had collectively taken the name of the Sword of Saladin—to wrest the world from the grip of godless capitalism, just as their heroic medieval namesake had sent the brutal Frankish invaders reeling back from the gates of the Holy City of Jerusalem. Apart from that, he seemed to have boarded the plane with only the vaguest intention of causing trouble for the French (because they had profaned the Mosque of Omar in the eleventh century and were supplying arms to the Iraqis in the present one), the Americans, and the Japanese (as the two bodies politic in which the infection of godless capitalism was most advanced at present), as well as focusing the world's attention on the Sword of Saladin and the righteousness of its cause.

After his infernal machine had switched on, automatically, and it was clear to everyone on board that they were drifting helplessly through the skies, he had intended to get up and address some sort of harangue to the passengers, attempting to make it clear to them that they had been tragically mistaken to entrust their lives to fallible mortals and soulless machines, which could not save them from destruction when the will of Allah had decreed otherwise. The Soviet fighters had turned up, however, before he had had a chance to deliver this timely and philosophical message.

By this point, or so it seemed to Grigoriev at any rate, the suitcase full of *elektronika* seemed like a much more promising subject for investigation than the demented dervish Mohammed Khomsi, who initially claimed, rather proudly, to be entirely ignorant of such matters, then immediately retreated to the position that he lacked the technical vocabulary to discuss them intelligibly in Russian. It was then that the colonel finally chose to show his true colors—to strike the red flag, as it were, and run up the green—by addressing Khomsi with a burst of some sort of uncouth Transcaucasian jargon that Grigoriev could only suppose was Azerbaijani, the mother tongue of both the KGB colonel and the Islamic commando. Bronski, obviously overwhelmed linguistically, closed his notebook and sat back to enjoy the captain's discomfiture.

Soon the colonel and Khomsi were chattering away quite affably, like a couple of carpet peddlers in the bazaar, when the door opened and Captain d'Orbat was brought into the room. The colonel instantly switched over from Azerbaijani to French (every incomprehensible word of which was as coals of fire on Grigoriev's close-cropped head).

"It is this man," said Akhmedov, gesturing toward Khomsi, "who has brought you here, Captain. Apparently his luggage contained a powerful transmitter that jammed all your radio frequencies and a gamma-ray source that erased the memories of your computers. Both were triggered automatically, and all in a single suitcase, Captain. It seems to me that you have a bone to pick with the security detail at your Paris airport. I'm sure you'll agree that they have behaved with abysmal laxity. A suitcase containing radioactive material was brought on board your plane, after all. If the political situation had been a little less, how shall I say, *relaxed* than it is at the present moment, this violation of our airspace could have involved you in very serious difficulties. Under the circumstances, however, now that the mystery's been solved, you and your passengers are perfectly free to resume your journey."

D'Orbat smiled involuntarily, wondering what sort of accommodations might have been found for them if the political situation had been, as he said, less relaxed. "I'd be delighted to, Colonel, but without instruments—"

"I'm sure you'll find that all your instruments are working perfectly now, Captain. Of course, you'll be expected to return to the authorized commercial flight path by the shortest possible route, and we'll be pleased to provide you with a fighter escort to make sure that you encounter no further difficulties of this kind. I must insist, however, that the passenger Mohammed Khomsi and his bag of tricks both remain in our custody."

D'Orbat was about to utter a protest, when it dawned on him that he had been assuming that the skyjacker would automatically return with them, "back to civilization" in effect, for a thorough investigation of his case. However, as he realized somewhat sheepishly, the Soviets had also signed the various international antiskyjacking conventions and were entirely within their rights in detaining Khomsi. Khomsi himself, who did not appear to understand French, had been sitting quietly through all this, but when d'Orbat nodded his agreement to this arrangement and turned toward the door, the Iranian leapt to his feet, clutched at d'Orbat's sleeve, and began another impassioned oration, this time in a mixture of Farsi, Azerbaijani, and a language that Grigoriev was proud to identify as English.

Though he lacked Akhmedov's gift of tongues, it still seemed strange to him that Khomsi, who spoke no French, had been chosen as Islamic emissary to people who were traveling on an Air France flight from Paris. Before Grigoriev could pursue this point, however, two of Akhmedov's plainclothes "inspectors" appeared to take the prisoner into custody.

D'Orbat looked questioningly at the colonel. "So, you might say that it was a sort of clock bomb that made such a royal shambles of our instrument panel?"

But Akhmedov did not appear to be disposed to offer any further explanations. "So far we have only the suspect's word for that. I must tell you that he does not appear to be very well versed in scientific matters. The contents of the suitcase will be examined by specialists in

Moscow, and the results of their investigations will be communicated to your government in due course. Meanwhile, the only thing we can conclude from all this is that religious fanaticism poses a terrible threat to all of us, to the citizens of all civilized countries."

In fact, the final phase of Khomsi's confession, when the two of them had spoken in Azerbaijani, had been much more informative than that. The "clock bomb" in the suitcase consisted of three separate devices: first, a gamma-ray source with an effective radius of several dozen meters—10 grams of radioactive cobalt 60 that was mechanically extruded from its lead shielding for no more than a couple of seconds—sufficient to erase the memories of the plane's on-board computers; second, a multifrequency transmitter to jam all radio communications to and from the ground; third, an electromagnet powerful enough to bring about a magnetic compass deflection of no less than 30°, just enough to send AF-270 winging toward its nonscheduled destination on the shores of Lake Baikal.

Soviet fighters escorted the Air France jetliner in relays as far as the southern tip of the island of Sakhalin. All instruments were fully operational, and no problems developed during the rest of the flight. Still, the three men on the bridge only began to breathe normally again when they saw the fifth pair of MiGs peel off from alongside them and disappear into the west.

Faremoutiers, 4:55 A.M.

Wendy had scarcely had time to catch her breath before hurrying off to the chapel for prime, the first service of the day. The file of nuns processed slowly across the stone floor of the chapel; the small group of novices with their starched white veils went in ahead of the postulants, and Wendy was about to take her place behind them. She turned involuntarily as she felt someone come up beside her and was surprised to be confronted with the face of Mother Marie-Bernadette. The mother superior signed almost imperceptibly for her to come closer. Wendy obeyed and, to her even greater surprise, saw Mother Marie-Bernadette spread her arms wide to give her the kiss of peace. Wendy responded with two respectful pecks at the nun's black-clad shoulders.

"I was about to compliment you on how fresh and rosy you look this morning, my child," Mother Marie-Bernadette remarked. Wendy just bowed her head and said nothing. "But I must say," she went on, "now that I look a little closer, I see that your face is very flushed and you seem to have dreadful rings under your eyes. Have you been sleeping poorly?"

"*Ma mère*, it's just that I was up all night meditating . . . trying to master my thoughts," said Wendy shamelessly, "and I had the window open."

"And who asked you to do anything of the sort? It's been thirty years now since I took my vows, and I've yet to hear of anyone being any easier in her mind from leaving the window open on a cold October night." The mother superior continued in a softer, less reproving voice, "You must learn to be more temperate, my child. And you mustn't deprive yourself of rest. Also . . . I want you to come see me today at lunchtime. There is something I have to tell you."

"Very good, *ma mère*." Wendy went into the chapel and immersed herself in the ancient melodies of the liturgy, though she discovered that she was not quite capable of raising her eyes to the altar. A little less than five hours later, she and Mother Marie-Bernadette were about to continue their conversation in the mother superior's office. This was a long, narrow room with casement windows that overlooked the garden; a small vase of flowers was the only ornament. As Wendy came in Mother Marie-Bernadette was seated at her desk, her hands folded across a letter or document of some sort. The expression in her eyes was lively and compassionate, somewhat at variance with the tightness of her skin and the austerity, almost harshness, of her features. Wendy had never been able to gauge her intelligence or the generosity of her heart, but thus far she had been careful not to underestimate the former or to overestimate the latter.

"Do you know what we should probably conclude from these excesses of yours?" Mother Marie-Bernadette began abruptly. "That you were not made for the contemplative life. You have doubts about yourself, about your vocation, and you attempt to make too much of them. And you mustn't think that what you imagine to be humility is anything but pride and presumption. I'm afraid you're simply not capable of examining your thoughts in a humble and penitent spirit."

"Oh, *ma mère*!"

Mother Marie-Bernadette fluttered the ample pleats of her black robe. "Alas, everything changes, everything is always in the process of becoming something else. Our abbey is a good example. Fourteen centuries ago, this place was called Eboriacum, which meant that there were many oak trees here, as I'm sure was the case. Then along came our patron, Saint Fare, and founded a convent. Did you know that one of Charlemagne's daughters was abbess here? And all of it was destroyed during the Revolution and had to be built again from the ruins, from nothing really, during the last century.

"It seems to me that in an abbey such as ours, which has been so cruelly cut off from its origins, deprived of its traditions, even stronger faith and greater fortitude are required than in former times. These walls are of old stone, but they are like the walls of any old house you might find in the town. I think you have made a mistake in coming here. . . . Yes, I feel I must say it, even if it gives you pain. You thought that instead of renouncing the world you could bring your whole little world in here with you—your books and your science and your passionate concern for things that can have no meaning for us here."

"But, *ma mère*, haven't people always studied in monasteries?"

"We are here to study and meditate on the Holy Scriptures. That is our vocation. Yours is different. You must believe me when I say that I am not questioning the ardor of your faith or the sincerity of your convictions. However, there is a place for everything . . ."

"*Ma mère*, does this mean I'm not going to be allowed to stay here any longer?"

Mother Marie-Bernadette held up a restraining hand whose parchment flesh was virtually transparent. "First, you must remember that God is everywhere, and wherever you go, His comforting presence will find you there—as long as you remain worthy. Also, there are certain places where one is closer to Our Lord than elsewhere, to be sure. I have a letter here"—she scooped up the document in question from her otherwise empty desktop—"from the Pontifical Academy in Rome. It appears that our Mother Church has need of those who possess the sort of scientific qualifications that you do and at the same time, if possible," she added with a sort of wintry smile, "are strong in their faith. Am I right in remembering that you have a doctor's degree in mathematics from Oxford University?"

Wendy nodded, as if confessing a grave fault; the feeling of exultation that had risen up within her had vanished. Mother Marie-Bernadette got abruptly to her feet to signify that the interview was at an end and followed Wendy to the door. She was taking very small steps, and suddenly seemed extremely old. When they reached the door, she said, her voice blurred with indecipherable emotions, "I think I shall be able to recommend you to a research institute in Rome where I'm sure you'll do very well. God be with you, my child." Then, seeing that Wendy was still hesitating in the doorway, she added, "Go now, it's time to eat."

Route de Compiègne, 5:30 A.M.

All sense of urgency had left him, and he had fallen into a kind of reverie that was tinged with melancholy but was principally inspired by the desire to avoid thinking about anything in particular, especially about himself or the future. Each time Michael had driven her back to the abbey, he had tried to avoid thinking that this might be their last meeting. This time had been more difficult than usual.

The Peugeot held the road smoothly, drifted a little too close to the median line, straddled it at times, but the road was deserted at this hour. *What amazing powers the girl had!* No one had ever compelled him to show so much weakness, such cowardice. There was something in him that recoiled from this, so much that when the thought suddenly came to him, *I'm not really like that,* he felt obliged to repeat it out loud, as if to convince some secret, skeptical part of his brain that it was true. At the moment he was feeling too spent and drowsy to advance this proposition any further. Instead, he flicked on the car radio to help deaden the emotional aftershock of this very eventful morning.

At 5:30 precisely a soothing yet authoritative voice announced that the Air France jetliner that had inexplicably vanished during a nighttime overflight of the Soviet Union was expected momentarily at Tokyo's Narita Airport. "For the two hundred and forty passengers aboard AF-270," the voice intoned solemnly, "the nightmare is over at last." The announcer took note of the fact that a militant Islamic group calling itself the Sword of Saladin had claimed responsibility for diverting the plane from its course, and read, in an audibly bored voice, a brief but incoherent communiqué to that effect. The breaking story, the highlight of the updated bulletin at 5:40, was provided by a Tass news dispatch.

The Soviet government had reacted with uncharacteristic promptness, condemning the attempted hijacking, or rather, "the fanatical outrage perpetrated in the name of the pirate regime in Tehran and abetted by the criminal negligence of Paris airport security." Only the vigilance of the personnel of Irkutsk military district had prevented this affair from ending in tragedy—the closest thing to an explicit reference to the KE-007 disaster that Tass would permit itself. Once the hijack attempt had been detected and foiled by Soviet authorities, the plane was safely escorted out of Soviet airspace via the authorized commercial flight path. The hijacker, if convicted, faced a possible sentence of twenty-five years. . . .

Michael grimaced and turned down the sound. The story of Muslim fanatics involved in furtive criminal high jinks only reminded him of Wendy and her mysterious phone calls from "Abdul." Instantaneously, a clutch of neurons exploded in some inaccessible memory file, and a rapid sequence of scenes—Oxford, London, Belfast, Malta, the abbey, and the forest—intercut with half-formed images of the runaway airplane and the bodiless voice on the telephone flashed by him on the grainy gray surface of the roadway before the conscious part of his brain could trace the logical, or possibly merely neurological, connection between them. He reflected, not for the first time, on how much easier it would be to keep track of these things if he had his brain hard-wired with the appropriate output leads, like the poor cats that awaited him in the laboratory at Compiègne with their skulls stuck full of electrodes.

This was a question that he was seriously very interested in—that is, whether the brain, in its dreamy, partially disconnected state (not unlike his current one) might not be capable of processing information more efficiently than during wakefulness, when the forefront of the conscious mind was almost continuously occupied with coding and evaluating the enormous quantities of irrelevant data that were being received at every moment. Perhaps, he had concluded, the conscious mind quickly reaches a state of supersaturation, of not being able to cope, which is simply another name for what we perceive as the passage of time.

Work expands to fill up the available time, according to the famous law, because time, as a function of our inability to cope, is almost infinitely expandable. With computers, of course, it was just the opposite—they could divide and subdivide the time line into almost infinitesimal segments, though humans could still experience the instantaneous elapse of time, as a foretaste of the Final Shutdown, simply by dropping off to sleep. . . .

The glare of the truck's headlights bearing down on him forced him to swerve back into his own lane, and to abandon his experiment for the time being. He should have known, as stated by an equally famous principle, that he would not come up with very good data if he tried to do double duty as experimental subject and experimenter. He had certainly not come up with anything that was likely to help him in his work, but he was not required to be quite as rigorous in thinking about his personal life. At any rate, he seemed to have reached an important conclusion that had to do with Wendy—he no longer had the right not to know, to pretend that something very odd was *not* going on. Otherwise, he was almost certain to lose her; perhaps she would be lost altogether.

It was too early to go into Compiègne, and he felt that he needed a shower, a hot cup of coffee, and an hour or two to pull himself together. What he wanted most, however, was to be in a place where she had just been, to be able to breathe the sweet fragrance of her presence, to soothe himself with the illusion that she might return at any moment. . . . The Peugeot turned off onto the forest track that led to the cottage; the leaves of the trees and the underbrush were just turning from gray to green in the early morning light. Suddenly, with a terrific roar like that of a great beast flushed from cover, a car came hurtling toward him down the narrow track.

It was a black sedan, with its headlights off. Michael just had time to shoot the wheel hard over and plunge the Peugeot into the deep ditch full of leaf mold and stagnant water at the edge of the track; even so, there was a hideous squeal of metal against metal, the Peugeot gave a shudder and lurched forward convulsively, and the other car disappeared in a cloud of dust and rattling gravel. Michael had been able to identify it as a BMW and had counted three heads inside; at any rate, there was no mystery about where they were coming from. Michael put the Peugeot into reverse; the car hesitated for a moment, then hoisted itself laboriously out of the ditch. Once past the next bend, Michael could see that the front door of the cottage was wide open.

He threw open the car door and ran inside, crunching through shards of broken glass on the doorsill. In the large living room, the stuffing had been plucked out of all the cushions, the chairs overturned, their upholstery slashed; the floor was covered with books and papers, record albums out of their jackets. The receiver of the telephone was dangling off the edge of a table, emitting a plaintive bipping sound. Three small coals were still smoldering in front of the fireplace, and Michael strode over to stamp them out; the chimney had been induced to vomit up its contents—what looked to be many decades of soot and creosote—onto the tiles and the carpet around the hearth.

He wheeled around slowly to survey the chaos on the lower floor, then made for the stairs with a kind of staggering gait, and climbed up to the bedroom. The bed had been stripped and the bedclothes strewn all over the floor; the mattress had been slashed up the side, with flecks of foam rubber spilling out from the edges of the gash. Nothing made him feel worse than the cold air blowing through the window, which had carried off all the fragrance of her skin and all the magic of the night before. He threw himself down on the shredded heap of bedclothes on the floor and lay still for several minutes, breathing in great gasps and trying to understand. Finally, he remembered the secret compartment under the sink in the bathroom, where he had £5,200 in cash, his emergency escape fund, hidden away.

They had found the money, but they had not taken it, simply strewed the notes all over the bathroom floor. Far from consoling him, this discovery only reawakened his rage—and behind his rage crouched the hulking shadow of terror. It was Wendy that they had come for; they wanted to steal her from him. Nothing other than that. And he hated them in a way that he would never have believed he could hate anyone.

3

Baku, Azerbaijan SSR
KGB Residency
October 8

Colonel Akhmedov followed Gaydar Aliev with admiring eyes as Aliev took his place behind his desk, facing the two envoys from Moscow. The chief had got what he was after, and in record time; only three days ago it might have seemed that Aliev had staked everything, including a career that he had been building for forty years, on an outside chance. Akhmedov supposed that his own career had been at stake as well, something that might easily have caused him some anxiety if he had not had total confidence in his chief's abilities. In any case, the period of uncertainty had not been a long one.

Aliev could hardly have been called headstrong or impetuous, and his reputation in Moscow was such that he was allowed, with no discredit to himself, to take an occasional plunge—of the sort that in a man of less prudent impulses would be condemned out of hand. Aliev, however, was not the sort who would ever be condemned without being given a chance to present his own defense. The colonel watched Aliev with something of the feeling that the still clumsy apprentice might have for the deftness of the master. Whereas Aliev was straightforward, direct, and firm, he, Akhmedov, always gave the impression of being arrogant and inflexible. Aliev's gestures were fluid and easy; his, brusque and mechanical.

Certainly Aliev seemed very much the master in Baku, the capital of his little Caucasian fiefdom—or sheikhdom, he supposed some would call it. This was doubly appropriate, since Baku was an oil boomtown that had experienced a remarkable growth in recent years. It was what Comrade Lysenko would have ended up with, someone had said, if he crossed a mushroom with a nice fat olive. Aliev rarely left the city and almost never by choice, generally only for meetings of the dozen full members of the Politburo. His critics reproached him for being Azerbaijani first and Soviet second (by which they meant a Russian, of course), and Aliev certainly did nothing to relieve them of their suspicions. He claimed to be nothing other than what he was, after all, and he certainly had some grounds for complacency in that respect, since if the socialist paradise truly existed, it was surely to be sought in the little Muslim (but definitely not Islamic) republic on the shores of the Caspian Sea.

If it was suggested to Colonel Akhmedov that a man of such exotic origins would probably never make the climb all the way to the top, Akhmedov always replied that what was possible for a former seminary student from Tiflis—namely, Stalin—might also be possible for a mullah's son from Nakhichevan. Aliev could scarcely be said to have reached the pinnacle of supreme power, yet certainly he was already among the twelve most powerful, not to say formidable, men in the Soviet Union, with his KGB legions at his back in addition to a little band of zealous collaborators and compatriots in Baku.

In the eyes of his detractors and competitors, Aliev's greatest defect was that he had none, no infamous vices, that is—like his predecessor Lavrenti Beria's notorious fondness for red-haired underaged girls—or at least none that could be found out. Aliev, himself, however, seemed to take a more than professional interest in sniffing out the vices of others and had actively taken up the campaign against "social crime" and corruption in state services and in public life that had been promulgated by Yuri Andropov shortly before his death. Since then, Aliev had become the scourge of venal or incompetent bureaucrats, factory managers who had skimmed off a little too much of production for sale on the black market, high-ranking dignitaries with a few too many suburban dachas or official cars to their credit.

He was also believed to be the animating spirit behind the current crackdown on alcoholism in the military forces and among state workers. There were those who accused him of trying to "Islamicize" Soviet society—his campaign against public drunkenness being seen as just a prelude to an absolute ban on cigarettes, and pork chops as well. Even his colleagues in the Politburo were probably more concerned about the 60 million Soviet Muslims whose representative he could plausibly claim to be than about the 200,000 KGB men who were under his direct command.

Thus far, the most prominent victim of Aliev's crusade against official misconduct had been a fellow member of the Politburo, Grigori Romanov, once considered the odds-on favorite to succeed Konstantin Chernenko. The fact that Mikhail Gorbachev and not Romanov had actually done so was largely due to Aliev and an incident involving a state service of china and glassware that had originally belonged to Catherine the Great and had been borrowed from Leningrad's Hermitage Museum for the benefit of the several thousand guests at the wedding of Romanov's daughter, a festivity at which there had been much drinking of toasts in the hearty, old-fashioned style, and much breakage of irreplaceable glassware. It was Aliev who had given widespread publicity to this event (so much so that it had even been picked up by the Western press), inspiring predictable comments to the effect that Grigori was starting to take himself for a *real* Romanov. Aliev had also been responsible for the ouster of Marshal Ustinov, minister of defense at the time of the KE-007 incident; only the marshal's subsequent death, of natural causes, had saved him from total disgrace.

Nowadays, Aliev was widely spoken of as the number-two man in the new regime. He had been awarded Ustinov's former prerogative of keeping tabs on foreign air traffic and had largely been put in charge of the Soviet Union's often difficult relations with the Islamic world. Nevertheless, Gorbachev had no intention of relinquishing control of his foreign policy—even those aspects of it that involved Muslims or foreign airliners—or of allowing his talented deputy to engage in adventurist intrigues or to stir up international crises without prior consultation with other departments of government. The presence of Aliev's Aliev—Colonel Akhmedov—at the base in Irkutsk strongly implied that the two had foreknowledge of the hijacking incident, in fact may have had a hand in arranging it from the beginning.

Aliev's response to Gorbachev's outraged phone call was disarming, disingenuous. He had assured the first secretary that all proper procedures had been followed—those approved by Gorbachev himself in cases where a foreign aircraft deviated from the authorized flight path as the result of navigational error (genuine or feigned for purposes of espionage, which had never been conclusively ruled out in the case of KE-007), technical problems, or a hijacking. In any case, the detention of the passengers and the search of the luggage bays had been extremely fruitful—and he went on to describe the contents of Mohammed Khomsi's cardboard suitcase in some detail.

"That's all very well, Gaydar. You can stop pretending you're at a press conference—in one of your own interrogation rooms, for that matter. I just want you to answer me two simple questions. First of all, I want to know what Akhmedov was doing at the airbase, and second, I want to know precisely what you're up to. You can answer the second one first if you wish."

Aliev sighed, as if Gorbachev's brutal directness had bruised his devious Caucasian sensibilities in some way. "To answer *precisely*, as you say, Mikhail Sergeyevich, I'd have to sit you down in a briefing room for at least a couple of hours. And it's not so much what I'm up to as what *they're* up to, in the West I mean. I've uncovered evidence of a monumental . . . I can only call it a *conspiracy*, a kind of technological conspiracy against us and about as destabilizing as anything you can imagine short of actual war. There's not a great deal I can tell you about it over the telephone—even a line as secure as this one."

Gorbachev chuckled. Aliev's concern for the security of the workers' state was only slightly less obsessive than his concern for the security of his personal telephone lines. "Go on. Tell me as much as you can, Gaydar."

"It involves satellites, though not in the way you might think—nothing to do with Star Wars. The evidence is quite complete, and all in a single envelope. I have it right in front of me."

"And I take it you haven't discussed this with anyone but Akhmedov?"

"That's right. And now it will be our secret, Mikhail Sergeyevich. No one knows that we know—not even the Americans. I could bring it to you in a couple of hours, and you know how much it grieves me to leave my comfortable home and fly to Moscow. But in the present case, I am firmly convinced that time is of the essence."

"Perhaps at least you could tell me who's involved in this technological conspiracy, Gaydar?"

"All of them, all of the Western powers—plus several others that aren't even powers at all strictly speaking—with us, and the Arab states as well, as its intended targets."

"So it's Aliev and the ayatollahs against the world now, Gaydar. I trust you won't be offended if I don't invite you to Moscow just yet.

Perhaps we should wait on that until Grigori Romanov is resting a little more comfortably in oblivion."

"Nevertheless, Mikhail Sergeyevich, I assure you that this is a matter of the utmost importance—"

"Very well. Comrades Akimov and Vikhalev will be calling on you in the morning, and you can tell them all about it. Then, after they've told *me* all about it, I'll call you up and we can have another discussion, possibly somewhat more fruitful than this one."

Aliev was not entirely displeased as he replaced the receiver. Gorbachev was evidently skeptical—as he had every right to be under the circumstances. But that would only make his triumph all the more decisive when it was finally confirmed by the evidence.

The heraldic symbol of the Azerbaijan SSR, as featured on the official coat of arms of the republic, is an oil derrick, and there were many other, more tangible symbols of this national preoccupation along the highway from Baku international airport. Gorbachev's envoys were rolling along in a big black Volga limousine, past a landscape crowded with refineries and petrochemical plants, the orange flames of natural gas flares flickering garishly against the bright blue sky. From time to time, great billows of smoke drifted between them and the sun. Next came a lengthy sequence of tidily planned little suburbs, each with its own shopping district and municipal square. Baku was also called "the City of the Winds," as evidenced by massive dustclouds swirling over the construction sites and the broad trenches that had been dug for the new subway system. Finally, they passed through a kind of urban fringe pierced by broad boulevards lined with block-gray buildings in the postwar "Stalinist wedding cake" style. This brought them at last to the older quarters of the city, where the KGB residence was located.

Viktor Akimov and Andrei Vikhalev—one very thin and frail, the other more substantial, both seeming a little bulkier than normal in their tailored English tweeds—were ushered into a conference room with a long table. At one end Colonel Akhmedov was seated opposite two empty chairs; Aliev had drawn his chair back from one corner of the table, to enable him to survey all three of the others with a single glance. Aliev was smiling, relaxed, obviously very much at home, contrasting oddly with the fidgety, stiff-backed demeanor of his two guests from Moscow. Akimov and Vikhalev were clearly, and justifiably, apprehensive about confronting the beast in his lair—nor were they as well briefed on the habits and character of the beast as he was about theirs. Aliev had had a dozen hours in which to collect this information, and he had already discovered a number of things about them their own mothers would doubtless have been surprised to learn.

Akimov began the conversation. "First of all, Comrade General, the first secretary has asked us to tell you that, whatever the nature of the information that you have to tell us today, he is far from satisfied with the manner in which this operation was carried out—without consultation with any other authority—" He glanced over at Aliev and immediately stopped short, even though his host was still smiling and nodding at him in an encouraging way. The other envoy made as if to take up the complaint, but Akhmedov, superb in his bemedaled uniform, dissuaded him from doing so with an abrupt gesture.

"I'm afraid we've already gotten past that," said Aliev blandly. "There'll be a time for you both to speak, comrades, but that won't come till you're back in Moscow, ready to report to the first secretary. For the moment, the reason you're here is to listen, and serve as a conduit between me and the first secretary—to enable us to continue our conversation on what I can only regard as a matter of capital importance. I hope you will forgive my bluntness in pointing this out to you, but I thought it best that we waste as little of our time as possible in pointless discussion. . . ."

This speech seemed to have had the desired effect on Vikhalev and Akimov, who had begun to feel like ambassadors at the court of some cruel and capricious foreign potentate. They were willing to sacrifice a little of their dignity, for the moment, if that meant they would not have to sacrifice anything else. Aliev nodded approvingly and motioned for Akhmedov to begin his presentation. Akhmedov shuffled through his papers, as if to prolong this delicious moment as long as possible.

"First, comrades, I'd like to supply you with a bit of background," he finally began. "It's essential to bear in mind for purposes of this discussion that formal diplomatic relations between the Vatican City State and the United States of America were formally suspended between 1867 and quite recently . . . January 10, 1984. . . ."

"You should give us a few more of the details than that, Comrade General," said Aliev reprovingly. "Our guests are surely eager to share in your appreciation of the complete picture."

"Very well. Formal relations were suspended in 1867, after the United States Congress refused to vote any further appropriations for an embassy in the Papal States. Two years later, when the Papal States were annexed by the Kingdom of Italy, consular relations were suspended as well, and so the situation remained in 1939, when President Franklin Roosevelt dispatched a personal representative to the court of Pope Pius XII. After the war, President Truman planned to appoint an ambassador to the Vatican, but this was blocked by the rabid opposition of Protestant and Jewish pressure groups. He too was obliged to make do with a personal representative, General Mark Clark; Mr. Nixon was able to upgrade his representative, Henry Cabot Lodge, a descendant of a very prominent merchant family, to the status of personal *delegate*. . . . " Akhmedov paused for a moment, perhaps expecting a reprieve from Aliev. When none was forthcoming, he continued his recital.

"In February 1981, Ronald Reagan appointed his delegate, Mr. William A. Wilson, and on January 10, 1984, once again in the teeth of embittered sectarian opposition, Wilson was confirmed as America's first full-fledged ambassador to the Vatican in over a hundred years. This Wilson was a personal friend of the president's, deep in his confidence, a devout Catholic of the most reactionary stripe, and totally without previous diplomatic experience. Certainly it was to be expected that an emissary of this kind would be dispatched by the American president to the court of the Polish pope.

"What was not to be expected, however, was that this Ambassador Wilson had also been dispatched to the court of Colonel Qaddafi—since at that time, Mr. Reagan's now notorious penchant for secret diplomacy was still a secret. Ferried back and forth from Tripoli in an Italian private jet, Mr. Wilson had several personal conversations with the colonel, though at that time their two nations were virtually at war with one another. Later, it was pointed out that since Wilson had extensive personal interests in oil extraction and refining in his own country, it was simply a case of one big oilman talking to another. . . ."

"Now perhaps you'd better start getting to the point," muttered Aliev.

"The point," said Akhmedov promptly, "was that Wilson was compelled by his own State Department to tender his resignation and return to private life. In Italy, the scandal was immense, as scandals have a habit of being, particularly where the Vatican is considered. Nevertheless, there the matter rested for more than two years, until quite recently, when Wilson, whose official functions in Rome had since been discharged by a variety of other personnel, was formally replaced by an American 'special envoy,' a Mr. James Wilcox. This Wilcox is believed to be a career intelligence officer, now in his late sixties, who has previously served with some distinction in such capitals as Tehran, Havana, Kinshasa, Vientiane, once again in Tehran, Bangkok, Tegucigalpa. . . ."

The colonel glanced over at Aliev to make sure that the envoys had been presented with sufficient deep background before moving on to the real business of the day. "The sudden eruption onto the scene of such a personage naturally aroused our interest. At the comrade general's request, I went to South America to make contact with a number of our agents who had infiltrated militant Catholic organizations. . . ."

"Oh, yes," said Vikhalev brightly, "we're aware that the information of this network has been one of the comrade general's most impressive successes."

"That may be," Aliev replied, "but the only time we ever hear from the buggers is when they want more guns and more money. As an intelligence source, they're entirely worthless."

"It's true that my inquiries in that quarter were not very fruitful," said Akhmedov. "But as so often happens in these troublesome cases, it was right outside the lair of that old Barbary pirate Dom Mintoff on the island of Malta that we finally picked up the trail."

"He's retired from public life," explained Akimov knowledgeably, "though they still trot him out occasionally for official functions."

"I think you're burying the poor man a trifle prematurely," Aliev broke in. "It's true that he's allowed Carmelo Mitsad Bonnici to succeed him as prime minister, but his influence is still considerable. I'm convinced, for example, that he handles all negotiations with the Libyans. You'd have to be as clever as Mintoff to keep siphoning off Qaddafi's money without letting him set so much as one foot on Malta. . . . The man undoubtedly has a gift for it, also a gift for cultivating bad relations with everyone—but I'm sure Colonel Akhmedov would like to go on with the story."

"It was Dom Mintoff," Akhmedov continued, "who tipped off our ambassador in Valletta. There's nothing that happens in the whole Mediterranean basin, from Gibraltar to Tel Aviv, by way of Tripoli, that Mintoff doesn't find out about sooner or later. And when it suits him, he can be very chatty. It's curious that no one exactly trusts him, yet everyone seems to confide in him. He's the sort of person you might tell a secret to to spare the trouble of telling everyone else.

"At the end of 1984, shortly after Dom Mintoff had resigned as prime minister, he invited our ambassador to go out with him for a little deep-sea fishing—tuna is the prize game fish in those waters, and in spite of his age and the rather uncertain state of his health, Mintoff is still an avid fisherman. . . ." Aliev shot Akhmedov a warning glance, as if to imply that the background might be getting a little *too* deep, and the envoys from Moscow seemed lost in contemplation of Gorbachev's portrait, which was hanging on the opposite wall above a row of file cabinets.

"At any rate," the colonel went on, "an invitation of this kind was definitely to be regarded as an olive branch. At that particular moment, the Maltese were on the outs with Qaddafi and were casting around for a new protector and paymaster. At the same time, the Valletta government had just gotten embroiled in a controversy with the Maltese Catholic church, something having to do with public education. The Vatican came down heavily on the other side, of course, and Mintoff was still smoldering about that."

"Better get to the point, Akhmedov," Aliev said crisply. The two envoys looked on impassively, fully aware that Aliev enjoyed playing the role of the carefree, breezy autocrat, a sort of Caucasian Colonel Qaddafi, and that he and Akhmedov were merely going through a routine they had been polishing for many years, like a couple of old circus clowns.

"Very well," Akhmedov continued in a sort of gabbling, staccato voice. "What Mintoff told our ambassador was that, at the request of President Reagan, the Pentagon prepared an elaborate study of the political and geostrategic role that might be played by the Vatican, notably in the realm of global communications—"

"Again, Comrade Colonel, I must interrupt. Now that you've finally come to the point, it might be wise to stay there for a moment or two so our guests from Moscow will be able to make a *comprehensive* report to the first secretary."

"With pleasure, Comrade General. It seems that the White House's sudden interest in this arcane topic was spurred by a previous study, commissioned by the Pentagon's Institute for Defense Analyses. The contributors to this study were asked to describe what the world would be like in several years when the majority of the industrialized and the more prosperous developing countries have acquired their own direct-communication satellites. The maps that accompanied this study made it clear that the boundaries of the current spheres of influence of the superpowers were about to be radically redrawn by the forces of technological change, or, to put it another way, that the Yalta accords are soon to be rendered null and void—"

"What!" Vikhalev exclaimed.

"I'm sure the comrade colonel was only indulging in a flight of rhetorical exaggeration," said Aliev soothingly.

The comrade colonel was busily polishing his glasses with a handkerchief he had pulled out of an inner pocket of his tunic. Clearly, such moments were all too infrequent in his career. All the good lines generally fell to Aliev. "I merely meant," he went on, "that the proliferation of these satellites is going to have an enormous impact on the world's political boundaries. At first, the system of alliances and power blocs will remain just as it is, but the real stability of this system will be considerably eroded. In fact, the authors of the Pentagon study went so far as to conclude that the nation-state as we know it would actually wither away, to be replaced by a very different sort of a creature altogether, for which they have coined the term *logical state*. . . . Now this hypothesis, while not fully in accordance with the tenets of Marxism-Leninism—"

"And of course you're only talking about the *capitalist* countries now," put in Akimov hastily.

The colonel made a sweeping gesture, as if to relegate all such doctrinal niceties to the dustbin of history. "Traditionally," he said, "a nation of any kind has been a mosaic cemented together by the state, which strives to accommodate the interest of each particular racial, religious, cultural, and of course *economic* group, as far as it is consistent with the greater good of the community. That, at any rate, is the way it's supposed to be. A *logical state*, on the other hand, is an assemblage of individuals who already share the same interests and aspirations, who subscribe to the same values and are acting toward a common purpose, wherever they might be found on the planet. *Wherever* they might be found, comrades—but still acting in concert to carry out the same political program, or to follow the same directives from on high, if it came to that. Do you begin to see the point?"

Neither Akimov nor Vikhalev showed any signs of failing to see the point, but Akhmedov went on anyway. "Today, the citizens of these logical states are dispersed all over the surface of the globe, sometimes isolated. Take the example of the world's fifteen million Jews—one that's figured very prominently in our propaganda over the years. There are three and a half million Jews in Israel, another six million in the United States, three million here in the Soviet Union, another couple of hundred thousand in the people's republics, perhaps a million and a half in Western Europe, and a couple of hundred thousand here and there all over the rest of the world.

"This famous Diaspora is the one thing that keeps those Zionist plots, if any, from becoming a reality. However, a single communications satellite could conceivably weld these scattered communities into a single logical nation, which would occupy a single logical space—as the terminology has it—irrespective of their geographical separation from one another. All you'd need is a transmitter, an antenna, and a fraction of a second to transmit a piece of information, a message, or an order, to the citizens of this Jewish—or Armenian, Muslim, Communist—logical state all over the world."

"We simply wouldn't permit the Zionists, or the Armenians for that matter, to beam their transmissions toward our territory," said Vikhalev.

"Very likely," said Akhmedov, "but nothing could prevent them from broadcasting in such a way that a very sophisticated antenna that was operating clandestinely in our territory could intercept the very fringe of the transmission."

"But you still need to have the antenna," interjected Akimov, "and some sort of special television set as well, I would expect."

"How many years will it be before the possession of a satellite-dish antenna *and* a television set equipped with a signal decoder will be new high-status staples for the comrades of our *nomenklatura*? I'd say ten at the most—about the amount of time it will take for the Japanese to start turning them out at a price that even we can afford. Just like the Beatles, the Walkman, those little electronic calculators. The ayatollah found it easy enough to walk right into power after twenty years of exile, and after a couple of million cassette tapes of his speeches had been smuggled into the country to serve as his reactionary vanguard. And with something like this, there'll be no way we can close our borders to the intruder."

"Why couldn't we simply jam their broadcasts with a powerful transmission of our own?"

"If we did," said Akhmedov, "we'd be jamming our own internal television broadcasts as well, since most of the frequencies we use are identical to those assigned to certain Western states by the ITU. There'd be no way of undoing these arrangements without causing considerable tension—and, in effect, bringing the situation out in the open. . . ."

"And what about the Vatican, Comrade General?" asked Vikhalev. "So far we've been discussing Malta, the Jews, the ayatollah, and television sets. You'd better tell us what the Vatican has to do with all of this."

"First," said Colonel Akhmedov, a little stiffly, "I thought it was important to develop this concept of the logical state—a supranational community that bears some resemblance to those nations that have been dispersed by historical forces but which have preserved their national identity—in order to convey some idea of what a terrible threat this idea can represent. . . . What we are faced with here is not just the usual sort of problems of social adjustment that arrive in the wake of any new technology. This represents a serious threat to the basis of all civilized societies, to the most essential ties between individuals that are represented by the authority of the state—"

"I think our friends have taken your point, Akhmedov," interposed Aliev, "but what they're interested in hearing about now is the Vatican."

"I was just getting to that," said the colonel. "To summarize, then, these various studies commissioned by the Pentagon converged on a unified vision of the future, of the political landscape of our planet as it very well may be in the year 2000."

Akimov sat bolt upright in his chair and gave a little shudder, as if someone was trying to make him swallow a spoonful of some particularly nauseating substance. "You mean to tell me that this is all about some sort of science-fiction *simulation* or *scenario*? That sort of thing is nothing but internal propaganda. I'm astounded that you could be capable of taking it seriously! They have several thousand so-called specialists churning it out for the State Department and the Pentagon, all very adept at proving why more millions should be appropriated for more preposterous simulations and scenarios." While his colleague sat red-faced and seemingly exasperated beyond further words, Vikhalev returned to his careful contemplation of the portrait of Gorbachev on the opposite wall.

"Colonel Akhmedov," said Aliev after a brief pause, "it's clear that you've expressed yourself poorly. Our guests seem to think that we're in the habit of killing flies with a bazooka. Perhaps you'd better try a different approach."

Akhmedov opened one of his folders and brought out a photograph, which he slid across the table to the two visitors from Moscow. "This man is called Father Nicholas Resaccio," he said. "Likewise Professor Resaccio—a priest, a Jesuit, a computer specialist, a passenger on board AF-270, occupied a seat in the first-class cabin next to the American envoy, James Wilcox, who was also on board that flight. Father Resaccio was carrying with him two highly confidential documents, one of which contained a detailed abstract and analysis of the two Pentagon studies of which Comrade Akimov appears to have such a poor opinion. This was addressed to Father Giuseppe Pitta, Jesuit provincial of Japan. The other document contained Father Resaccio's personal instructions—issued under the signature of John Paul himself—which confirmed that the massive destabilization campaign that we first got wind of from Dom Mintoff was, as they undoubtedly say in the Vatican, about to come to pass.

"The fragmented future society envisioned in these studies is evidently regarded, by the Vatican and by the more temporal powers of the West, as a consummation *devoutly* to be wished—a kind of TV millennium in which there will be no room for the principles of democratic centralism, or centralism of any kind, in which the bourgeois-individualist sheep will ascend ever upward while the poor old collectivist goats will be obliged to take the downward path. Or, to put it in more familiar terms, the Americans have the idea that just as the past decades were dominated by energy and transportation, the decades to come will be dominated by communications; the distances between cities and nations have already been vastly diminished, and now we are on the verge of abolishing them altogether. This TV apocalypse that our adversaries are already preparing—or should I say girding their loins?—for is none other than the age of instantaneity—"

"In any case," said Vikhalev, "you'd think that as the largest country in the world, which has probably spent a greater percentage of our energies surmounting these barriers of climate, terrain, and distance, you'd think that we'd have the most to gain from the age of instantaneous communication—it would be as if a terrible handicap we'd been struggling with all this time were suddenly removed and we were free to go toe to toe with the other fellow on our own terms. . . ."

Akhmedov merely shook his head—whether at Vikhalev's political naïveté or at the homeliness of his rhetoric was not clear—and picked up his discourse where he had left off. "When the authors of the first Pentagon study tried to represent what they imagined would be the effects of this proliferation of telecommunications satellites and fifth-generation computers in graphic terms, they arrived at this projection—literally a planar projection of the globe envisioned as an overlapping patchwork of logical states—in which, as you'll see in a moment, the regions of least and greatest political stability and instability are defined in terms of a series of *telematic poles*. . . ."

After these mystifying words of explanation, the mystification of the visitors from Moscow was only increased by the sight of the multicolored chart that Akhmedov slid across the table to them, emblazoned with the eagle-headed emblem of the CIA and the bold printed legend TOP SECRET—DEFENSE. The "map" was composed of a complex geometric construction, which looked like nothing more than a kaleidoscope pattern or perhaps the rose window of a cathedral. Five partially overlapping petals had been inscribed inside a slightly deformed circle (slightly broader at the bottom than at the top); a pentagon had been inscribed inside the circle, its center more or less at the center of the circle.

Each of the five vertices of the pentagon had been provided with a label—*Liberal Democracy, Judeo-Christian Tradition, Marxism, China, Japan*—and the bottom three vertices had been flipped over to provide a sixth point inside the pentagon that was labeled *Islam*. To further complicate matters, three contiguous pairs of vertices had each been chosen as the focus of an ellipse—making four in all, two of which had been drawn in with a solid line, two with a dotted line. The diagram was descriptively, if not very helpfully, labeled THE TELEMATIC PLANISPHERE.

"To think that we came all the way from Moscow for this," muttered Akimov in a voice that was clearly audible across the table. The colonel, as usual, took no notice and went on with his recital.

"The overlapping zone divisions on the telematic map attempt to represent both the sources and principal points of impact of those factors that can be described as *immaterial*—the information transmitted by satellites, computer programs, plus the more traditional vehicles of human culture, the world heritage of religion, ideology, and tradition, this informational ebb and flow that laps like a great ocean against the most distant shores of our planet. The projection is based on the assumption that the inhabitants of the more advanced regions of the globe are already able to make their own selection from the ideals and values on display in this televised marketplace and thus, in effect, to offer their primary allegiance to a *logical state*, a supranational community of like-minded individuals, rather than to the nation-state in which they happen to reside. I should mention—and this is a very important point—that the obvious language problems involved in such an undertaking would be at least partially resolved by the simultaneous-translation capabilities of this latest generation of computers. . . ."

Akimov was fidgeting in his chair, though without quite being able to commit himself to another verbal outburst. Aliev smiled to himself; perhaps Mikhail Sergeyevich's emissaries, in spite of their best efforts, were beginning to get the point.

"Each of the ellipses marked on the map represents what the Americans have chosen to call a *logical continent*, a region of the globe, not necessarily contiguous, which shares a similar orientation toward the twin foci of politics and religion. The premise is that an individual's cultural environment is defined by the preponderant influence of two of these, so that we have an ellipse drawn around the foci labeled *Liberal Democracy* and the *Judeo-Christian Tradition*, which roughly corresponds to the West, likewise *Liberal Democracy* and *Islam*—not a very extensive continent at the moment—*Marxism* and the *Judeo-Christian Tradition*, which seems to make for a very harmonious blend in a country like Romania, far less so in a country like Poland. . . ."

"I see that the fellows who drew this chart left plenty of room for the Jews and the liberals and the Japanese, but I'm afraid I don't quite see where we fit into all this." This was from Vikhalev, who was stabbing impatiently at the map with a wizened index finger.

"That's precisely the problem," Akhmedov replied. "Our logical continent is actually composed of three separate sociocultural plates, if you will, with *Marxism* at one pole, of course, and *Judeo-Christian Tradition*, *Islam*, and *China* at each of the others. The fellows who drew this chart were merely taking note of something that we've all had good reason to be aware of in recent years, and that's the revival of interest in religion, in all religions, throughout the Soviet Union. Of our two hundred and fifty million citizens, over half are either Christians or Muslims; there are currently twice as many *practicing* Orthodox Christians as there are Party members, and forty percent of the children in Moscow are being baptized these days.

"Clearly our two million Buddhists, like our three million Jews, have a significance far beyond what their numbers would suggest, since no one can deny that a great many of the inhabitants of our eastern territories have their eyes firmly fixed on China. That's what all this is really about." He tapped the stack of documents that was lying in front of him on the table. "The Americans are determined to exploit this religious revival for all they can, especially since recent events, in Poland for instance, have shown how easy it is for a believer, when confronted with vigorous opposition, to turn into a fanatic. They also place a great deal of confidence in their little band of archangels—I mean the ones that are hovering up above in geosynchronous orbit—and their ability to weld these scattered communities of believers into a powerful political faction, something on the order of what the so-called electronic ministry has achieved in the United States."

"But there," Akimov objected, "they have a government favorably disposed toward that sort of thing, which we definitely do not. You haven't really explained how these 'scattered communities' are going to get hold of these sophisticated electronics and how they're going to use them without our knowledge and consent. . . ."

"That's all right here," answered Akhmedov, not without complacency, "in this envelope, the second of the two envelopes that Nicholas Resaccio was carrying with him to Tokyo." He produced a reproduction of the second chart, identical in outline to THE TELEMATIC PLANISPHERE but filled with intricate cross-hatchings that were explained in a key below the drawing. Here the title read RELATIVE STABILITY OF LOGICAL STATES.

"As we've just noted," said Akhmedov, "the authors of this study have also assumed that there is a high correlation between political instability and sociocultural 'overlap,' repesented graphically in this case by the overlapping of the various geometric figures on the graph—in other words, those areas where there are a number of conflicting ideologies competing for the loyalty of the individual. The regions of the highest stability—Level One as it's called here—are those, like China and Japan and much of the industrialized West, where the only apparent tensions are those between the two poles of the traditional values of the region and the prevailing political ideology—liberal democracy in the case of Japan, Marxism in the case of China.

"Next, we have Level Two, as in South America, where the situation is slightly more complicated; here, we have Christianity on the one hand, and a conflict between Marxism and liberal democracy (or possibly among all three) on the other. We ourselves are on Level Three, where the situation is still more complex, not to say critical, and so on until we come to a place like Lebanon, where we have a fivefold cultural

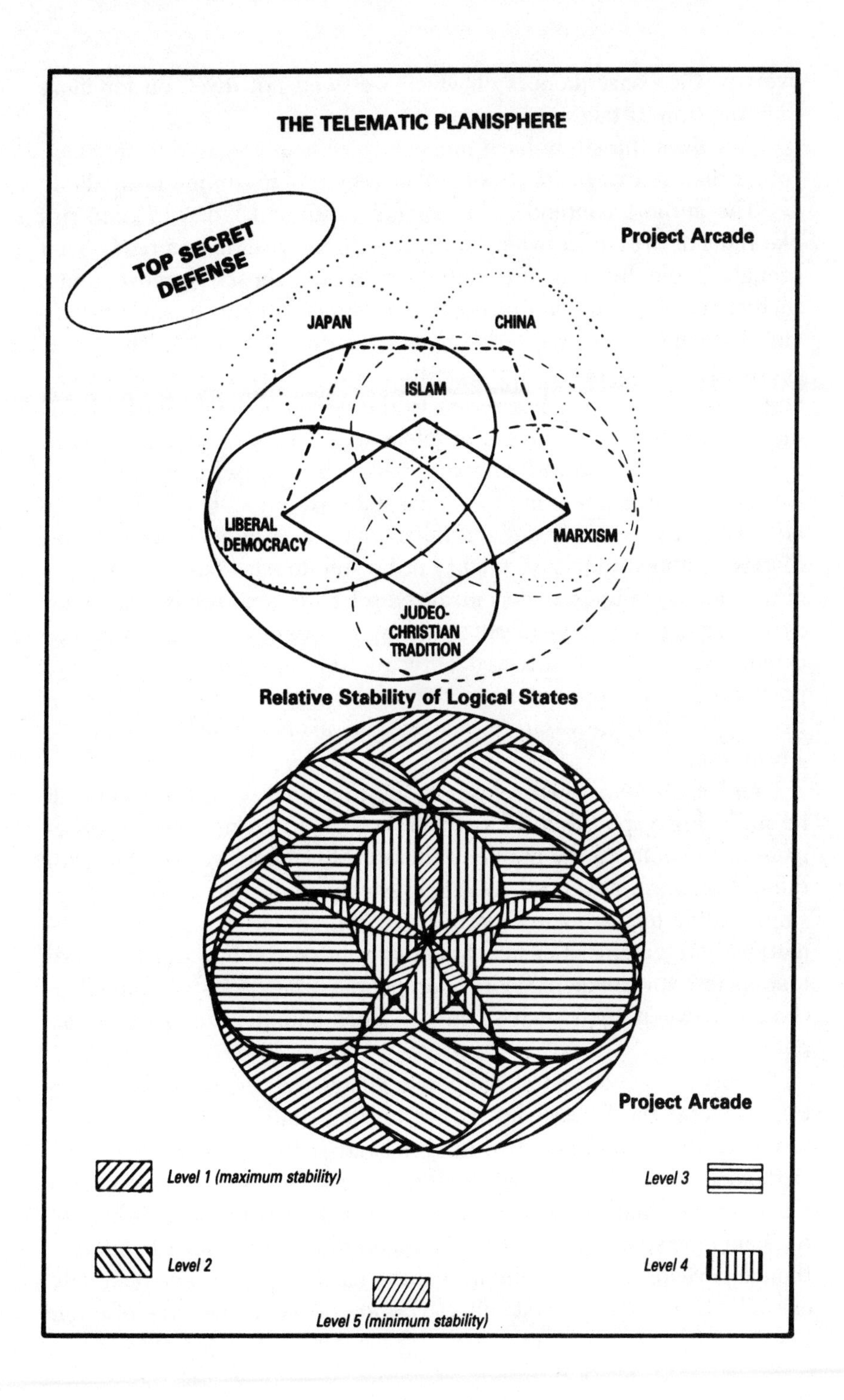
THE TELEMATIC PLANISPHERE
TOP SECRET
DEFENSE
Project Arcade
JAPAN
CHINA
ISLAM
LIBERAL
DEMOCRACY
MARXISM
JUDEO-
CHRISTIAN
TRADITION
Relative Stability of Logical States
Project Arcade
Level 1 (maximum stability)
Level 3
Level 2
Level 4
Level 5 (minimum stability)

overlap, the consequences of which we need not dwell on for more than the time it takes to mention it. . . ."

"Nor does the study have much to say about India," put in Aliev, "other than to categorize it as another region of maximum instability."

"The authors contend," the colonel continued, "that in countries like India or Sri Lanka, where several political crises have already been brought about by religious conflicts or ethnic separatist movements, such crises may only be exacerbated as direct satellite broadcasts provide local minorities with a stronger sense of cohesion—assuming of course that they choose to regard themselves as an extension of some larger community that has access to these facilities. Obviously this is much more likely to prove a problem with Catholics and Baptists in our own country than with militant Sikhs or Naga headhunters in India.

"The threat is that a multinational state like ours, which could only be created by the powerful centralizing forces of industrialization and Marxist-Leninist ideology, might not be able to withstand the stresses of this new age of highly decentralized telecommunications, *telematics* as the jargon has it. If the loyalties and aspirations of a significant number of our people are all directed outward, this automatically creates a powerful internal opposition to the sort of highly centralized system that is absolutely necessary to manage the affairs of a nation as vast as a continent.

"And if the individual refuses to act in solidarity with the state, if he shirks his responsibilities as a worker and citizen in order to participate in the cultural life of one of these artificial enclaves created with the aid of these advanced satellite systems, then our Soviet state is simply going to shatter into dozens, possibly hundreds, of counterrevolutionary fragments. I'm sure I needn't remind you how quickly these tendencies can develop among our people when they are forced to choose between their own spiritual values and the authority of the state.

"Perhaps you've read of the whole villages of Old Believers in the time of Peter the Great who set fire to their houses, with themselves inside of course, and perished in agony rather than accept the revised Orthodox prayer book in which the name of Jesus was spelled in a different way than the one they were accustomed to. The authors of the Pentagon study seem to have had something very similar in mind—though perhaps they were unaware that such a useful precedent already existed. 'During the forced collectivization of the 1930s,' one of them writes, 'the kulaks rose in rebellion because Stalin wanted to take their little garden plots away from them. In the 1990s, it may be the entire nation that rebels if the Soviet authorities are forced to confiscate their prayer rugs and the icon hanging in the corner of the room.' "

Akimov shrugged his shoulders, to make it clear he was not necessarily impressed by Colonel Akhmedov's daring ascent into the higher reaches of strategic planning. "It seems to me, Comrade Colonel, that as the old expression has it, what is true in all this is not necessarily new and what is new is not necessarily true. It's obvious enough that there's always going to be conflict between state power and religious fanaticism, and the West is always going to use these anti-Soviet elements, like the Zionists or the Siberian Baptists, as pawns in their propaganda struggle against us. And it also seems incredible that in the real world, as opposed to some professor's 'projection' or 'scenario,' things could ever be permitted to go that far. . . ."

"Read the *conclusion* of the report, why don't you, Comrade Colonel?" said Aliev.

This time, with no preliminary wiping of lenses or shuffling of papers, Akhmedov plunged into his text. " 'Every month,' " he read, " 'new geostationary satellites will be injected into orbit, at a rate that, though closely monitored by the ITU,* will undoubtedly continue to accelerate. The content of the broadcasts themselves will necessarily be, implicitly or explicitly, political; in the context of a radically different political or cultural context, they will quite correctly be construed as aggressive assaults on the integrity of that culture or polity.

" 'This conjures up the idea of an international race to develop a sophisticated battery of *ideological* weapons that we will all have to reckon with in the future, and for which, needless to say, the appropriate countermeasures will have to be devised. In the future, these informational weapons, both offensive and defensive, will have to stand beside our present alphabetic array of ABC weapons† in the arsenal of every nation that is eager to protect not only its terrestrial, maritime, and aerial but also its "informational" borders from the depredations of aggressive neighbors or its ideological adversaries.' "

**International Telecommunications Union:* Direct descendant of an organization founded in 1865 to standardize and regulate an international system of telegraphy, its mandate later broadened to include the telephone (1885), radiotelegraph (1906), radiotelephone (1927), and telecommunications satellite (1977). The ITU is now an agency of the United Nations.

†ABC weapons: Atomic, biological, and chemical weapons.

Akhmedov stopped reading and riffled through the next couple of pages. "I'll skip over the technical background to get right to the heart of the matter," he announced dramatically, and then, rather less dramatically, continued reading. " 'The evidence suggests that, as far as we in the West are concerned, the best strategy for the defense of our own informational borders would involve the cultivation of closer relations, in effect, between the two logical poles designated *Liberal Democracy* and the *Judeo-Christian Tradition* on the accompanying chart. In spite of credible challenges to the economic supremacy of the West—mounted first by the OPEC countries, more recently by the Japanese—it seems that a far more serious threat of destabilization exists in the realm of personal values and beliefs than in that of mass politics.

" 'Far from being the rock on which our civilization was founded—the main cohesive force which enabled it, contrary to the prediction of Marx and others, to survive the shocks and tremors of the Industrial Revolution—this *ideological* pole would now seem to require considerable shoring up, and free peoples everywhere stand desperately in need of a common moral standard and a shared vision of the future, possibly the only things that will enable our civilization to survive the current crisis.

" 'While we are hardly suggesting that the Vatican is the *only* rock on which we should build our church, it is certainly worth noting that Roman Catholicism remains the sturdiest of all Christian denominations, with respect to both the number (and extremely broad geographical distribution) of its adherents and the solidity of its organizational structure.

" 'It is also the only Christian sect that is headed by a man of genuine charisma, in the purest sense of that term, as well an international media celebrity. A man whose *image* and *voice* can not only draw crowds, but move multitudes. A man who, with the assistance of the appropriate communications infrastructure, may not only enable us to guarantee the integrity of our own ideological frontiers but even to move over to the offensive in the coming ideological conflict that we have described in the previous pages.' "

Akhmedov raised his eyes from the printed page. "The Vatican has its own satellite," he said, "but the Americans have since decided that that would hardly be sufficient for what they have in mind, and in any case, its broadcast area would hardly have extended beyond the frontiers of Italy. Instead, the Americans are planning to ask each of the

Western allies to reserve one of its assigned satellite frequencies for the use of the Vatican. This is what is meant by 'the appropriate communications infrastructure'—in fact, nothing less than a global communications network conceived with no other purpose than to enlist the world's seven hundred million Catholics, and millions of other believers of other denominations, as loyal subjects of this ancient, militant 'logical state.' "

"The Vatican City State is the smallest country in the world," said Aliev, "but if this project succeeds, it may end up as the capital of the largest and most powerful of these logical states. Comrades, if Stalin were alive today, he wouldn't ask how many divisions does the pope have, but how many satellite channels."

Even this amusing topical variation on an old and venerable anecdote failed to raise a smile on the faces of the envoys from Moscow. "I know," said Aliev, "that all of this must still seem a little disconcerting, even, as Comrade Akimov has said, fantastic. I can tell from your reactions that you are still not fully aware of the seriousness of the stakes in this matter. Nevertheless, everything suggests that Mr. Reagan is taking this very seriously indeed; copies of these two Pentagon studies have been dispatched to the appropriate departments of all the Western governments."

"Obviously," chimed in Akhmedov, "Dom Mintoff is not included on the normal distribution list for strategically sensitive material, but he was able to take advantage, as he usually does, of an indiscretion on someone's part. We have also learned that Mr. Reagan's proposal has been accorded a remarkably respectful hearing by his European allies—especially remarkable for an American defense initiative of such an unconventional character, which thus far has provoked neither howls of protest, like the Pershing missile, nor peals of undisguised merriment, like the Star Wars proposal. . . ."

"In other words," said Aliev, "they seem to have an idea that it just might work. That brings us to the question of ways and means, and to the contents of Father Resaccio's *second* envelope." He smiled a thin smile. "It may seem incredible to you that we've been talking all this time and hardly said a word about it." He nodded to Akhmedov, who held up for their inspection a slim folder with a red cover inscribed with a single line of print that read PROJECT ARCADE.

Faremoutiers
October 10

They were walking slowly around the tiny cloister, with Mother Marie-Bernadette taking two steps for every one of Wendy's. Wendy's head was bent slightly forward, as if she was straining to hear, but at the moment the mother superior was quiet, preoccupied with her own thoughts. After discussing a few of the practical details of Wendy's departure from the abbey, she had lapsed into silence, and indeed the dark-gray, moist-looking stones of the cloister were not a great stimulus to conversation.

Wendy felt both anxious and excited; a pulse was pounding in her temples, and it was almost painful to her to be walking in silence, with such tiny, mincing steps. She felt like a Chinese slave girl with bound feet or a convict dragging his ball and chain. She was almost convinced by now that something had gone wrong, that her application had been rejected. She could think of innumerable reasons why this might have been so—the only question was how many of these, if any, might have come to the attention of the Pontifical Academy of Sciences in Rome. And if not, there was always the danger that she might be summoned—ordered—to go to Rome immediately and would have to give up her trip to Tokyo, which would be no less catastrophic.

Finally, Mother Marie-Bernadette removed several folded sheets of paper from the depths of her wide black sleeve, unfolded them carefully, and glanced over them for a moment, slowing her steps even more as she did so. "This is a letter, for you," she said. "It was forwarded to me by the diocesan offices at Meaux. It was they who were kind enough to bring your application to the attention of the academy." She looked at Wendy very closely, but without giving her the letter.

"I know nothing of all this, you understand, but it seems that you've been asked to take part in a very important project. All I know is that it will be your duty to prove yourself worthy of the trust that others have placed in you, that you go with our blessings—or we would not have sent off such an excellent recommendation—of course that we expect to hear very good things of you, though I must say we hear very little of the news from Rome around this part of the world."

"But I'll write to you, *ma mère*, and tell you about it. . . ."

The mother superior smiled. "As I'm sure you would, my child, but I was forgetting that quite soon that won't even be necessary. This letter tells me that you are to take part"—she glanced back at the folded sheets of paper in what Wendy took to be a practiced pantomime of unworldliness and forgetfulness—"in the design and installation of an ultramodern telecommunications network. I suppose that soon enough all the world will be hearing of your exploits, and in any case, why take the trouble to write a letter when I'm sure you'll be able to push a button of some sort."

"I have the feeling that you don't precisely approve of all this, *ma mère*."

"It's not for me to approve or disapprove, my child. I don't think I should say any more about it, since I prefer you didn't remember me as an ignorant, reactionary old woman—which is what I undoubtedly am. . . . I'm sure the Church stands to benefit a great deal from these developments. They tell me that every diocese will be able to communicate directly with the Vatican and that this will only increase the authority of the Holy Father throughout the world. It's what they call the 'permanent ecumenical council,' if you can imagine such a thing." Mother Marie-Bernadette handed the pages over to Wendy with a weary gesture. There was a brief covering letter followed by three more pages of closely printed text; Wendy's eye was immediately struck by the phrase "Project Arcade—Not to be Copied—Most Confidential" that appeared at the top of these pages.

The mother superior gave her a dry smile. "It seems that your new employers are counting on your complete discretion in this matter. They'll be expecting you in Rome in the middle of November; the letter will tell you all about it. . . . I suppose you're still planning on going to Tokyo?"

"Oh yes, *ma mère*."

"To play that beautiful game of yours, is that it?"

"For the Japanese go championships, as you well know, *ma mère*. There'll be players from all over the world, and I've been chosen to represent the Irish federation—not a very formidable group of players, to be sure, but it's still a chance I've been waiting for for at least three years."

"I understand that this is very important to you. . . . And I think we're both forgetting that you're no longer a postulant at Faremoutiers—you no longer have to seek my approval or my consent. You must go where your spirit calls you, my child—Mlle Keenes as I must remember to call you now. . . ."

"But I shall always remain your obedient daughter, *ma mère.*"

Just then, a nun appeared at the entrance to the little courtyard; she glided toward them and, when Mother Marie-Bernadette nodded for her to speak, she explained to Wendy that a young man had brought an urgent letter for her. "He said he'd wait for an answer," she added before gliding away again.

"Bad news?" asked the mother superior after Wendy had torn open the envelope and read the few lines on the note inside.

"I'm afraid so, *ma mère*. It's a friend of mine, a professor at Compiègne. . . . His father's just died; it says the funeral's today, at Coulommiers. . . . I wonder, do you suppose—"

"Certainly, my child. You must go at once. Though I must say it's a little peculiar of this young man to come routing you out at the last possible moment like this . . . but that comes of his being a professor, I suppose. . . ."

Wendy bobbed her head and kissed the hand that Mother Marie-Bernadette extended to her, seemingly with some reluctance, then hurried off to the visitors' parlor. She found Michael waiting for her, staring out of one of the high grilled windows. When he heard her soft footsteps on the carpet, he wheeled around to face her; he made no attempt to conceal his astonishment.

"You must be out of your mind! I thought just a word or two—one word would have done quite well. There was no need for a personal appearance—"

"Never mind about that now," she said. "I have to go back to your place to pick up a few things. There's nothing more for me here. We can talk in the car. You're supposed to be taking me to your father's funeral in case anyone should mention it."

For the first time they walked out to the Peugeot together, in broad daylight. Michael looked haggard, as if he hadn't been sleeping well; his cheeks and eye sockets were hollow, and he kept shooting furtive, almost fearful glances at Wendy as they walked down the drive in silence. When they reached the car, Michael said to her, his face twisted as if he wanted to scream out the words, "And after all these months of slinking around like thieves, you're ready to chuck it, just like that?"

"I told you, it's finished for me. Do you expect me to sit here and molder—and I mean that quite literally—while you're lolling about like a cannibal king on your island in the sun?"

When they were driving along the Route du Compiègne, she asked suddenly, "Is your da really dead then?"

"Yes, he had a heart attack."

"That was his specialty, wasn't it?"

"He was a heart surgeon, if that's what you mean. . . . He collapsed in his clinic in Valletta as a matter of fact, fifty feet from the operating room. There was nothing that could be done."

"It's crazy, something like that happening, isn't it?"

"Nice of you to pretend that you actually give a fuck."

"For God's sake, Michael, don't be like that." She squeezed his arm. "Why don't you tell me about him. . . . Did you favor him very much—were you very much alike, I mean?"

"Not really. He was a local notable, something of a big shot, one of those larger-than-life personalities; he had a constant parade of VIPs and cabinet ministers through his surgery, and not all of them came to have their EKGs taken."

"What were his politics exactly?"

"Exactly is not the way we do things on Malta. I think he preferred the socialists, but only socially—Dom Mintoff always called him 'my dear good friend'—and as far as I know he invariably voted for the nationalists. *That's* the way we do things on Malta. . . . I liked him. He was a remarkable man. He never lost an argument, particularly with me—that, as I recall, was one of the main reasons why I left Malta."

"And what will you do now? Stay on and look after the clinic?"

"That's what he would have wanted, of course, though I'm not exactly sure it's what I want at this particular stage of my life. Still, it's what I feel I *ought* to do, and I suppose that for the time being that will have to suffice. . . ."

They drove along in silence for several minutes, Michael taking nervous, deep drags on a cigarette, the ashes of which were soon scattered all over the front of his shirt. "About these few things, that we're going back to get I mean, there's nothing specially fragile or irreplaceable I hope. . . ."

"No, not really. Why?"

"Well, the fact is that I haven't been having a very good week, so far at least. I had the burglars in. They did a very thorough job—one would have thought it was the Gestapo, except they were in a BMW instead of a Mercedes."

"You saw them?"

"Just as they were leaving. It was right after the last time I drove you back to the abbey. They really ransacked the place—tore open the sofa cushions, slashed the mattresses—but they don't seem to have taken much of anything. . . ."

Wendy's face was dead white, with two bright spots of color just below her cheekbones. "What do you mean 'ransacked the place'?"

"I mean that they were clearly looking for something, and they kept at it for as long as time pemitted. . . . I don't suppose you could shed any light on this murky business?"

Wendy slumped back against the seat, making a kind of sibilant whistling sound between her teeth. "Are you all right, love?" asked Michael.

"Be quiet now. . . . I'll tell you in a minute."

Michael had long since been conditioned out of the habit of asking direct questions, but now he found it impossible to resist. "And while you're waiting, try thinking about what we're going to do, the two of us I mean, as an entity. . . . If I stay on in Valletta, where are you going to be?"

"I'll be in Rome—even though Sister Wendy is no more. No more of those romantic moonlight flits, no more midnight drives, but perhaps we'll be able to work out some other arrangement. Tell me about this burglary of ours—are you sure nothing was taken, for example?"

"Nothing that belongs to me—which includes £5,000 in cash, I might add. . . . They must have been real up-market criminals to look down their noses at something like that. Is there anything of yours there that might have interested them more—the plans of Maggie Thatcher's next holiday hotel at the seaside? A nice fresh batch of gelignite perhaps? A passbook for the IRA's Swiss bank account? Exclusive videotapes of Tim Finnegan's wake?"

Michael seemed very manic, even slightly unhinged, and it was clear that he was not joking. Wendy flirted briefly with the notion of telling the truth, then decided to take refuge in one of her typical evasions. "Just some things of mine, I told you." Then they both lapsed into uneasy silence for the rest of the drive.

As soon as the car had come to a stop in front of the cottage in the forest, Wendy made a dash for the front door. The broken lock had still not been fixed. Michael had wedged the door shut with a few scraps of wood, and Wendy tugged on the wrought-iron latch with all her might and sent them flying. By the time Michael caught up with her, in the big downstairs room, she was kneeling by the hearth, rummaging through the mossy-looking old chest where Michael kept firewood and kindling and a great many items of miscellaneous debris that he could not quite bring himself to throw away.

A moment later, she had upended this venerable article of furniture and discharged its contents all over the goatskins in front of the hearth—a couple of logs, a cloud of sawdust and fragments of bark, a pair of blue jeans stiff with paint, an Air France traveling bag, a disintegrating straw mat, yellowing back numbers of the *Guardian*, the desiccated corpses of a pair of running shoes. . . .

"It took me at least three days to get this place tidied up the last time!"

"You're a great one for accumulating old rubbish, you know," she replied, trying—rather idiotically under the circumstances—to make her voice sound casual as she took the lid off a crumpled cardboard box that had been lying flat at the bottom of the chest and was now on top of the heap. The box was empty.

Everything was gone. Everything that Abdul had given her, the instructions for her trip to Tokyo, the detailed dossier on the man she was supposed to contact there. Michael was wandering around the room, prodding with one foot at various objects that she had tossed back over her shoulder in the initial stages of her search, trying very hard, she imagined, not to walk over and send her sprawling with a single well-placed kick. "Now that that's over with," he finally said, "can I possibly know what this is all about?"

"No, you can't," she said. "I'm sorry, Michael, I just can't tell you. Listen, I'll take care of everything, like I did the other time. Remember, I was the one who brought us back together again."

"I do remember. But that was then, and this is now. I don't even know if you just found what you were looking for, or if they did. . . ." He bent down and picked up a scrap of paper that had lodged behind the folds of the decayed straw mat. "Has this got something to do with it, by any chance?"

It was a photograph that had been clipped from an Italian newspaper; a photograph of some official function at the Vatican. The name of one of the guests of honor, "S. Eccellenza James Wilcox," the American envoy to the Holy See, had been circled with a red pencil; the face of one of the others in attendance, a priest, had been circled with an arrow pointing to a name that was printed in the margin: N. Resaccio.

"Give that to me," said Wendy fiercely. Michael reluctantly complied. He did not especially feel like fighting over a scrap of paper, not that this seemed any less absurd than a number of other things that had happened in his life lately.

"Our friends, like you, seem to have an aversion to accumulating bits of old rubbish."

"Nevertheless, they got what they wanted," Wendy replied. "I can assure you that they found more than enough to satisfy them." The bleak despair in her voice suddenly reminded him how entirely separate their lives were. She had reacted to the news of his father's death with the sort of polite simulation of interest that people normally assume when their friends are recounting their dreams, and the frenzied search through the wood box, which to him had all the elements of knockabout domestic farce, was to her a tragedy—if the newspaper clipping really had something to do with it—of international proportions. And now their physical separation, the one enduring constant in their life together, was going to resume, with him on Malta and Wendy in Tokyo or Rome or God knew where. . . .

Wendy got up, walked over to him, and clutched at his arm. Michael put his arms around her and drew her to him; she opened her eyes wide, surprised by the violence of his embrace.

4

Tokyo
October 31

What a curious species we are, thought Wendy. *They've all come to watch the* gaijin *playing go—playing* at *go is the way they probably think of it—just the way the English would turn out to watch a Martian mixed-doubles team at Wimbledon.* At the moment they were all taking part in a simultaneous match being held in an enormous room on the second floor of the Imperial Hotel. Their opponent was to be Father Nicholas Resaccio, one of the best-rated foreign players in the world, who had recently distinguished himself by an upset victory over a couple of Japanese and Korean masters at a tournament in Rome.

This was not an exhibition match, strictly speaking, since those who acquitted themselves well against Father Resaccio would be permitted to compete in the elimination rounds of the Japanese amateur championship. The nine other foreign players present were French, German, English, and Dutch; Wendy was the only representative of her sex and nation (as a Republican, she preferred to play, however badly, on behalf of all of Ireland, not just the Six Counties).

Father Resaccio had been assigned a different handicap for each of his opponents, according to their *kyu*, or formal ranking in the hierarchy of the game. In Wendy's case, this amounted to the maximum handicap of nine stones, which had been placed on her *go-ban* before the competitors filed into the hall. She had a slightly irrational feeling of having been slighted, on account of both her sex and her nation, but was forced to concede that the organizers of the tournament could not possibly be aware, especially on the basis of her rather spotty record in official match play, that all her most brilliant games had been played against herself. And besides, this fell in very well with her objective of upsetting—though possibly not in the sense of "scoring an upset victory over"—one of the few fifth *dan* players from outside Japan.

The decor of the hall was elegant, the lighting hushed and decorous, the Japanese spectators hardly less so as they followed Father Resaccio from one table to the next, sometimes emitting an appreciative murmur as another stone took its place on the *go-ban* with a dry little click. She felt slightly sheepish that she had almost failed to recognize her quarry when she was finally confronted with him. In his photographs—including a few better-quality newsmagazine photos in the wake of the temporary disappearance of AF-270—he seemed stiff and self-conscious, a little severe, like a terrorist or an unsuccessful artist in a passport picture. In person, he was disarmingly attractive; he looked a great deal younger than she had expected and surprisingly "worldly," as Mother Marie-Bernadette would have said, in his tailored gray suit, black turtleneck, and lustrous Italian shoes.

As far as she could tell, she had made no initial impression on him whatsoever; a two-hour clock was running on the match, and a player who was expected to dispose of ten opponents in two hours, even simultaneously, would have been ill advised to linger over the opening moves. It occurred to her that a player in this situation, striding rapidly from one board to the next, playing coldly and automatically and surrounded by a worshipful little entourage, would have some difficulty in *not* appearing arrogant and self-absorbed. She decided to file these reflections away in one small corner of her mind, since the rest was urgently required by the search for some brilliant, or merely astounding, strategy that would make him start to take notice.

As the match progressed, and the young priest began to stop and consider his moves for a minute or two, Wendy stood patiently waiting her turn at the last board but one. By now, she had acquired a modest entourage of her own, a very old man with a wispy white beard who stared at her intently as she made her play, then either squeezed his eyes shut very tight or opened them up very wide. It did not take very long to figure out that the first of these was a sign of contentment and approval, the second a sign of disapproval and disbelief. The instantaneousness of these reactions seemed to suggest a considerable familiarity with the game, perhaps, judging solely by his appearance, the better part of a century.

She had finally decided on a defensive maneuver called *hasami* to repel the attack launched by black along the right side of the board. When Father Resaccio returned to her table, he countered with a deft sacrifice of a couple of stones in order to consolidate his advanced position. The spectators bobbed their heads in agreement; this time, he raised his eyes to meet hers and smiled slightly, which seemed to convey respect for the soundness of her move as well as the tranquil conviction of his own invulnerability. After that, a few confident strides propelled him to the next table.

At least, she thought, *that was better than nothing. I must do something to frighten him. Make him stop and think for a moment, make him bend over and pretend to be tying his shoelace. As long as he remains the master of the situation, he'll just keep on looking right through me, I'll just be another one of the harmless victims he requires for this public demonstration of his prowess.* By this point, the audience had split up into three large groups, clustered around the three *gobans* where Father Resaccio seemed to have encountered his only serious opposition. Apart from the hundred-year-old master of go, who remained steadfast at his post, few spectators paid much attention to Wendy, and of those who took the trouble to glance occasionally at her board, she doubted that any would risk so much as a single yen—if there was such a thing as a single yen—on her chances at the moment.

Moments later, as if she were still back in her cell at Faremoutiers, she suddenly saw it all very clearly. Resaccio had been able to envelop an entire corner of the board by means of a maneuver called *sente*. He would have to regain the initiative, go over to the attack. But where exactly? It would have to be *kikashi*, a breakout in force; there was an area where black seemed poorly developed. . . . Then, just as at Faremoutiers, she could see it no longer; the modest flare of intuition was quickly succeeded by indecision and self-doubt. Tentatively, almost surreptitiously, she touched a fingertip to the coveted intersection, then glanced over at the master of go. His eyelids were screwed up tight, like those of a Bedouin waiting out a sudden sandstorm, the rest of his features composed in an expression of serene enjoyment. *Thanks, O ancient of days, that's one I'll have to owe you—and what's a little cheating between friends? After all, it was only an idea. . . .*

At the end of the first hour of play, the situation was serious but not entirely hopeless. She had captured a couple of stones and had succeeded in loosening the vise by a couple of turns. Resaccio seemed unaware of this, or if he was, he gave no sign of it. He carried on with the same brisk, decisive style of play, as if there were no other possible move than the one he was about to make. Wendy found this very irritating and started clicking her stones down on the board with exaggerated ferocity, in order to remind him that he had another opponent besides the clock. This too seemed to make no impression.

After an hour and a half, he seemed intrigued to discover that this time there were thirty or forty spectators at his back when he came around to Wendy's board. He stroked his cheek with the back of his hand and appeared, for the first time, to be really concentrating on the position. Wendy found herself, also for the first time, to be suffering from terrible stage fright. The stone felt warm and smooth in the hollow of her hand. *Once more unto the breach, my girl. Let she among ye who is without sin cast the first stone. . . .*

She slowly unbent her right arm; one short, pink fingernail grazed one of the cells on the board, and at the same moment the eyebrows of the master of go disappeared like moles into the deep brown creases on his forehead. Then, with a kind of hectic, impulsive gesture, she jerked her hand over to one corner of the board and plopped down a white stone. The master's eyes shot open wide, then relaxed almost instantly into an ecstatic squint; the crowd started to make a gentle rumbling sound, and some of its more excitable members even burst into articulate speech. "*Tesuji!*" she heard one of them say, which she knew to be the Japanese for "Hear! Hear!"

Resaccio was actually staring at her. He seemed surprised, not devastated or cut to the quick exactly, but interested, challenged. *Has it finally dawned on him that I'm a woman?* She did not return his smile, but lowered her eyes demurely, just as if she were back at the abbey. By this time four of his other adversaries had capitulated, and of those who were still holding out, Wendy was the only one who was not at an obvious disadvantage. Slowly, incredibly, the balance had begun to shift in her favor.

Each time Resaccio came back to face her across the board he seemed less sure of himself, less in control. With barely twenty minutes left on the clock, he reached over to select a black stone but did not pick one up; he studied the position for all of seven minutes, his lips moving slightly as if he were trying to multiply large numbers in his head. Finally he shook his head, looked over at Wendy, and bowed stiffly from the waist in a way that seemed partly ceremonious and partly ironic.

"I think you have a won game, Miss Keenes," he announced in almost perfect English.

The spectators broke into applause; the other players joined in or crowded around the table to offer their congratulations. Wendy rose to her feet, then grasped the edge of the table with both hands to steady herself. She felt a strong, immediate need to make contact with the object of her pursuit, like a lovesick schoolgirl or an assassin—in spirit, she supposed she was somewhere between the two. Sidestepping to avoid the outstretched hands of a pair of effusive Germans, she lurched back against the table, obliterating the position on the board, and practically clutched at Resaccio's sleeve to restore her balance.

"Father," she said, "I have a confession to make."

A voice called out to them, and they turned to face a photographer's dazzling flash. Resaccio turned back toward her, still blinking, and gave her an encouraging look. "But not here," she added hastily. "I couldn't talk about it here."

"Surely it can't be as serious as all that."

"I'm beginning to think it might be."

The crowd had begun to disperse, clearing a path for them toward the entrance to the hall. "But not so serious that we couldn't discuss it over a plate of tempura, I hope. The events of the last two hours have given me a fearful appetite, and I understand there's an excellent Japanese restaurant on the premises—six of them in fact."

"Tempura would suit me very well, I think," said Wendy with a smile.

They walked down to the main lobby of the hotel, which was swarming with nattily dressed travelers and porters pushing enormous baggage carts. This scene, reminiscent of the set for an extremely high-budget musical comedy, was dominated by a great world map made out of a row of white and black vertical panels, to indicate which parts of the globe were in sunlight or in darkness at any particular moment. As Wendy and Resaccio paused to watch, one of the panels swung around, presumably just as the dawn was breaking on a cluster of little islands in the south Atlantic.

The elevator took them up to the restaurant, actually the only one of the six that served traditional Japanese fare. They sat down cross-legged on tatami beside a low table that was scarcely larger than the *go-ban* across which they had faced each other a few minutes earlier.

"Now," said Resaccio, "are you ready for your confession?"

"I just felt compelled to tell you that I really didn't deserve to win, not entirely, at any rate. . . . It was . . . I suppose you could call it a kind of divine inspiration."

"But all our victories are achieved with God's help," said Resaccio, looking at Wendy a little curiously.

"That's not exactly what I had in mind. The divinity inspiring me was actually standing right next to me. He'd taken the form of a very old Japanese man with a little chin beard. . . ."

"That seems only fitting under the circumstances."

"And he had the most amazing eyes; that was how he signaled to me. He sort of squinched his eyes up when I hit on the right move, and then he opened his eyes wide if he thought I was about to go wrong. I must admit that I came to depend on him at some fairly critical junctures in the game. . . ."

"I very often feel," said Resaccio, "that God makes some little sign to me when I make the right move, and opens up His eyes very wide in the opposite case."

Oh, Lord, said Wendy to herself, *spoken like a pale young curate . . . like a pale young curate who's convinced he's talking to a lunatic, in fact. I only pray he's not really like that. . . .* "But the little sign seems to come after the fact in your case," she said, "so you wouldn't actually call it cheating. I knew I shouldn't have done it, but I did so much want to win, you know. And you did beat all the others . . . the ones who played fair, I mean."

"Very true, though after the fact, as you say, I find it much more stimulating and enjoyable to have played against someone who was able to defeat me by supernatural means."

A waiter had materialized at their table, and Resaccio ordered tempura and *yosenabe* for both of them. The tension generated by the match had completely dissipated by now, and they had begun to feel a little more comfortable together and were able to observe each other more directly. Wendy felt that this was particularly true in Resaccio's case, since the white linen skirt she was wearing was fairly short, and even with her knees clamped together in a sort of modified crouch on the tatami, somewhat as if she were riding sidesaddle, she could not avoid showing a great deal of thigh. Resaccio seemed neither embarrassed nor especially impressed by this display, though she felt that it did seem like a rather odd introduction to what she was about to tell him.

"Now that that confession's out of the way," she said, "I'm afraid

I've got another one for you." He nodded encouragingly, but Wendy spent a moment tugging, in vain, at the hem of her skirt above her right knee before she went on. "I know you didn't know me from Adam—I saw you glancing at the little nameplate on my table just before you called me 'Miss Keenes'—but when I found out you were going to be playing in the tournament, I was really very much hoping I'd get a chance to meet you."

"So you could make mincemeat of me—is that the expression?"

"That's the expression, all right, but that's not the reason. It has nothing to do with go at all really. . . ." At that moment a large platter of tempura—shrimp and vegetables deep-fried in batter and garnished with little sprigs of parsley that looked like bonsai trees covered with golden frost—was set down on their table. A young Japanese waitress dressed in traditional costume knelt beside their table and served them both, first Resaccio and then Wendy (a much smaller portion), set out the little bowls of soy and ginger dip and all the rest, then folded her hands demurely inside the broad sleeves of her kimono. *Just like a nun,* thought Wendy, *and him just sitting there, getting an eyeful, like one of those lecherous priests in Boccaccio. . . .* Self-consciously, she arranged her napkin to cover most of her right knee while Resaccio looked on impassively, as if trying very hard not to laugh.

"What does it have to do with really?" he finally asked. "Your other confession, I mean."

"Oh, it's just that I already knew all about you, because I'm a computer person as well, only in not nearly so grand a way as yourself of course. You see, I've been asked to go to Rome next month, to start working on the same project that you'll be working on—only of course you'll be at the head of it, as I understand, and I expect I'll be somewhere rather near the other end. . . ."

Resaccio looked frankly astonished at this, though whether by the information itself or by the form of words in which she had chosen to impart it was not entirely clear. "What I mean is," she went on, "it seemed like too good a chance to pass up, since I wasn't sure that I'd ever get an opportunity to talk with you in the ordinary course of things. . . ."

Resaccio nibbled meditatively on a morsel of tempura before he replied. "And it was only my good fortune that you chose to introduce yourself in such a bold and decisive manner—and maybe it will also be my privilege to face you across the board one day, in Rome perhaps, when your Japanese divinity is no longer present." He laughed. "You know, this project is entirely new to me as well, and it all still seems quite unreal to me—though I'm not sure that meeting a colleague in such unforeseen and exotic circumstances actually helps to make it seem any less unreal."

He reached for the little porcelain sake jug so he could fill Wendy's cup, but the waitress, who seemed to have been hovering by their table with this exact purpose in mind, picked up the jug herself and poured out a cup of warm sake for Resaccio, then another for Wendy. A glance of amused complicity passed between them before they went on with their conversation.

"And if you've been asked to join us," he said, "then you must have some connection with the Church."

"I was a postulant at the Abbey of Faremoutiers. When the mother superior got word that recruits were wanted for something called Project Arcade, she was kind enough to recommend me—in part, as she more or less admitted, because she didn't think I'd make a very good nun. I was certainly planning to give it a try, but I can't pretend that I really hesitated for very long when the other thing came up. And of course I'd already practically memorized your book—*The Immaterial Revolution* I mean."

Wendy took several quick gulps of sake, in hopes of concealing what the Jesuits would have called a grave mental reservation. In fact, she had first seen a copy of Resaccio's book—subtitled *The Impact of Technological Change on Spiritual Values*—in a Paris hotel room some ten months earlier, and it was Abdul who had given it to her. "If you expect to seduce this priest," he had said, "then you first have to impregnate your mind with his thinking—somewhat the reverse of the usual process, I agree. . . . I'm not asking you to actually memorize this silly rubbish, but I want you to learn to think like he does. Pretend you're playing that game of yours, so you can be both yourself and your opponent at the same time."

Now she had the feeling that even the waitress thought she was despicable. *Probably thinks I swill it down like this all the time*, she said to herself. Resaccio had put down his chopsticks; the last piece of tempura was getting cold and sodden on his plate. He seemed to have embarked on a monologue of some kind, perhaps a more sophisticated variant on his standard after-dinner remarks on the subject of the New Technology: Good for the Church? Bad for the Church? She had already missed the beginning, but apparently he had not said anything thus far that required a reply.

"Considering your background," he was saying, "I have to assume that you're more comfortable with the idea of being a denizen of the so-called Information Age, or if it comes to that, a participant in the Postindustrial Revolution, than most of the rest of us in the Church—the ones who are even aware of the fact that such things are already upon us. In one sense, of course, this revolution can hardly be regarded as threatening, since it's merely the culmination of a very long, slow process of development that began with Aristotle's two-valued, linear system of thought and is solidly grounded in Cartesian logic and, in modern terms, the practically reactionary notion of cause and effect. To my mind, that makes it all the more tragic that with all these vast new territories to conquer, the Church has chosen to remain the mistress of a very narrow—I might almost say one-dimensional—space, and we, who have chosen to remain within the Church, end up as prisoners within that space. . . ."

"Yes, but at one time," said Wendy, who felt compelled to sustain her role of wily, intelligent listener instead of merely sinking into a sort of hypnotic torpor, as she otherwise would have been tempted to do, "it must have seemed as though it was a choice between that and nothing at all, and the Church's main job, after all, is to continue to exist."

"True," he replied, "but as a great theologian once said, God is a circle whose center is everywhere and whose circumference is nowhere. That seems like a very good way of expressing the idea that God Himself cannot be confined in such a one-dimensional space. Our faith is in no way smaller than or *circumscribed* by the linear evolution of our secular culture, which has been steadily building upon itself for several centuries now; it simply does not occupy the same dimension. Certainly God reveals himself to us in the material world through certain signs, but His true dimension is by no means to be found in the signs themselves."

"One might even be inclined to say," Wendy suggested, "that God occupies a zero-dimensional space, where we can never expect to find him, at least not by looking in the ordinary way."

"Again very true," said Resaccio, "though I expect it might be better to start looking around in time, or in space-time as the quantum people say, rather than in space. . . ."

"Which brings us right back to computers, in a roundabout sort of way."

"Right again, though I hope I haven't given the impression that I expect that computers, or anything in physics or mathematics, are ever going to *prove* to us that God exists, or that our faith has a rational basis. The task that I've set for myself, I admit, is highly presumptuous, but not quite *that* presumptuous—I hope to be able to help those who have already found the gift of faith to make the transition from the nineteenth to the twenty-first century, to enjoy some of the benefits of this Postindustrial Revolution without sustaining too much damage to their spiritual values or, as the Americans say, 'culture shock.'

"You see," he went on after a pause, "I worked with computers for fifteen years before I became a priest. I started out by trying to analyze the effects that the various modifications in my technological environment were having on my judgment and behavior. There were times, I must tell you, when I got very scared. I could see such frightful storms looming on the horizon that I began to wonder if my simple Christian faith might not be scattered before them like a heap of straw. Nevertheless, I'm glad to tell you that I emerged from these small tribulations convinced that our faith would prove strong enough to sustain us through the even greater ones that were to come. . . ."

"Like Saint Anthony after his temptations, do you think?" asked Wendy with a slightly malicious smile.

"Like anyone," he said, "who thinks that he has finally come to an understanding of something that is very important to him. It seems to me that we are about to say farewell to an age of pure materialism and enter another age in which even the idea of three dimensions and all the rest of it will no longer have very much meaning. And I'm firmly convinced that spiritual values are going to be back at the center of things—by definition, in fact, since, if you don't mind my quoting my book to you for a moment, they occupy the center of what I called 'immaterial space.' "

A waiter brought the *yosenabe*, Japanese bouillabaisse, full of shrimp and crabmeat and pieces of fish garnished with bean curd and a forest of thin transparent noodles that reminded Wendy, not unpleasantly, of some form of delicate submarine life. Resaccio and Wendy watched delightedly as the waitress ladled out two unequal portions into deep porcelain bowls.

"We mustn't forget that the basic stock-in-trade of the computer scientist," said Resaccio, after a mouthful or two of *yosenabe*, "is time, measured out in almost infinitely small amounts, millionths of a second at present, and perhaps we'll be doing better very soon. . . . The infinitely small, the infinitesimal, as I probably don't have to remind you, at least according to Pascal, is one of two things that make men yearn to know God—the other one being the infinitely great, which of course these days we must acknowledge to be the special province of the physicists."

"In other words," said Wendy, "you're thinking of the computer as a kind of time machine, one that will allow us to retrace our steps all the way back to the Beginning, is that it?"

Resaccio grinned a little sheepishly. "That's not quite what I had in mind. . . . And I'm a little disappointed that you're still taking a linear, two-valued, on-off, right-left, up-down Cartesian approach to the problem—"

"Like a computer," said Wendy promptly.

"Like the way that computers have functioned until now. But what I object to is that you're looking at time in the old one-dimensional way, as a step forward in experience or backward in memory and along a single line, starting out at coordinate zero, which is the present moment. But who's to tell us that computers couldn't just step off that line, so to speak, and spread out along some other axis, into some other dimension of time—or why not a whole vast empty plane that extends out infinitely in all directions but, from our perspective, has a thickness of only a billionth of a second on the real time line?"

Wendy nodded enthusiastically. "I think I see what you're getting at. It's like the new generation of computers that are supposed to be capable of working on hundreds of different but interrelated problems—what they call relational multiprocessing—instead of concentrating all the force of their giant brains on one little problem at a time."

Just then she noticed out of the corner of her eye that the waitress was giving off unmistakable if almost imperceptible signs of exasperation; the fact that Resaccio was sitting in front of a brimming, almost untouched bowl of *yosenabe* was probably even less irksome to her than that Wendy had devoured hers greedily while Resaccio had been talking and was now sifting through the bed of noodles in the broth at the bottom of the bowl.

"It's sometimes useful to recall that ENIAC," said Resaccio, "the machine designed by von Neumann, contained more than thirty-six thousand vacuum tubes and weighed eighteen tons. . . ."

The waitress was positively scowling now, possibly at the mention of ENIAC, which had been instrumental in the success of the Manhattan Project and thus had contributed directly to the flattening of two large Japanese cities in August 1945, more probably because Resaccio had picked up his ceramic soup spoon and toyed with it for a moment before putting it down again.

"And now," Resaccio was saying, "after forty years and countless technical improvements, the majority—I won't quite say all—of our computers are really not up to much more than a poor dumb behemoth like ENIAC. That is, they can function in a purely sequential mode; they can compare two bits of information, or they can add them together. It's only because we've gotten so much better at writing programs, as one generation of computers succeeded another, that we've acquired the naive and pompous delusion that we've actually created a form of 'artificial intelligence' that can mimic the functions of the human brain, which of course is absolute nonsense. . . . And that brings me back to what we were talking about a moment ago, about one-dimensional, sequential, linear thought—this narrow little furrow that we've been tirelessly plowing for a number of centuries now, plodding along behind our faithful axiom of the excluded middle, which states that there are only two possibilities as far as a given proposition is concerned—"

"—that it's either true or false," Wendy put in helpfully. "And why do you suppose it is," she went on eagerly, "that we haven't learned to be a little more flexible after all this time?"

"All modern science owes its existence to a single invention, writing, and there you have the perfect prototype of a linear, sequential operation; it seems quite natural that we would have designed our 'electronic brains' in accordance with the same universal prototype. What's more, the computer's electronic circuitry is nothing but hard-wired Boolean algebra, which in turn is nothing more than an elegant mathematical abstract of Cartesian logic.

"It's not that the machines have gotten any smarter, it's just that they've gotten so much faster. It's a certain kind of giddiness triggered by rapid technical advances that has started all this talk about artificial intelligence. I'm afraid we have yet to come up with a genuine time machine, which I imagine as something that would actually reverse or at least dramatically accelerate the flow of time. What we have at present is a machine that's merely very effective at slowing it down for us—a sort of temporal version of the electron microscope, or as the mathematicians used to say, a 'calculating engine' that can carry out as many as a billion operations in a single second. Even within the confines of the old binary logic, a machine that can count that quickly may very well give the user the impression that it *thinks* before it speaks, but even at that level of proficiency, it's no more than a glorified version of the poor old chess-playing program that can only come up with the 'right' move after it's gone to the trouble of playing through all the wrong ones."

He paused impressively, picked up his chopsticks, selected a plump pink shrimp from his bowl, and popped it into his mouth.

"The natural consequence of our having restricted ourselves to a single sort of logic is that we eventually came to forget that there *were* any other kinds, or that the human was a much more impressive resource than von Neumann's poor old ENIAC. The real technological revolution that we should be preparing ourselves to cope with will be based on a totally different approach to the problem—it's somewhat analogous to the way we've continually had to revise our way of thinking about the atom. You remember that Democritus and Lucretius, in their respective centuries before Christ, announced that 'nature is composed of little particles that are irreducible by any process of division, solid, and eternal.' We've spent most of the present century coming to grips with the idea that those little indivisible particles were atoms, then the nucleus of the atom, then the proton and the electron, and finally the quark—which may or may not exist. . . ."

"Perhaps that was the one that Democritus and Lucretius had in mind all along," suggested Wendy. "The quark, I mean."

"Very possibly," Resaccio said. "But the point I'm trying to make is that a great deal of the technology, the science, and the economics of the next century is going to be involved in the attempt to isolate and exploit the resources of the minutest particle of a second—not that we have any reason to believe in this case that there is such a thing. In the sciences we've already abandoned the old linear mode of thought, at least to the extent that prediction—the unraveling of a single thread, chosen more or less at random—has been replaced by *simulation*, so that virtually all the implications of a particular set of data can be evaluated at once. You might liken it to the difference between groping your way from one blaze mark to the next along a rather daunting mountain trail and being presented with a satellite montage of the entire region—or being privileged to stand with Moses on the mountaintop if you prefer."

"Either one will do, for a metaphor," said Wendy, a trifle severely, "or you might even want to call it 'the conquest of immaterial space,' I suppose." Their waitress had already poured out their tea and disappeared; only two other tables were still occupied, one by a pair of Europeans, or more probably Americans, the other by two Japanese. She was beginning to feel a little uneasy and impatient, in spite of the fact that all four of the others seemed to be dawdling over their food in an even more scandalous fashion than Resaccio (though the conversation at the other tables seemed to be much more desultory than their own). She was uneasy because all four of them seemed to be watching their table, watching Resaccio as much as herself, though their interest in him was unlikely to be sexual, still less philosophical. It was just beginning to dawn on her that Resaccio might very well be the sort of person who would be provided with *security*.

"Since you don't seem to be impressed by my metaphors," Resaccio was saying, "perhaps I should switch over to the quantitative approach. I'm sure you're prepared to concede that if a computer can perform a billion operations in a second, that would be roughly as many as a single unassisted human being could perform in an entire lifetime. Now, do you have any idea how many human beings have lived on earth, from the dawn of time to the present day?"

"No idea," said Wendy. "I couldn't even guess."

"Eighty billion, more or less. . . . Now, I won't take you through all the calculations on this, but it would be fairly easy to demonstrate that we, the human race I mean, have had to process approximately the same number of bits of information in order to reach our present level of civilization as we *will be able to process*, by electronic means, over the next ten years or so, by the end of the present century. I'm not trying to suggest that we're actually going to end up being twice as civilized in a dozen years as we are right now—though you might say that that seems like little enough to hope for in any case—I'm merely suggesting that the *potential* is already there.

"And in qualitative terms," he went on, "I'm sure you'll agree that the effects of this almost inconceivable expansion of our computational abilities are going to be felt far beyond the sciences. Time, particularly at the level of the billionth part of a second, is an inexhaustible resource, after all, and one of the results of this technological revolution will be to guarantee the economic supremacy of whatever nation learns to make the best use of those billionths. The computational resources of the United States can already be reckoned in billions of human lifetimes, and it seems likely that the surest index of the power of any country will be expressed in terms of billions of operations per minute, or per annum, instead of per capita income or the number of warheads or pounds of plutonium on hand or millions of barrels of oil. . . ."

"Or you might make it the number of lifetime brain equivalents, LBEs, just like the energy resources of a country are currently expressed in PTEs, petroleum ton equivalents," Wendy suggested.

"An excellent idea," said Resaccio, smiling, "and I predict that soon after you start in on your new job, you'll be dividing your time between the Club of Rome and our humble institute. Now, if we're prepared to think of time as a precious natural resource, then we must naturally conclude that, like most other resources of this kind, it is not available to everyone equally. Some will be going after it with picks and shovels, while others already have access to the latest thing in robotized strip-mining equipment.

"The Japanese, of course, are currently in the lead insofar as the design and production of the latter are concerned. You and I are going to be privileged to be working on, or perhaps I should say *with*, a revolutionary new machine, the PSI-100—the first machine that actually incorporates the kind of brand-new, nonlinear, nonsequential logic that we have been agitating for for such a long time . . . virtually the entire time that we've been sitting here, in fact."

Wendy was amused by this, and more than a little intrigued. It seemed that Resaccio was a somewhat different sort of person than Abdul, or a very close reading of *The Immaterial Revolution*, had led her to expect. "Then I'd call that pretty quick work in fact," she replied. "Can it actually be that the famous fifth generation is already upon us?"

"I'd have to say that the PSI-100, though hardly more than an infant, is decidedly fifth generation, the result, if not necessarily the culmination, of a process that's been going on for some years, ever since our colleagues who were so desperately determined to write 'artificial intelligence' programs figured out that they were never likely to get anywhere as long as the computers they were using were so patently inferior in design to the human brain."

Wendy was already familiar with the basic problem, the solution to which had been eagerly anticipated for a number of years now (and she was grateful to Resaccio for not attempting to explain it to her all over again). Even the most elaborate of conventional computers consisted of a single processor, which was able to cope with a single bit of information at a time, albeit at a rather impressive rate. The human brain, on the other hand, consists of a complex network of synapses linking a total of 10 to 20 billion neurons, *each* of which is in effect a separate processor that can handle, by electrochemical means, about a thousand bits of information per second. This gives the brain the capacity to process roughly 10 to 20 *trillion* bits of information in a single second, and the idea had naturally suggested itself of designing a computer that really was the functional analogue of the human brain—that is, a complex of thousands, if not millions or billions, of separate processors linked together and organized into sectors—rather than just a single highly overdeveloped neuron.

While Wendy was pondering all this, Resaccio had signaled for the check and signed for the meal. He rose to his feet, if not quite effortlessly at least gracefully enough. Wendy, with both legs asleep, did her best to follow his example. The restaurant was dimly lit and silent as they walked slowly toward the entrance.

"I'm sure we'll meet again very soon," said Wendy.

"We will indeed. I don't have to tell you how pleased I am that you're joining us. Most of the researchers I met at ICOT—the institute here in Japan where the PSI-100 was designed and built—were under thirty. I'd hoped that for our institute in Rome we'd be able to recruit a certain number of people who were young, enthusiastic, imaginative, and free from the grosser sorts of prejudice that come with age and self-satisfaction. . . ." He looked vaguely troubled or distracted for a moment, then went on. "I realize that I've said a great deal about what you might call the material side of our enterprise and very little about the spiritual side. I assure you, first of all, that there is one, and, second, that to my mind at least it's rather critical. There are wolves prowling around, Wendy Keenes, pretty much everywhere you look nowadays, and that means that it's time for us to be looking after our flocks."

He waved one hand in a noncommittal sign of farewell and walked rapidly down the corridor. The two Japanese had gotten up from their seats at about the same time as Resaccio had signed the check, but Wendy had made up her mind to stop noticing such things.

Valletta, Malta
November 2

It was more than a little discouraging. On the long marble-topped table in the large sunlit room that had been his father's office for so many years, Michael had arranged five piles of file folders. Each was about a foot and a half high; each contained numerous items that would have to be read, pondered, answered, put off, or otherwise acted upon by the new administrator of the Albert de Bonno Clinic. It had already cost Michael two afternoons of pitiless triage to reduce the files from their original, considerably vaster bulk; the first of them dealt with cardiology; the second with neurology and neurosurgery, in which the clinic had specialized for the past ten years; the third with financial and administrative matters. The fourth, the untidiest, dealt with personal and family business; the fifth, which contained everything that could possibly be grouped under the heading of politics, was the most surprising. His father had played an important part in the movement for full independence from Britain, finally achieved in 1974 with the proclamation of the Maltese republic. After the last British troops had left Malta in March 1979—and the island was free from foreign occupiers or overlords of any kind for the first time in almost three millennia—Michael had been under the impression that his father had gradually retired from political life.

Nevertheless, eight years later Michael had come across a number of reasonably important state papers and confidential reports in a locked file drawer, all dealing with matters of recent or current importance—unemployment (which affected no fewer than 20 percent of Malta's 350,000 inhabitants), the "scholastic quarrel" between the government and the Catholic church, and foreign affairs. The island's strategic location—"the lock on the door to the Mediterranean," Churchill had called it—was its only valuable resource. In spite of Albert de Bonno's close personal connections with the Maltese Labor Party, Dom Mintoff's extravagant flirtations with the Eastern bloc and the Libyans had not been much to his liking, and—judging by a number of letters from ministers, ambassadors, even several chiefs of state—his advice and assistance had repeatedly been sought by those who were determined to steer a more moderate course—or, at any rate, not to sail so close to the wind.

Michael read the letters with a mixture of apprehension and embarrassment, though, realistically speaking, there was not much chance of his being expected to succeed Albert de Bonno in the role of gray eminence or elder statesman. The island was a small one, the political balance between the thirty-three Labor MPs and the thirty-two Nationalists was generally precarious, and his father had been an energetic and influential man. He could hardly see himself haunting the corridors of the House of Representatives, as his father had certainly done, slapping backs or standing drinks and saying things like "A word in your private ear if I might, Minister." He noted, without great interest, that there was an empty red file folder labeled "PSI-100"; he could make nothing of this cryptic designation, and he put the folder aside in case its contents should happen to turn up later on.

At five o'clock precisely Mrs. Benzequen, his father's personal secretary, brought him his tea and half a dozen newspapers on a silver tray. The *Bulletin*, the Maltese afternoon daily, instantly reminded him of most of the more depressing aspects of life in what was, in spirit if not in fact, a small provincial city. *Le Monde* and the *International Herald* seemed considerably more promising; the official Vatican paper, *L'Osservatore Romano*, seemed a good deal less so, and he wondered why his father—who had shared Dom Mintoff's opinion of the Church if not of the Russians and the Libyans—had bothered to subscribe to it at all. He was about to dispense with *L'Osservatore* altogether when his eye was caught by a provocatively titled article on the front page. "The Prophecies of Malachi—The Pontificate of John Paul II Unexplained."

When he turned to glance at the continuation on page 4, his eye was caught once more, this time in a much more abrupt and astounding fashion, by a photograph of Wendy on the opposite page. It had been taken not in Rome but at the go tournament in Tokyo, and the accompanying article was concerned exclusively with the doings of the owner of the other face in the picture, a Vatican functionary of some sort called Nicholas Resaccio.

Resaccio was the "Holy Father's chief councillor on matters pertaining to the sciences and the new technology" and had recently been named to the Pontifical Academy of Sciences. He had also been a passenger aboard AF-270—which triggered off a series of disturbing recollections that Michael was determined to suppress—in the company of the American special envoy to the Holy See. The article concluded, somewhat anticlimactically, "Those who have been wondering why our brilliant computer expert was flying off to Tokyo in such distinguished company now have their answer: to contend for the amateur championship of the ancient game of go."

There was no mention of Wendy in the article, and it was possible that she had only wandered into the frame by accident—perhaps on the well-known photographic principle that a picture of a priest with an attractive redhead standing beside him is much to be preferred to one without. In Wendy's case, however, Michael had long since learned that there was no such thing as an accident. He had forgotten all about the prophecies of Malachi and was still staring at the picture when the telephone rang.

It was his father's secretary. "It's the prime minister's office, Dr. de Bonno," she announced cheerily. A firm but deferential male voice informed him that the prime minister would like to have a word with him, immediately if possible. Michael decided to go at once, more out of restlessness than curiosity; he was not looking forward to another evening rooting around in the mound of folders on the marble table. The clinic was in Floriana, one of the rare garden suburbs that actually lives up to its name, and the road downtown was lined with exuberant foliage. He drove past the outer ramparts of Valletta, the most visible relic of the Knights of Malta—the last of the great crusading orders, who had been chased out of Rhodes by the Turks and had settled on Malta for a two-hundred-year campaign of privateering and pious brigandage directed, for the most part, against their ancient enemy.

He turned onto Duke of York Avenue, where the old town was beginning to come to life again in the cool of the late afternoon. The last of the season's tourists were being trundled up and down the steep and narrow streets in horse-drawn cabs called *karrozins*. A number of old ladies were opportunistically engaged in lace making and other traditional pursuits in the doorways of their houses, and potters and other craftspeople had spread out their wares along the narrow sidewalks.

Michael parked the Volvo on a side street just past the Castile Gate; the prime minister's administrative offices were housed in the former Houses of Castile and León, a sort of palatial barracks once occupied by the knightly donors of the celebrated Maltese Falcon. The row of cannons outside was most impressive, as was the bust of Manuel Pinto de Fonseca, grand master of the Knights of Malta, over the entranceway. Michael was swallowed up by the cool, shadowy interior of this magnificent baroque building. He stated his business to an usher in the corridor and was shown to the office of the prime minister's chief of staff.

The chief of staff was a vigorous little man with a gleaming bald head, a beautiful tan, and an antique marquetry desk, behind which he plumped himself down once Michael had had his hand firmly shaken and been seated in a squashy leather armchair.

"What splendid weather we've been having," said the chief of staff, beaming. "One would almost think we were still in the midst of summer instead of early November." He paused for a moment while his features rearranged themselves into a mask of solemn woe. "But I hope you won't think it presumptuous of me, my dear Dr. de Bonno, when I say that all of us in the government feel that we've suffered a terrible loss, and I know that the prime minister especially feels that he has lost an old and valued friend. . . . I trust you'll allow me to add my own condolences to those already expressed on behalf of the government and the nation."

Michael merely nodded in acknowledgment. He felt ill at ease and was beginning to wonder why he had received such an urgent summons and what else the government and the nation, in the person of this sleek little man in this large, elegant office, could possibly have to say to him. For the moment, the chief of staff seemed intent on adding his impromptu funeral oration to those that had gone before.

"Albert de Bonno," he was saying, "did so much for his country, was never sparing of his own time or energy, and left virtually no stone unturned—and I'm sure I don't have to tell you that on Malta we have a great many stones—where the welfare of his fellow countrymen was concerned. For those of us in public service, the Floriana clinic will always remain a shining example of modernity and efficiency, of supreme administrative competency as well as compassion and concern. . . ." By the end of this little litany of bureaucratic virtues, the period of official mourning had apparently run its course; the prime minister's chief of staff was beaming once more.

"And of course," he went on, "we were not only pleased but relieved to hear you'd agreed to take over the reins yourself." He paused, and Michael knit his brows in slightly suspicious acknowledgment.

"And finally," said the chief of staff, "I have the honor of telling you something that you don't already know. Several months ago, your father agreed to collaborate with us on a project of the utmost importance for the political future—I am tempted to say the survival—of our country. I hasten to add that this is a project that falls far beyond the normal purview of the hospital administrator, and I hope this also explains the rather unseemly haste with which you've been summoned to this interview."

"I'm afraid it doesn't," said Michael, "at least not yet."

"In all fairness, I probably should begin by explaining that the role you'd be playing—as yet unspecified, as you've pointed out—will undoubtedly have certain drawbacks. You'd certainly be admitted to what are called the highest councils of state, and at the same time, you'd be held accountable for the performance of your duties in much the same way as any high-ranking government official. Security will be of the very tightest, which may well mean that your private as well as public life will be subject to a degree of . . . official scrutiny which you may not find particularly congenial. . . ."

"And you still haven't told me what any of this is all about."

"I do hope I've made it clear that I'm offering you an opportunity to perform an extraordinary service to your country. And while I'm sure you've already heard enough silly talk about following in your father's footsteps to last a lifetime, that is precisely what you'd be doing in the present case. . . ."

"Forgive me, but my father was a man of many talents and many interests—a number of which, admittedly, were 'well beyond the normal purview of the hospital administrator' or however it was you put it a few minutes ago. I'm hardly to be compared with him, with respect to either his talents or his ambitions. In the first case, I'd be foolish to try and follow in his footsteps—any more than a step or two at a time at least—and in the other, I simply don't have all that much interest in politics. I'm convinced that the best way I can serve my fellow man is simply to carry on with my own work in neurology, and of course to try to look after the clinic as best I can."

The sleek little man spread his palms apart in a broad, mercantile sort of gesture, like a street vendor offering reassurance to a skittish customer. "In that case, Dr. de Bonno, I'm sure we still have a great deal to talk about. As you've obviously gathered, there's very little that I'm authorized to tell you about this famous project of ours just at first. About the only thing I *am* authorized to tell you, in fact, is that your father signed a purchase agreement several months ago in which the clinic and the university each agreed to contribute half the cost of a high-performance computer.

"The clinic's share of the purchase price would be made up by a substantial but strictly unofficial government subsidy, thereby reducing the real cost to the clinic to nil. The computer itself is extremely advanced in type, one of the very first production models of the PSI-100, which the Japanese have been kind enough to sell to us—for an astronomical price, I might add—on a sort of trial basis. Its quarters are already being prepared, as I understand it, on the campus of the College of Arts and Sciences in Msida, in the medical school to be precise."

"So that the clinic—"

"The clinic will enjoy a direct linkage to the computer and virtually unlimited access. I understand that your father was contemplating a very ambitious research project, also having to do with neurology, and that he believed his work would be enormously facilitated by the use of such a device. I imagine it would have a great many applications to the day-to-day business of the clinic as well."

"But I won't get a chance to play with it unless I agree to help out with this highly confidential project of yours, which is so confidential that you can't even tell me what it is until I've actually agreed to do it."

The little man nodded. "Wiser heads than yours or mine have decided that some sort of formal assurance on your part would be necessary. I trust I've made it clear that the prime minister is very eager to secure your cooperation in this matter. I'm sure you've already received your invitation to the reception at the Soviet embassy the day after tomorrow. I encourage you to accept—the prime minister himself will be there, and I know he'd prefer to hear your answer in person."

"I hadn't planned on it, but I've never been to the Soviet embassy, and I suppose we mustn't disappoint the prime minister."

Michael had been looking forward to spending a few more hours in the paneled solitude of his father's third-floor office at the clinic, meditating on this bizarre and unexpected turn of events. He was therefore surprised, and a little disappointed, to find his father's secretary—now his—still waiting for him, even though it was after seven, just as she would have waited for his father. He stepped into his office, glanced at the great unlovely pile of folders and documents and dossiers on the marble table, and remembered the empty red folder labeled PSI-100. He summoned the secretary and showed her the folder. "Do you have any idea why this folder has nothing in it?" he asked.

"I'm sorry, Dr. de Bonno, I should have mentioned it to you. Your father had a certain amount of confidential material that he locked up in the office safe a couple of days before . . ."

"Before he died. Did he seem to be worried about it particularly?"

"Your father never seemed to be worried about anything," she replied, proudly. "Would you like to see the PSI file? There's a lot if it, I'm afraid."

He nodded, and a few minutes later he was sorting through another fat bundle of documentation, which began by telling him that PSI stood for "processing by sequential inferences" and continued on through numerous charts and graphics and technical appendices, as well as an offprint dealing with a French programming language called PROLOG, another on recent experiments in speech synthesis, and an organizational chart of ICOT, which Michael knew to be a prestigious research institute in Japan much concerned with matters of this kind.

Next, there was a brief note from Dom Mintoff to Dr. Albert de Bonno, informing him that the computer was expected to arrive in Malta at the beginning of December 1987; this was stapled to a copy of the joint purchase agreement signed by his father and various representatives of the government, as well as a memorandum signed by the minister of the interior and describing the various "nonbudgetary funding sources" by which the clinic would be reimbursed for its share of the purchase price. There was also a photocopy of a long handwritten letter from his father to Dom Mintoff describing certain anticipated "problems in the conduct of the operation" in terms that Michael found largely incomprehensible. Mintoff's reply, on the other hand, was extremely enlightening.

"In response to your very sensible inquiry regarding the means by which computer program material originating in Rome is to be furnished directly to us," Mintoff had written, "we have recently been informed of the identity of the person who will be responsible for this critical phase of the operation. She is described as a highly competent young computer scientist who is regarded by the Colonel's special services as being absolutely steadfast in her political convictions and perhaps only slightly less desirable as far as the purely psychological dimension is concerned. A Roman Catholic by upbringing, a militant Irish nationalist by conviction, she has recently completed an intensive training program in Libya and has accordingly been 'reinserted' as a novice at a convent in the Paris region. You should be encouraged to know that Miss K— also enjoys the distinction of being the first woman to receive a doctorate in computer science from your own alma mater. . . ."

Michael read a few more lines, which supplied additional details of Wendy's background with which he was already familiar. It was a little too much to take in all at once. During all those months he had tormented himself with erotic, masochistic fantasies of Wendy's life without him—but not one of them, and there were thousands, had ever taken place in a terrorist training camp in Libya! Perhaps in a way it was reassuring to know that these mysterious, unspeakable entanglements of hers were political and not emotional. But there again, he was not entirely certain. He did not have to close his eyes to see her rifling through the wood box in the forester's cottage, her eyes ablaze with fear and anger, then throwing herself on the torn scrap of newsprint on the floor—a photograph of Father Nicholas Resaccio.

He rang for his secretary. "Mrs. Benzequen, I need your advice. I've been invited to a reception at the Russian embassy on the day after tomorrow. What would you recommend I wear?"

"Your father had several very handsome dress suits, Dr. de Bonno. Of course, he was a little wider through the hips and shoulders, but in two days' time, I think we should be able to come up with something that would do very well."

5

Tokyo
November 3

Rather than seeking out the relative tranquillity of lesser streets, the driver resolutely thrust his cab into the arterial torrent of the expressway that ran down to the river en route to Narita Airport. The pace and volume of the traffic, even by Roman standards, was a little intimidating. Nicholas felt as if he were trapped in the midst of a whole nation on the move, not just a late-morning rush hour. It was ten o'clock in the morning. It was raining, and a cold gray wind was lashing against the low buildings of the city.

The driver had his white-gloved hands draped over the top of the steering wheel in a highly professional manner. The address, Nicholas had been relieved to discover, was an easy one, on the broad avenue called Umamichi-Dori in the heart of the Asakusa quarter, and not one of those where additional cross-references, in the form of monuments, parks, and government buildings, had to be supplied to make up for the notorious shortage of street names and street numbers in Tokyo.

He had called the Jesuit provincial as soon as he got back to his room after his dinner with Wendy. He was eager to meet with Father Pitta, whom he barely knew and who clearly was destined to play an important role in Project Arcade. As for Wendy Keenes, he still felt a little bewildered by their encounter. She seemed perfect for the project, of course, and there was one position in particular for which she was well suited. As a general rule, Nicholas was inclined to agree with the ingenious Frenchman who asserted that "God is in the little details," but he felt that even the Good Lord rarely took the trouble to make sure that things worked out so perfectly.

Not only had she contrived a chance meeting over the board, she had also contrived to beat him soundly—both of which said a great deal for her audacity and tactical sense. She had apparently been playing well above her usual form, since while Nicholas went on to the semifinals and took tremendous pleasure in being beaten by one of the greatest players in Japan, Wendy was eliminated in her very next match, only the second round of the preliminaries.

After the match Nicholas had really learned very little about her, apart from the obvious facts that she was quick and intelligent and addicted to the milder forms of irony. He had been so overwhelmed by running across a colleague and a fellow enthusiast that he had scarcely given her a chance to say more than a word or two at a time. Now he would have to do penance for this bit of self-indulgence by an extra two weeks of gnawing curiosity, the feeling that something was not quite right—or rather, that everything was too perfect.

The gardens of Asakusa Kannon Temple were bathed in thin yellow light. It seemed as if the sun was all ready to set again after having shone for only a couple of hours. The other lane of traffic was filled with fog lights groping their way through the rain, which was heavier now. The taxi cut itself loose from the pack and came to a stop in front of Father Pitta's apartment building. The driver pulled the lever that automatically opened the passenger door.

Father Pitta met him at the door of his small apartment, which was furnished sparsely, even austerely, in a kind of Japanese-Jesuit style. Nicholas took off his shoes as soon as he was inside.

"You know," said Father Pitta, "that modern young couples can hardly wait to clutter up their houses with microwaves and dining-room sets and all that sort of business. I feel it's up to foreigners like me to preserve the old traditions." He paused at the door of an inner room. "There's someone here whom I understand you've already been introduced to."

Nicholas walked into a room with bookcases and file cabinets, but no chairs, which evidently served as Father Pitta's study or workroom, and saw to his surprise that James Wilcox was sitting cross-legged on a tatami on the floor. He seemed ill at ease, his pose rather reminiscent of Wendy's on the previous night, only what the American diplomat was trying to conceal from view was a pair of attractive plaid socks. "Don't bother to get up, Mr. Wilcox," said Nicholas as he crouched down on an adjoining mat.

Father Pitta was a short-waisted man with long, gangling limbs, which he arranged on his tatami with considerably more agility and comfort than either Nicholas or Wilcox. His cheeks were flushed, his face pale and curiously asymmetrical; his nose appeared to be tilting gently to one side, and there was a pronounced cast in his right eye. Nicholas suspected that the provincial had a great deal to tell him and that the presence of a third party, even such a distinguished one as the American envoy, might make it a little difficult for both of them to express themselves with the necessary frankness.

"I don't choose to live in the Japanese style for the sake of courtesy," said Father Pitta, "and certainly not for the sake of comfort, or even to suit my own personal taste. It simply seems to me that to live in the same style as one's hosts is a way of reducing one's debt to them. No one has to put himself out on my account, and I require neither toleration nor understanding."

"I see your point," said Nicholas. "And I'm sorry I haven't had the chance to promote myself from the status of tourist, or at least temporary visitor. Here in Tokyo it's difficult not to feel like a lost child in a gigantic amusement park. One always has the feeling of having strayed away from one's mother."

"Your situation is rather different from mine," said Father Pitta. "You're an invited guest in this country. The Japanese have agreed to furnish you with matériel and information, to educate you, in effect. That represents a debt that is incurred by the Church, on your account and on account of this project."

"What are you implying? What will I have to do to repay this debt?"

"Nothing whatsoever. That is not your responsibility." Father Pitta turned toward Wilcox. "The essential purpose, in my opinion, is to maintain a certain balance of payments between the Vatican and its various trading partners." He thrust both hands into the pockets of his rumpled gray suit jacket and came up with a pack of cigarettes. He lit one and took several deep drags in rapid succession. Nicholas, who had never smoked, envied him the luxury of this gesture; the American's silent, looming presence was beginning to get on his nerves.

"And I surely don't have to remind you," said Father Pitta, "that as far as our project is concerned, we have adversaries and competitors, both within the Church and without, as well as partners. Individual motives are of no account. What matters is the success or failure of the project. That is why I've been charged with the task of watching over you, of making sure that there are no unsuspected obstacles in the path of Project Arcade. In particular, we have to make certain that there is no *personal* interference—"

"On whose part?"

"Anyone's. I'm simply asking you, in a roundabout way I must admit, not to make my task overly difficult."

Nicholas stiffened for a moment in a small, polite gesture of exasperation. "Perhaps if you'd care to be more specific."

Father Pitta and Wilcox exchanged glances. "There can be no doubt," said Father Pitta, "that the purely technical side of the project has been entrusted to your exclusive care. Naturally, you're expected to choose the sort of colleagues and subordinates who seem best qualified to assist you from a purely technical standpoint. Nevertheless, there are other criteria, which was why you were asked to confine yourself to a list of preselected candidates." It was clear enough what Father Pitta was getting at, but Nicholas made no attempt to break in before he had completed his peroration. "It's a problem of security, quite simply. We can't allow anyone to join us whom we're not absolutely sure of."

"Then you must be aware of something that I'm not."

James Wilcox suddenly rose to his feet with a great creaking of joints and began to walk briskly back and forth across the room. Father Pitta remained silent for a moment.

"It has to do with Miss Keenes, I think," said Nicholas. "You'd better tell me whatever it is you've found out about her."

Father Pitta lit a fresh cigarette from the glowing stub of the last one. "The young woman who gave such an excellent account of herself during the go tournament—or during its initial stages, at any rate—has naturally aroused a great deal of curiosity."

"Especially such an attractive young woman," said Wilcox, who had finally come to rest over by the window. "I've seen her picture."

"We won't insult Father Resaccio by assuming he might be . . . susceptible in such a way," said Father Pitta, not without a trace of amusement. He turned toward Nicholas. "Since Miss Keenes was suggested as a candidate for the program by the mother superior of Faremoutiers, one or two other pieces of information concerning her have been brought to light."

"It doesn't look too good," said Wilcox, who seemed to be admiring the traffic in the street outside. Nicholas glanced at Father Pitta, who nodded slowly in confirmation.

"As in the case of many who seem to be attracted by the contemplative life, Miss Keenes has apparently had a very eventful past. As a student, she was very active politically—"

"She was a radical," put in Wilcox firmly. "She was *active* on behalf of the IRA, which practically makes her a terrorist, in my opinion."

"However," said Father Pitta, "on the basis of the record, it might seem fairer to classify her as a *militant*—she was twice arrested in Belfast and once in London, each time as the result of a so-called peaceable demonstration. But as often happens in such cases, her record at the university was otherwise blameless—indeed, quite brilliant."

"But isn't it rather usual," said Nicholas, "for students in Ireland, even the brilliant ones—especially the brilliant ones—to get involved in radical politics, even to take part in anti-British demonstrations from time to time?"

"There are other ways," said Wilcox, "of getting involved in politics, even radical politics, besides overturning cars and throwing rocks at the police."

"And is that what she was arrested for?" asked Nicholas.

"Actually," said Father Pitta, "on each of these occasions, she seems to have been arrested, in concert with a great many others, for 'failure to heed a lawful order to disperse.' We don't have too many of the details, admittedly. There's also a report that she was involved in a hunger strike, in 1979—she gave it up after three days. . . . I'll grant you that none of this appears to be too serious."

"Then what exactly is the problem?"

"It's just that there's a gap of two years in the story of her life. She was awarded her doctorate, then a one-year teaching fellowship at the University of Belfast, then dropped off the face of the earth. Then some sort of mystical crisis appears to have brought her back, clamoring for admission to the gates of Faremoutiers."

"You talk as though everyone who's had some sort of conversion experience should be suspected as a security risk. What about Saint Paul? What about Loyola?"

"Exactly," said the American as he came back and crouched down on the mat. "She just seems like a bit too much of a godsend—if you'll excuse the expression, Father."

"But wasn't her candidacy approved in Rome?" asked Nicholas.

"Possibly, before these additional facts were brought to light," said Father Pitta. "It's true that she was given an excellent recommendation.

The report from her mother superior was extremely favorable, and there can hardly be any question concerning her aptitudes and abilities. . . ."

"I certainly have none," said Nicholas.

Wilcox was plucking at his right sleeve to attract his attention. "Just understand one thing, Father. We have nothing against this young woman, and I'm sure she's as talented as everyone says she is. It's just a question of how you go about these things. You really haven't gone about this the right way, Father. You no longer have the luxury of putting all your trust in just anyone who comes along, anyone who talks a good game. From now on, you're going to have to limit your social encounters to people who've been checked out, people who haven't been compromised in any way. If you have any questions about the procedure, Father Pitta and I are at your complete disposal."

"Procedure? Why not hire two large gentlemen in trench coats, one to stand on either side of me, and let that be the end of it?"

"Actually, Father," said Wilcox, "that's only the beginning of it. Two of our people from the embassy have been looking after your security since our arrival in Tokyo."

Nicholas felt his face flush with rage and humiliation. Father Pitta hastily stubbed out another cigarette just as the filter tip was beginning to smolder. Nicholas rose quickly to his feet, and Wilcox followed suit, unfolding slowly to his full height.

"You seem to have forgotten all about the little adventure we shared in Irkutsk, Father. If you could be sure that the papers in your attaché case *weren't* photocopied and returned to you, that they don't have any idea of how important you are to us, then I'd say we could all rest easy. However, I think you'll agree that the character of this entire episode suggests a very different conclusion."

"But surely you don't believe," said Nicholas, "that the plane was hijacked just so the KGB could go through my attaché case!"

"I think you're far too modest, Father."

"And the large men with the trench coats—where are they?"

"They were at the go tournament, they had dinner in the restaurant with you and Miss Keenes. They're there to protect you, Father. And as you see, they're very discreet."

Nicholas spread wide his arms, palms outward, as if calling on the Hosts of Heaven, or just Father Pitta, to bear witness to this perfidy.

"These things aren't really for us to decide," said Father Pitta. "I think you should trust the embassy to do the job properly."

"Does the Holy Father realize," shot back Nicholas, "that he's got the CIA working for him now as well?"

"The fewer there are that know it," Father Pitta replied mildly, "the better for all concerned."

"And isn't it for us to decide," pursued Nicholas, "whether we're old enough to look out for ourselves?"

"In your case, no, Father Resaccio. You must learn to put aside your personal feelings in this matter, or perhaps you might console yourself with the reflection that these measures have not been adopted for your personal protection but for the sake of Project Arcade. And if Miss Keenes is going to participate in the project, she'll have to be kept under surveillance as well."

"The telex," prompted Wilcox.

"We've just received word from the office of the nuncio on Malta," said Father Pitta. "It seems that Colonel Akhmedov has been in Valletta since yesterday afternoon."

"You remember Colonel Akhmedov?" said Wilcox. "You remember Irkutsk? The Russians are up to something, Father, you can be sure of that."

"Malta?" said Nicholas. "How does Malta come into it exactly?"

Rabat, Malta
November 4

Michael felt as if he had been transported to some parallel dimension where the Russian Revolution had never occurred and Lenin had spent his last days in a lonely exile's cabin in Siberia. The Soviet embassy was housed in a sprawling Edwardian villa on a hilltop in the little town of Rabat, a mile or two outside of Valletta, bathed in soft exterior lights and soothed by fragrant sea breezes. Inside, it was all gilt and crystal and slightly superannuated luxury and—apart from the fact that the glittering, gabbling crowd in the ornate reception hall was predominantly Maltese rather than Slavic in appearance—very much in keeping with his idea of one of the less ambitious functions at the Winter Palace in the days of old Petrograd. Between the floodlit façade and the reception hall, a more contemporary note was struck by the bulletproof glass in the lobby, the blunt, wary faces, and, if not exactly a security checkpoint, at least a very close scrutiny of his invitation.

Michael guessed that a large percentage of the couturier clothes and real diamonds on the island were in attendance, along with the island's leading artists and intellectuals, politicians and diplomats, bankers, arms dealers, and military men, plus the sturdy wives or young and attractive girlfriends of all the above. Michael also felt somewhat at a loss. The last reception of any kind he had attended had involved a group of graduate students and faculty members at Compiègne and not enough bottles of cheap white wine. He was not really prepared for anything like this, particularly in his tight new shoes and one of his father's old dress suits that had been taken in in a great many places and let out in several more by a tailor in Valletta.

There was no one there he really knew well, nor even anyone he recognized except a few of his father's medical and political cronies, friends of the family, and a handful of Malta's top-ranking celebrities. As nearly as he could tell, the celebrants, including the wives, the girlfriends, and the Russians, had already sorted themselves out by categories. As he edged through the crowd, none of the fragments of conversation he overheard made him feel disposed to linger on the fringes of any group. Attracted by the clinking of glassware, he found his way to the buffet. He was not very hungry, and decided it made much better sense to have a drink or two instead.

Henry Zubbieq—which was the name, he had discovered only that morning from Mrs. Benzequen, of the prime minister's chief of staff—had not yet materialized or, more probably, was still trying to hunt him down in some other corner of the hall. The idea of simply fleeing from the sight of the little man and melting into the crowd when he arrived was an appealing one, though also one that he might prefer to contemplate rather than actually carry out. He picked up his drink and moved away from the bar.

As he did so, he became aware of people nodding and smiling at him, waving or beckoning to him. A great many of these people seemed to know who he was, or at least to recognize him as his father's son, "young Dr. de Bonno." He returned these greetings with nods and smiles of his own, plus flustered motions with his free hand indicating that, regrettably, he was expected elsewhere. He returned to the buffet, vaguely aware that he was being talked about; he swallowed his whiskey quickly and took another.

The moment that he had been dreading finally arrived when a sort of informal delegation of his father's old friends brought him to bay between a ficus tree and a corner of the buffet table. Nodding and smiling like an imbecile automaton, he accepted their compliments, condolences, words of encouragement. They reminded him what promise he had shown, even as a very young boy, and what great hopes they all had for him. He thanked them and made his escape. This time he made it all the way to the other end of the buffet, past the silver and the crystal and the subtropical flower arrangements to the bar, where he went in search of his third whiskey.

He heard voices speaking Russian right behind him and was suddenly reminded of the real purpose of his visit to the embassy. He felt impatient to get it over with, preferably before he got completely drunk and made some sort of spectacle of himself, but Zubbieq was still nowhere to be seen. Instead, at the edge of the crowd that surrounded the bar, he caught the eye of a very attractive young woman with the voluptuous figure and provocative-pouty expression of an Italian film starlet of the old school; Michael decided she might actually be Italian. He turned his head away, took a few more gulps of whiskey, and turned to look at her again; she was staring back at him blandly, with neither flirtatiousness nor curiosity.

Who was she? Almost certainly not another old friend of his father's, much less likely to be a wife than a girlfriend, or a gossip columnist, or a beautiful spy queen who had sold herself for Soviet gold. He held up his glass, as if to inquire if she would care for a drink, but before she had time to reply, a solid phalanx of German diplomats, East and West, had pushed their way through to the bar and set up a clamor for "fodka." She had disappeared from sight, though not without giving him a tantalizing smile (unless he had imagined it). He stood indecisively for a moment, then decided to cleave a passage through the dense crowd that had collected around the pyramids of caviar sandwiches, the shashlik, and the attractive little hillocks of crystallized fruit on the buffet table. She was nowhere to be seen.

Someone laid a hand on his sleeve, and he gave a start, thinking for just an instant that it might be she. But it was Zubbieq, affable, animated, his cheeks flushed and his forehead glistening. "I'm so glad you've come, Dr. de Bonno. Quite an elegant gathering, don't you think?"

Michael did not reply, still scanning the room for a glimpse of the elusive brunette.

"If only the nations of the world could get on as well as some of their representatives appear to be doing tonight," said Zubbieq.

"Given a limitless supply of caviar and vodka," said Michael, "perhaps they would."

"You'd better come with me. . . . It looks as if the prime minister may not be able to join us, but there's someone else here who can fill you in on what this is all about." Michael noted with interest that Zubbieq seemed apprehensive about something—perhaps that whoever was delegated to stand in for the prime minister wasn't going to turn up either—and he allowed himself to be herded toward the door to a narrow hallway, like a ship's companionway, at the other end of the room. Zubbieq continued to talk to him in a low, urgent voice, as if every moment of their encounter was too precious to be wasted.

"The gentleman I'm about to introduce you to—who is not affiliated with the government of Malta, as you'll soon discover—is nevertheless going to explain to you the exact nature, and importance, of the mission that your country has entrusted you with. You mustn't think I'm merely being rhetorical or sentimental when I assure you that this is what your father would have done. I merely state it as a fact . . . and I leave it to you to decide whether it's what he would have wanted you to do as well."

Just as they were about to step out of the heat and tumult of the reception hall, Michael caught sight of the brunette standing by a palm tree set in an immense marble planter. She seemed totally self-absorbed, her face impassive, but she swung her long dark mane from side to side, which Michael took as a sign that she had at least taken note of his departure.

Zubbieq led him to a small library a few steps down the hall, a sort of Edwardian smoking room full of old oak paneling and soft brown leather. The sight of a Soviet officer standing in the middle of the room instantly relieved Michael of the last comforting remnants of his drunkenness. Colonel Akhmedov (Michael was told his name but nothing more about him) was standing by an armchair, his right hand extended stiffly toward Michael, as if he were about to hand him a package, his jowls compressed into a bristly pinkish ruff by the stiff collar of his tunic, his face round and frowning like a disapproving moon.

Three commodious armchairs had been arranged in triangular formation, and the colonel motioned for the others to sit down. To Michael at least, his armchair smelled as if it had recently been sprayed with some sort of aerosol essence of Napoleon brandy and clear Havanas. Zubbieq began the conversation with a number of vaguely phrased but ominous predictions that the young Dr. de Bonno's eventual success in carrying on his father's work in the fields of medicine and public health might in some way be connected with his evident willingness to emulate his father as a patriotic Maltese and a helpful friend of government. Zubbieq was no less prolix and portentous than before, but his speech was halting and indistinct, perhaps, Michael thought, because he did not much relish the task of warming up his audience for the Soviet officer—who was obviously the headline act—but more likely because he was terrified.

"I think we'd better get on with it," the colonel broke in after several minutes. "Dr. de Bonno, quite simply, I am going to acquaint you with the situation as we see it and the reasons your government has requested your cooperation in this matter." The colonel leaned back against the headrest of the armchair and continued speaking while staring up at the ceiling. Unlike Zubbieq, Michael felt perfectly calm. The unreality of the situation—highlighted by the colonel's stiff, professorial manner, his precise, peculiarly cadenced English, and his unlovely, almost grotesque physical appearance—and the nostalgic recollection of three stiff whiskeys in rapid succession had induced in him a certain philosophical detachment.

"First of all," the colonel was saying, "you must understand that I am not speaking from a standpoint of political partisanship and that what I am saying ultimately has little to do with the rivalry between my country and the United States of America. The world today is divided into a number of different blocs—socialist, capitalist, neutralist, Islamic, the rich nations, the poor nations, and all the rest. Normally, when we speak of some new political development or weapons system as 'destabilizing,' we mean that it threatens to upset the balance of power between the two superpowers. But in this case, we're talking about something quite different—a situation in which the balance is tipped decisively in favor of one of these blocs, the Western capitalist bloc, and to the detriment of all the others . . . a situation quite comparable to the years after World War II, when only the United States possessed the secret of the atomic bomb, except that those who have developed this new technology need not trouble themselves with any strategic or ethical restrictions on its use." The colonel smiled wistfully at this vision of unrestrained, all-out global conflict, then removed his wire-framed glasses and peered at Michael myopically but intently. "Has anyone spoken to you of Project Arcade?"

Michael shook his head.

"Its objective, essentially, is to provide the pope of Rome and the Catholic church—historically, the most effective apologists and propagandists for so-called democratic capitalism—with the means necessary to speak directly to an audience of 700 million Catholics all over the globe. The United States and its allies have agreed to contribute a network of telecommunications satellites and several hours of broadcast time each day so that the pope and other princes of the Church can communicate, simultaneously and almost instantaneously, with every diocese in the world, and thus to the broad masses of the faithful. *Arcade* means exactly what it says." The colonel traced a succession of little parabolas in the air in front of him, as if to illustrate the continuous broadcast range of a series of geosynchronous satellites circling the globe.

"As for the reception equipment," the colonel continued, "all that's really required is a parabolic antenna, ninety centimeters in diameter, aimed toward the closest satellite in the network. These would cost several hundred dollars apiece, so that all of the roughly twenty-five hundred Roman Catholic dioceses in the world could be equipped for less than a million dollars. This may seem like no great matter to you, but I assure you that it is something that its sponsors and organizers, as well as all other interested parties, are inclined to take very seriously."

Zubbieq, who had been listening in fretful silence, selected a thin, golden-brown cigar from the humidor on the table, then offered one to Michael, who accepted gratefully; the cigar seemed perfectly suited to the atmosphere and decor.

"But America isn't Ireland or Italy," protested Michael a few moments later while exhaling a great cloud of pungent blue smoke, "and Catholicism isn't the established church of the United States. I can't see why the American government, particularly the elected officials in Congress and whatnot, should be all that keen on helping out the pope, even to the tune of a paltry million dollars."

Even as he said this, Michael had an obscure foreboding that he was stepping into a trap. It seemed to him that to take part in a discussion of this kind somehow constituted an agreement that he would abide by its conclusions. Zubbieq had half taunted and half tempted him into agreeing to cooperate with this bizarre project. Like a perfect twentieth-century Faust, he seemed to have come very close to selling his soul (and without really knowing why, or even to whom) for a few thousand hours of computer time.

"The eventual plan," the colonel was saying, "is that this religious channel will be parceled out among the various Judeo-Christian sects and denominations, so that the Jews and the Protestants will stand to benefit directly from it too. But for reasons that are quite basic to the logic of this operation, the Vatican is uniquely qualified to serve as base of operations and generalissimo of Project Arcade; the non-Catholics who might be in a position to approve or impede this program will undoubtedly fall in line. Perhaps it's merely a case of 'the devil that one knows.' You'll agree, Dr. de Bonno, for all its famous diversity and cultural pluralism, the West always seems ready to pull together—to regain, in fact, a monolithic and virtually medieval sense of solidarity—whenever it's called upon to deal with the Arabs or the Reds."

"Perhaps," said Michael. "But I'm still not sure I understand why you're both so concerned about this."

"What we're concerned about," said the colonel, "is stability and world order, which we equate, quite simply, with the survival of this planet. We are convinced that Project Arcade will have a tremendously destabilizing effect, since it consists of nothing more than an attempt by nonmilitary means to extend the sphere of influence of the Western bloc—far beyond the utmost frontiers of the great colonial empires of the past. We are also concerned that such an attempt would be regarded as so provocative that it would ultimately have to be met with force."

"In other words," said Michael, a little incautiously, "you feel yourself incapable of fending off an all-out assault on the part of the College of Cardinals."

This seemed to be the sort of joke the colonel could appreciate; he smiled briefly. "In the course of the last thousand years, the peoples of Eastern Europe have had to repel many such attempts at conquest or forcible conversion inspired by the Catholic church. The supposed defender of the weak has always been a great exploiter of the weakness of others. For the moment, we are more concerned with certain states on the fringes of the Islamic world that seem to be particularly at risk."

"And with Poland?" said Michael.

At the mention of Poland, it seemed to Michael that the pinkish fold of flesh above the colonel's collar had acquired a sort of dull-red glow. "As I've told you, that is merely part of a historic pattern. In this case, however, the aggressor is equipped not merely with lances and prayer books but rather with a string of satellites and an ultra-high-powered computer of radical new design. We have heard a great deal in recent years about the power of advanced telecommunications to erase both geographical and political frontiers—but this is not a process that we regard as progressive or desirable when carried out in the service of an ancient bigotry or an even more primitive greed for power and conquest. The Americans seem intent on deploying this technology of the future in order to advance the great political ideal of the Middle Ages; simply stated, they are preparing to launch a new Crusade, a holy war."

The colonel shook his head rapidly from side to side, as if to ensure that some delicate but refractory mechanism was in proper working order, then strode over to one wall of the library, lined from floor to ceiling with venerable leather-bound volumes. It was clear from his professorial stance that he would have preferred a blackboard.

"I'll cite you another commonplace of history, Dr. de Bonno—an imperialist state that is forced to make war on its neighbors, to continue to gorge itself on conquest and plunder until it occupies what it regards as its 'rightful' sphere of influence, as a remedy for its own internal chaos and disorder. The Nazis provide a striking example of this phenomenon—the lust for conquest that seems to provide its own unique psychological dynamic, which frequently overrules the councils of political and strategic common sense, even the basic human instinct of self-preservation.

"Let us suppose, for the moment," he went on, "that the nations of the Western bloc are currently in the throes of a spiritual and economic crisis. They feel the need to get a grip on themselves, an impulse that in such great states as these is often translated into the need to get a firmer grip on their neighbors, their vassals and poor relations—to regain their former sense of solidity and cohesion by administering discipline to whichever regions of the world seem to be threatening to shake off their political influence. As historical examples, you might consider the Americans in Vietnam, the French in Algeria, the British in Kenya and Malaya, at Suez and in Cyprus and a half-dozen other places around the globe.

"The current battlefield is and will continue to be South America, which is the home not only of the majority of the world's Catholics but of at least a dozen armed liberation struggles. The collectivist ideal is gaining ground there every year, most notably among the clergy. It seems clear enough that the Vatican and the United States can assist each other in damping the flames of so-called liberation theology and stamping out the threat to American economic hegemony over the region. The Americans provide the technology; the pope provides the authority of Saint Peter's throne as well as his personal charisma and the light of his telegenic countenance."

The colonel raked his finger along a line of books, suggesting that he was about to pass on to the second stage of his discourse. "This sort of collusion between the capitalist system and the guardians of Judeo-Christian morality is not a recent invention, though perhaps it is more flagrant in a case like this than ever before. Like the thousands of living corpses being sustained by purely mechanical means in American hospitals, these so-called traditional Christian values, now moribund, even moldering, are ready to be retrieved from the valley of the shadow—by purely electronic means this time—infused with new life, and set off on their triumphal march into the twenty-first century. What we're concerned with here is the fate of almost a billion people all over the globe who, on account of their simple, unquestioning faith, may be susceptible to this sort of cynical propaganda, may be taken in by such a trick and induced to set off on all sorts of reactionary adventures, to betray the objective interests of their class and country, to heedlessly trample and despoil the fruit of decades of struggle against exploitation and injustice."

Zubbieq brandished the glowing tip of his cigar to indicate that he would like to say a word. Perhaps, Michael thought, he was concerned that the colonel was laying it on a bit too thick. "I have no idea what your own religious convictions might be, Dr. de Bonno, but I'd like to clarify one point here if I might. First, the monstrous conspiracy that the colonel is speaking of has absolutely nothing to do with what we conventionally mean by such terms as *evangelism* or *religious revival* or *the propagation of the faith*, except perhaps in the corrupt and shabby way that these first two terms are sometimes used in Britain and in America or that the other is sometimes used as a sort of clerical euphemism for the clandestine espionage undertaken by the Vatican . . . as against our own country, for example.

"What we are talking of here has nothing to do with individual human spirituality and everything to do with mass political manipulation of the grossest sort. This Crusade that the colonel refers to is none other than an unholy alliance of the most conservative social forces in the capitalist world—including Japan, a nation with its own 'traditional values' that are about as far removed from Roman Catholicism as it's possible to be. The Japanese have agreed to *donate* a prototype of what is undoubtedly the most advanced computer in the world today, which represents no small investment on their part in the project—in addition to symbolizing, if I may say so, the incalculable advantage enjoyed by a tiny technocratic elite with respect to the rest of humankind."

Michael had been listening to all this with a growing sense of bafflement and impatience, wondering what it could possibly have to do with him. During the previous several minutes, an alcoholic mist had risen to obscure some of the murkier portions of the colonel's discourse, but at the mention of Japan, he was suddenly rapt with attention. The colonel's talk of these high-level machinations involving the United States and the Vatican had naturally suggested *Resaccio*, and Resaccio plus computers plus Japan had suggested *Wendy*.

It seemed for the moment, however, that the mystery was not to be clarified. The colonel produced a briefcase from the shadow of his vast armchair and from it removed a map, purportedly of U.S. origin, which showed how transmissions from the Vatican could be beamed back to every Catholic community on earth, from Alaska to New Zealand, with the help of a small satellite flotilla. The PSI-100 computer, the colonel explained, would be used not only to coordinate these activities but also to compile a massive data base, containing extensive demographic information on all these communities and a kind of potential order-of-battle roster in expectation of the day, according to Akhmedov, when all of Christendom would be transformed into a militant strike force of bigoted, battle-ready fanatics. Then the colonel lapsed into silence as Michael studied the map and Zubbieq began to expound the Maltese government's point of view.

"Here on Malta," he began, "we have benefited from the influence of many different cultures, as evidenced by the architecture of our cities and the character of our population. I love our island, Dr. de Bonno, and one of the things I love best about it is its sense of balance and harmony. It seems to me that our mongrel origins—through which we have inherited not only what is hardiest but also I believe what is best in many different peoples—impose upon us certain responsibilities as well, not only to preserve our island's heritage but also to fight on behalf of tolerance and cultural diversity throughout the world.

"You've undoubtedly heard news of what's been called the 'scholastic quarrel' between the government and the Church. It took many years of struggle before the Church accepted the principle of free public education, as well as the addition of laypersons to the admissions panels of our educational institutions. In return, the government agreed to make no attempt to secularize the school system or to confiscate Church property and accepted the appointment of a papal nuncio to represent the interests of the Vatican on our island. This seems to represent a sane and very sensible compromise.

"But you mustn't by any means think," he went on, "that the government's position in this matter has anything to do with its past political differences with the Vatican, which we must now regard as being settled. Quite the contrary. If we have adopted the position just expressed by Colonel Akhmedov, it is simply because we believe that the effects of Project Arcade would be profoundly destabilizing, and our own strategic position is likely to excite the cupidity of one or the other of the powers during a time of heightened global tensions.

"We believe that anything we can do to contribute to the failure of Project Arcade will also represent a positive contribution to the cause of world peace, and that we therefore have almost a moral obligation to do so—and not merely for the selfish purpose of keeping our island out of harm's way. This is something that your father believed very strongly, Michael, and I hope that now you understand why he did. I realize that what we're asking of you is no small thing, and I also suspect that some of the measures that will have to be taken to assure your protection may not be entirely to your liking—"

"What sort of measures?" Michael knew perfectly well that it was too late to quibble about things of this kind. Until now he had simply wanted to find out more about what his father had been up to, and about Wendy. In fact, he had found out very little and landed himself in a substantial mess. Zubbieq had made it quite clear that there would be no future for him on the isle of Malta if he failed to carry out whatever task it was that they had picked for him, and Akhmedov did not look as if he had very much respect for the principles of collective bargaining.

"Colonel Akhmedov will be responsible for your security," said Zubbieq unhelpfully. The colonel himself was fidgeting in his armchair, clearly reluctant to descend from the level of global strategies and world-historical forces to a discussion of mere trivialities.

"You'll be informed of the details as and when the necessity arises," said the colonel. "Rest assured that you'll be well looked after. Your

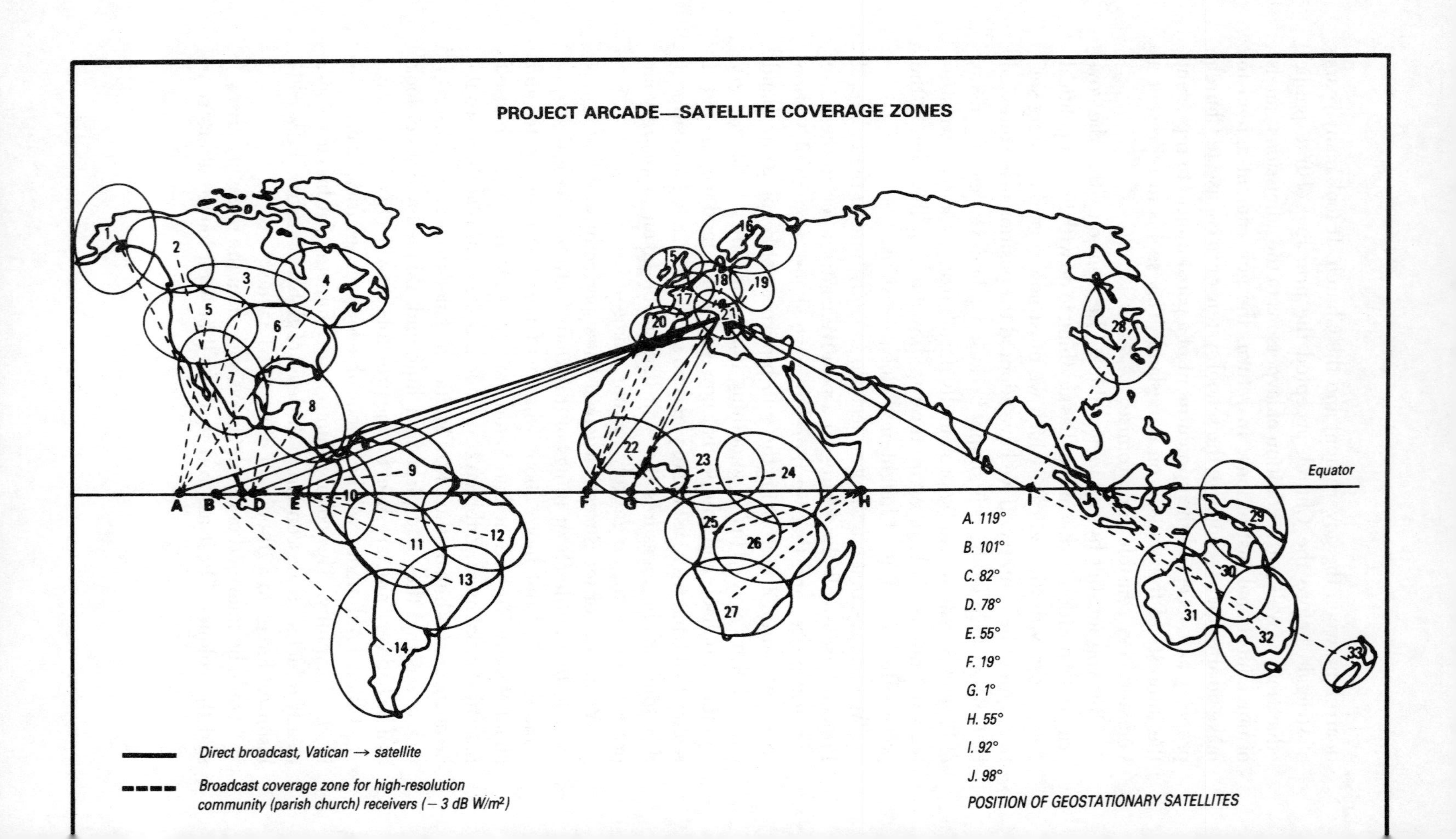
PROJECT ARCADE—SATELLITE COVERAGE ZONES
Equator
1
2
3
4
5
6
7
8
9
10
11
12
13
14
15
16
17
18
19
20
21
22
23
24
25
26
27
28
29
30
31
32
33
A
B
C
D
E
F
G
H
I
J
A. 119°
B. 101°
C. 82°
D. 78°
E. 55°
F. 19°
G. 1°
H. 55°
I. 92°
J. 98°
POSITION OF GEOSTATIONARY SATELLITES
Direct broadcast, Vatican → satellite
Broadcast coverage zone for high-resolution community (parish church) receivers (– 3 dB W/m²)

Individual Broadcast Zones

1. U.S.—CANADA
2. CANADA
3. U.S.—CANADA
4. CANADA—U.S.
5. U.S.
6. U.S.
7. MEXICO
8. GUATEMALA—MEXICO—EL SALVADOR—NICARAGUA—COSTA RICA—PANAMA
9. VENEZUELA—GUYANA—SURINAM
10. COLOMBIA—ECUADOR—PERU
11. BRAZIL—PERU—BOLIVIA
12. BRAZIL
13. BRAZIL—PARAGUAY—URUGUAY
14. CHILE—ARGENTINA
15. GREAT BRITAIN—IRELAND
16. NORWAY—SWEDEN—FINLAND
17. FRANCE—BELGIUM—LUXEMBOURG—SWITZERLAND
18. GERMAN FED. REPUBLIC—NETHERLANDS—AUSTRIA—GERMAN DEM. REPUBLIC
19. POLAND—CZECHOSLOVAKIA
20. SPAIN—PORTUGAL
21. ITALY—VATICAN CITY-STATE—MALTA
22. IVORY COAST—GHANA—TOGO—BENIN
23. CENTRAL AFRICAN REPUBLIC—CAMEROON—EQUATORIAL GUINEA—GABON—CONGO—ZAIRE
24. ZAIRE—UGANDA—KENYA—RWANDA—TANZANIA
25. ZAIRE—ANGOLA—ZAMBIA
26. ZAMBIA—ZIMBABWE—MALAWI—MOZAMBIQUE
27. BOTSWANA—SOUTH AFRICA—SWAZILAND—LESOTHO
28. JAPAN
29. INDONESIA—PAPUA-NEW GUINEA
30. AUSTRALIA
31. AUSTRALIA
32. AUSTRALIA
33. NEW ZEALAND

first briefing session will be in approximately one week's time . . . but not here."

"Not here at the embassy, you mean?" asked Michael.

"Not here on Malta. In Libya. At a training camp near Tripoli, in fact. . . . For the present, I can only sketch in the broadest outlines what will be required of you. As I think you know, another PSI-100 computer is to be installed on the premises of the university in Msida, an exact duplicate of the machine that is shortly to be employed by the Pontifical Academy of Sciences, under the direction of Father Nicholas Resaccio."

That name! The scrap of yellowed newsprint that had fallen out of the wood box in the cottage in the forest of Compiègne, the photograph of the priest in *L'Osservatore Romano*.

"I believe that Mr. Zubbieq has already explained the arrangement by which the computer will be made available to you for the furtherance of your neurological research, or for whatever purpose you may desire. In return, you will supervise the transfer of all data bases and programs developed on the duplicate machine in Rome—everything, in other words, essential to the operation of Project Arcade—into the files of your machine on Malta."

"But how do you expect me to do a thing like that if I don't even—"

"We expect nothing of you that's unreasonable, Dr. de Bonno. Your task will be a very simple one, and the process of copying these files in the ordinary manner will be carried out with the assistance of one of Father Resaccio's associates in Rome. You will be meeting this person face to face when you get to Tripoli, and I have no doubt that this encounter will furnish you with ample motivation to begin your work with us when you return to Malta." On this cryptic note, the colonel collected his map and briefcase, rose to his feet, nodded curtly to both Michael and Zubbieq, and disappeared through an inner door behind them that Michael had not even noticed as he came in.

After several long moments of silence, Zubbieq rose to his feet, seemingly ill at ease, and suggested to Michael that he should return to the reception hall "and enjoy some more of the magnificent hospitality of our Russian friends." Michael interpreted this to mean that the future would look a great deal brighter after four or five more scotches, but he was unwilling to let the sleek little man get away so easily. He had had enough condescension and obfuscation and insincerity and pomposity, and he felt like getting a little bit of his own back.

It seemed obvious enough now, for example, that it was Zubbieq who had sent him a copy of *L'Osservatore Romano*, in the hope that he would stumble across that photograph of Wendy with Nicholas Resaccio . . . and that this would prove decisive in convincing him to cooperate, as indeed it had. He suddenly recalled something else he had seen in the Vatican paper and decided to take it up immediately with Zubbieq.

"You realize, Mr. Zubbieq, that you're asking me to be the agent by whom the prophecy of Saint Malachi is to be fulfilled—I'm not sure that's a very enviable position."

"I beg your pardon?"

"You're not familiar with the prophecies of Saint Malachi? There was a lead article about them in *L'Osservatore Romano* the other day—I assumed that that was why you had it sent to my father's office."

"You'll have to enlighten me."

"Most certainly. Saint Malachi was an Irish bishop of the twelfth century who composed a series of one hundred Latin prophecies concerning the popes who would reign in the centuries to come. The earlier ones proved sufficiently accurate that the Church could never quite bring itself to have them suppressed; many of them turned out to be quite flattering, and thus had a certain public relations value."

"And the particular prophecy that you were referring to just now?"

"It's the one that's supposed to pertain to the current pope, John Paul II. Like the others, it's just a single phrase—*De labore solis*, which means 'Of the troubles of the sun,' a phrase that has defied all attempts at interpretation thus far; that's basically what the article was about. The prophecy for his predecessor, John Paul I, was *De mediatæ lunæ*, 'Half a moon,' which clearly refers to the fact that he reigned for no more than a few weeks. Now, you may well wonder what sort of troubles the sun might have, in connection with the Polish pope or otherwise, and it seems to me that Project Arcade might very well have given us the answer.

"In Malachi's day, the sun was still believed to be a satellite of the earth, so perhaps the prophecy refers to an *artificial* satellite of the earth, which sheds its beams—or in this case, the light of Gospels—over all mankind. In a word, the Vatican satellite. And *De labore solis* is usually taken to mean 'Of the troublesome *course* of the sun,' but I believe that since the prophecy is supposed to refer to John Paul II, the troubles are going to be experienced by him rather than by the satellite itself, and all because of me. In other words, I'm going to be personally responsible for the worst thing that happens to him, maybe to all of Christendom, during his entire reign, which sounds very destabilizing indeed. Frankly, Mr. Zubbieq, I'm not sure I like the sound of it."

Zubbieq did not appear to be amused. "I'd advise you to come down to earth, Dr. de Bonno. And I don't think it would be very wise to let Colonel Akhmedov or any of his friends hear you going on like that. In any case, we're not asking you to do anything of the sort. We're simply asking you to do your duty as a Maltese citizen—as a citizen of the nonaligned world if you will—just exactly as your father would have done."

"And would you have sent my father off to Tripoli?"

Zubbieq looked down at the floor for a moment before replying. "Quite possibly not." He shook his head. "No, almost certainly not."

"So that as far as you're concerned, his death came at quite a convenient time . . . his death and my return to the island." Without waiting for a reply, Michael turned his back on Zubbieq and strode off down the corridor.

When Michael returned to the reception hall, there were just a few stragglers picking over the remains of the buffet. He had no difficulty in getting served at the bar and decided to try champagne this time. The bartender proved cooperative, and he was on his third glass when the brunette turned up again.

"And where did you disappear to?" she asked him, her eyes open very wide as if she were surprised that he was still among the living. She also seemed a little drunk.

"They had to let me go," he replied. "A case of mistaken identity. Happens quite often, I understand."

She let out a snort of laughter to acknowledge the joke. "Oh, really?"

"Really. And why are they hanging on to you, may I ask?"

"It's not them so much. It's him." She thrust out her chin in the direction of a tall, silver-haired man across the room. "I follow him everywhere and he never pays any attention to me. Why, if I left this minute, he wouldn't even notice I was gone."

"In that case," said Michael, "have you ever seen the Roman villa by moonlight?"

"He's an MP, in the House of Representatives," she added by way of explanation. "And no, I've never been. It might make a nice change from the *Russian* villa."

Michael drove slowly, but they still had to circle Rabat three times before they spotted the Roman villa, crouched in the shadows of the archeological museum. Then, very slowly, they drove through Mdina; Michael's companion was a very appreciative tourist, exclaiming with pleasure and clapping her hands like a little girl. She said that her name was Leilah.

"You know what that one is?" asked Michael, pointing to an old stone building.

"No."

"That's the old Benedictine abbey. It was a convent actually, with nuns." He had been curious to see if he could say those words out loud without thinking of Wendy. He could not.

"Ask me another question," said Leilah.

"All right. . . . How many Libyan advisers are there on the island of Malta?"

"I have no idea. Giovanni would know. That's the name of my MP. I'll have to say . . . two hundred?"

"Close enough. Three thousand. Ready for another?"

"All right."

"Why is it, do you suppose, that the anchorage fees paid by Russian ships that lay over on Malta are three times as high as anywhere else in the world?"

"I have no idea. Why?"

"I'm not sure either, but I *think* it has something to do with the fact that everyone likes us so much—like the Libyans actually pay us to send their advisers over here, like a holiday camp or something. So it must be that everyone loves us because we're just so tremendously lovable."

"You ask very hard questions," said Leilah, "but now I have an easier one for you. . . . What were you doing when you left the party for all that time? Are you a spy?"

"I'm not allowed to tell you," said Michael, trying to keep his voice playful. "And I object to that line of questioning very strongly." This reminded him of innumerable deadly serious scenes that he had been through with Wendy. He had wanted to know everything, to know all her secrets, and he had suffered terribly for three years, but now that he had finally learned the one big secret, he could not see that this knowledge had made him any happier or easier in his mind, nor was it likely to in the future. He stepped on the gas pedal, the car lurched forward, and a sudden wave of nausea almost lifted him out of the driver's seat.

Now at least, he thought to himself, *it will all have to do with me as much as with you, Sister Wendy. You'll need me now. I'll be your equal. And maybe this business will be the death of me, but at least there'll be no secrets and no objections ever again.*

Leilah was saying something to him. "I think you are a Russian spy. Your name isn't Michael at all—it's Misha!" Michael sputtered with involuntary laughter, and then she added, "But to tell you the truth, I really don't mind."

He had pulled up in front of the villa, another of his father's legacies, a handsome three-story stone building surrounded by a little park. Leilah followed him up the front steps; she did not seem particularly surprised or impressed that he lived in such a place, and was certainly not the least bit nervous or reluctant. He took her to his little room upstairs, and they talked for quite a while. She had a frank and spontaneous way of talking that he liked very much; he could not imagine that she was capable of holding anything back or of saying anything simply for effect. *Why couldn't I have fallen in love with a woman like that?* Then life would be a very simple thing.

He encouraged her to talk about herself, he kissed her and caressed her. He forgot about *my dear Dr. de Bonno* and *I'd like to clarify one point here if I might* and *Colonel Akhmedov will be responsible for your security*; he forgot about Wendy. Leilah made love in the same way she seemed to do everything else—enthusiastically, unselfconsciously, all in a rush. She cried out very loud and then started to laugh. She was perfectly willing to start all over again, five times, ten times, but Michael, bone weary, had already collapsed into her arms.

Tripoli
November 10

It was hard to breathe. Two days earlier, autumn, with its endless rains and chilly winds out of the west, had finally arrived in Malta. The Tripoli airport was like a great slab of desert that had been baked into concrete by the desert sun. Michael's welcome as a guest of the nation had been very strange. Four men in uniform had surrounded him as soon as he stepped off the plane and guided him with abrupt mechanical gestures, stares, and nudges, like four very officious sheepdogs herding a single sheep. The other passengers disappeared inside the terminal; Michael walked on, empty-handed, toward a black Fiat that was parked some distance away.

The back door flew open and Michael got inside, sliding tentatively over the hot upholstery. The door slammed shut behind him; there were curtains on both rear windows, and a tinted glass partition separated them from the driver's seat. *Purdah*, said Michael to himself, though not out loud. "My name is Abdul," said a voice, and in a moment or two, Michael could just make out the features of the man sitting next to him—short curly hair, pointy chin, a face as sharp as a hatchet blade. Michael did not feel it necessary to mention that they had already spoken on the telephone, several weeks earlier. Abdul, with one hand resting on his knee and fidgeting nervously, seemed to have nothing further to say for the moment. Michael found himself sitting next to a certified international terrorist, but he suddenly realized that the only thing he was really concerned about was whether Wendy was sleeping with him.

As the car sped toward, or possibly through, the invisible city of Tripoli, Michael suddenly saw himself as a character in a comic book, not one of the fearless, supremely competent heroes but something more like *Tintin in Qaddafiland*, in which a boyish, bewildered innocent falls into the hands of cutthroats and thugs. He was ideally suited for life as it was, with his EEGs and stoical cats and root-mean-square deviations, for a life of order and method amid the tranquil hum of the laboratory. *Then why am I here?* "For love" did not seem an altogether satisfactory answer.

"Here we are," said Abdul as he pulled back the curtain beside him. Michael could see a tangle of barbed wire and a whitewashed wall. The driver braked abruptly, and Michael threw up his hands to keep from bashing his nose against the glass partition. A helmeted soldier's head appeared outside the window, gave a cry, and the car was in motion again. It gave a lurch and then skirted the edge of a kind of wooden stockade reinforced with sandbags and concertina wire. Then came a second checkpoint; three soldiers, one after another, examined the driver's documents. The third ordered them to roll down the window and stared at Michael for a good thirty seconds until Abdul lost patience with him and barked out something in Arabic. The soldier barked back but waved them on. After another fifty yards the driver slammed on the brakes.

"Get out," said Abdul.

Michael had half expected to be blindfolded after all that had gone before, but, on the contrary, Abdul was eager to show the place off. This, he explained, was the famous Al-'Aziziya barracks, Colonel Qaddafi's personal headquarters, a collection of low buildings in a stark utilitarian style that seemed like a compromise between corporate modernism and military necessity; there were few windows, a great many armored walls and doors and gun emplacements. The place was swarming with soldiers, all engaged in some purposeful activity, not in formation but individually or in small groups, like ants.

It seemed to Michael that there were at least two thousand troops within sight as they walked around a cubical white building and found themselves in an immense courtyard lined with rows of machine guns and in the center a large khaki tent. Michael had heard that Colonel Qaddafi, the son of a nomad family, still preferred to live under canvas, even though the rest of his impressive headquarters could hardly be described as portable. The tent was guarded by thirty soldiers. The three at the door, bristling with cartridges and side arms and grenades, subjected Michael to a final, extremely realistic pantomime of anti-imperialist vigilance. One of them patted down his pockets, then all three permitted him to enter with crisp, reluctant nods.

Inside the tent was no cooler than outside; the air was heavy, and it seemed very dark. Michael squinted and took a few deep breaths. In these surroundings, only Colonel Qaddafi seemed at all real or natural. The others, Wendy and Colonel Akhmedov, seemed purely hallucinatory, an impression that was heightened by the fact that Colonel Akhmedov stared straight through him and otherwise seemed to be, or to want very much to be, somewhere else. Wendy darted a nervous glance in his direction, which was all the welcome he received from anyone. "Sit down," said Abdul.

Michael obeyed, noting as he did that the goatskins on the Colonel's floor were in much better condition than the ones that had served as the hearth rug of his cottage in the forest of Compiègne. Abdul sat down between Michael and Wendy, an action in which Michael detected a certain hostility that seemed rather more personal than broadly anti-imperialist. Qaddafi was wearing a kaffiyeh and squatting tailor-fashion on the floor—like a sheikh of the desert hearing petitions from his subjects hundreds of miles out of reach of any more formally constituted authority—though the effect of this was partially spoiled by the rumble of the trucks and tanks outside. A soldier came into the tent with little cups of tea on a broad metal platter and handed them around; then he sat down, unholstered his revolver, and set it in front of him.

"Islam is the light of the world," said Qaddafi unexpectedly. "Its proper role is the education of mankind." He spoke a kind of elaborate textbook English, though somewhat haltingly; his accent was partly Arabic, and partly Italian, very much, it seemed to Michael, like a Maltese accent. The Chief of the Revolution looked at least ten years older, and a great deal less exuberant, than the television image Michael remembered. His face was puffy, his hair getting gray; he seemed a little tired and worn out, like a middle-aged schoolmaster or a bleary café intellectual beneath the sheikh's corded headdress.

"The Libyan revolution is the messenger of Islam, the standard and pride of Islam. Our task is to carry the message of Islam beyond our borders. Our mission must be to conquer the world by convincing it of the truth of Islam." He went on in this vein for several more minutes; Akhmedov, evidently a connoisseur of political harangues of this kind, seemed unimpressed to the point of torpor. Michael swallowed his cup of tea, minty and boiling, then reached out, very audaciously, and poured himself another. Wendy seemed to be watching Abdul rather than Qaddafi, perhaps merely as her model of correct revolutionary behavior. Michael was fascinated by Qaddafi, by the image of a desert sheikh who was not a sheikh but an ex–fighter pilot who had seen fit to prop up the twin pillars of the sheikh's traditional authority—the Koran and his strong right arm—with anti-aircraft batteries and mine fields and barbed-wire entanglements.

Meanwhile, the Colonel had moved on to a new topic. "The Vatican no longer exists as a moral or religious authority; it is only the plaything of the Americans. Today, Mr. Reagan is the temporal prince of Christianity. He has mistaken himself for Richard the Lion-Hearted, and he wants to lead his people on a new crusade—the Tenth Crusade. This time not to recover the Holy Places, for these are already in the hands of the Zionists, but to sow confusion and disorder among the nations of Islam. He has sent his emissary, the pope, into Morocco and other lands where the leaders of the people, like that contemptible puppet Hassan, have sold themselves for American planes and guns."

Once again Michael was fascinated, more by the man than by the contents of his diatribe, which appeared to be just another endless propaganda loop, suitable to be carved into thirty-second segments for the international TV cameras. Now, however, the Colonel's face was contorted with fury. "Reagan is determined to oppose the triumphal progress of the Islamic revolution. He knows that we propose to bring about the liberation of the peoples of the entire world. He wants to make certain that the people of the West are not released from their present state of captivity, and as his watchdog and slave master he has chosen . . . John Paul II."

Wendy nodded vehemently at this, which instantly brought Michael out of his reverie. He had been imagining, in some sense at least, that this undoubtedly picturesque spectacle had been arranged for his benefit. Abdul knew it all by heart, and Akhmedov was not the least bit impressed. But in fact this was all for Wendy; she and the Colonel were engaging in a sort of sacrament or ceremony, in which their solemn hatred of the common enemy was ritually affirmed. They had no intention of trying to win him over with the Colonel's involuted and obsessive oratory. They were simply providing him with a demonstration of the fact that Wendy was theirs and he would be ill advised to try to detach her from them. Instead, he was faced with the choice of cooperating with them, and on their terms, or of bowing out.

The ritual introduction was over. The next phase of the Colonel's address was more specific and a great deal more coherent. "The Church does not look favorably on the formation of personality cults, and this tremendous aggrandizement of the personal power of the pope is bound to encounter serious resistance. We can expect to see another outbreak of the perennial quarrel between the progressives and the conservatives within the Church, of much the same kind that followed the council of 1870. Our mission is to heighten the contradictions that already exist within the Church and to lend assistance, covertly of course, to the conservative faction, which is bound to be opposed to the implementation of Operation Arcade."

Michael had read that Qaddafi was fascinated by theology, but he had not expected that this fascination would extend so far beyond the teachings of the Koran and the law of the mullahs. After a few moments' hesitation, he started to reach over to set his teacup back on the low table beside him, but Abdul immediately checked him with a stiff-armed gesture. Evidently it was forbidden to fidget with one's teacup while the chief of the Libyan *Jamahirya* was still in full cry.

"We will lend our backing to the weaker side in this quarrel to ensure that the Church destroys itself from within. We have no hatred for Christians, and we recognize that there are many among them, persons of integrity, sincere in their faith, who could never be a party to the sort of shabby political trickery that Operation Arcade represents. All those who are stalwart in their faith are our objective allies. It is still not precisely clear to me what tactics should be adopted in such a case. I am only a frontline fighter, not a strategist." Then, for the first time, he turned toward Wendy and looked at her directly.

"When Miss Keenes begins her work for us in Rome, her first task will be to survey the land and report to us on the weak points of the project. She will be at the source, after all, from which all the computer programs will originate, the point at which the entire informational infrastructure"—he brought this fashionable word out with obvious relish—"of the project will be erected. Her main task of course will be to initiate the transfer of all primary data to the duplicate computer on Malta, in order to present us with an exact replica, if I may phrase it so, of the hideous creature that is taking shape in the Vatican."

Michael thought back to the aftermath of his encounter with Akhmedov at the embassy. He had told himself that he would be Wendy's equal, that she would need him. Now it seemed quite clear that she was to be the prime mover and he was to be a glorified switchboard or copy-machine operator, presiding over a sort of black mass parody or a looking-glass-world "simulation" of the real thing. From this, the Colonel went on to explain, would be distilled "the venom that will bring the great beast to its knees and reveal its weakness for all to see," or, alternatively, "the mockery of the beast that we have created in Malta will devour the original and destroy it."

After several repetitions of this theme, Michael finally grasped the essential point: namely, that after a papal address that had somehow—by this point the Colonel was much stronger on apocalyptic imagery than procedural detail—been doctored by Qaddafi's associates, perhaps including Wendy, was broadcast over the satellite network and the nature of the imposture had been publicly revealed, Project Arcade would be thoroughly discredited and the conservative, antitechnological faction in the Church would start howling for the blood of those responsible, possibly even the Holy Father.

Finally, according to the Colonel, a council of the entire Church would have to be convened, as a result of which John Paul would be thoroughly disgraced, perhaps even deposed, and with the discomfiture of its champion, the Western world would be plunged into a spiritual crisis from which it would be unlikely to emerge. "Think of it!" said the Colonel. "This great council—they will surely call it Vatican III—will also signal the triumph of the Islamic revolution! And this will all be accomplished—it must be accomplished—as a result of the glorious undertaking that we have joined in here today."

He beamed at Wendy. He seemed to be very pleased with her, even proud, as if she were the author of this eloquent harangue that had succeeded in converting him, the Colonel, to the cause of the Islamic revolution. However, as Michael was quick to observe with a small shudder of distaste, he also seemed proud of her in the way that one might be proud of a new possession or invention. Abdul was giving a very passable imitation of the disciple basking in the radiance of his master's presence, though still occasionally glancing at Wendy in a way that seemed both covetous and proprietary, as if he might almost be willing to contest the priority of the Colonel's claims to having discovered Wendy. Akhmedov was looking at no one; he seemed even to begrudge the contribution of his presence to this picturesque scene, though Michael imagined that he would have a great deal to say about it later on.

Now Qaddafi was showing signs of fatigue; there were rivulets of sweat running down his forehead, and he seemed to be having difficulty keeping his eyes open. "We are fortunate," he said finally, "that Miss Keenes and Dr. de Bonno have agreed to join us, and with their help there can be no doubt that the cause of freedom will continue its irresistible advance throughout the world." Then he spoke a few words in Arabic and gestured distractedly with his hands to indicate that the *majlis*, the audience, was at an end. Abdul and the soldier who had brought in the tea tray leapt to their feet. It was inconceivable that the Chief of the Revolution should be deprived of his well-deserved repose for an instant longer. Nevertheless, in the harsh sunlight of the courtyard, Abdul seemed somewhat apologetic.

"Colonel Qaddafi sleeps very little," he said. "He stays up every night working for the final victory of the Islamic revolution." He hooked his fingers familiarly around Wendy's arm. "The Colonel has asked me to convey to you his personal congratulations, for the excellence of your work in Tokyo as well as at Faremoutiers. He has told me that you are a brilliant underground fighter and that the revolution would progress at a much swifter pace if he had many more like you beside him. He has told me that he can sense that yours is an indomitable revolutionary spirit."

Wendy merely smiled and walked on. Michael was appalled, of course, and then, after a moment's reflection, a little encouraged. Discounting the possibility that the Colonel might really have said anything quite so fatuous, which seemed remote, it appeared that Abdul might have found himself in the position of a frontline fighter who has failed to achieve his initial objective and is forced to conduct a lengthy and humiliating siege operation. Akhmedov had already disappeared.

"With the computer on Malta and our two Arabsat satellites," said Abdul suddenly, "we are ready to move to the attack. We will beat the imperialists on their own battleground. The words of Qaddafi will prove themselves more powerful than the words of John Paul."

"You seem very sure of yourself," said Michael, who was a little taken aback by this. This was the first he had heard thus far of "our two Arabsat satellites." "Doesn't it seem rather imprudent to bring Wendy to Tripoli at a time when the intelligence services of all the countries involved in Project Arcade are undoubtedly running some sort of security check on her to make sure she's worthy of their trust? She has a police record in Britain, you know."

"Your concern does you a great deal of credit, Dr. de Bonno," said Abdul. "But we do know how to arrange these things, I assure you. And as far as these so-called intelligence services are concerned, Wendy Keenes is not in Tripoli but in Ireland, staying with friends in a little town some forty miles outside Dublin, where she will remain until it's time to leave for Rome and her new assignment. To make this little excursion, she had only to borrow the identity, and the diplomatic passport, of one of our embassy staff in Dublin two days ago. She will return in four or five days' time by the same means, and by then, surely your investigators will have reassured themselves as to her bona fides—is that the correct expression?"

Michael nodded slowly, and Abdul beckoned to him to move closer. "In the meantime," he said in a hoarse whisper, "I have a surprise for you, for both of you, and I trust a very pleasant one." After that, Michael was prepared to hear the worst.

Paris
November 8

The Vatican had long since recruited a cadre of scientific and political liaison officers for each of the sponsor nations of Project Arcade; in Paris, Michel d'Anglebert, the Jesuit provincial of France and professor of mathematics at the prestigious École Polytechnique, was the only conceivable choice. Highly placed in the hierarchy of the order yet still comparatively young at fifty-five, Father d'Anglebert was fascinated by the new technology, extremely sympathetic to the modernist program espoused by the papacy, and, unlike many of his fellow Jesuits, unconditionally loyal to the current pope.

Since the mysterious disappearance and reappearance of AF-270, Father d'Anglebert and his colleagues had been operating on virtually a wartime footing. The incident had been front-page news for several days, then been almost immediately forgotten, not because the mystery had been explained, but simply because there was no more to be said. The hijacker, Mohammed Khomsi, was still in the custody of the Soviet authorities, but it was unclear whether anything more had been learned about the real purpose of his terrorist mission or the origin of the sophisticated electronic equipment he had used to carry it out. The KGB had had ample opportunity to investigate the contents of Father Resaccio's attaché case, and one of the documents he had been carrying provided a complete exposition of the technological and political underpinnings of the project in just a few pages, including the roles to be played by the United States, Japan, and other sponsor nations in Europe.

There were a great many people in Rome, let alone in Moscow, that Father d'Anglebert prayed fervently would never set eyes upon this document, but when he confided his suspicions to Cardinal Ratzinger, prefect of the Congregatio Fide and the official of the Curia who was responsible for the overall administrative coordination of Project Arcade, he was encouraged to carry out a complete investigation—and assured that the project would under no circumstances be fatally compromised, no matter what the results of his inquiry. Naturally, he looked first to his old friend Giuseppe Pitta in Tokyo, where Nicholas Resaccio was still to be found. As it turned out, the American envoy, Wilcox, had decided to stay on for a couple of days as well, to ensure that Nicholas was properly looked after by the security staff of the American embassy. (The American diplomat had in fact been crouched convivially on Father Pitta's floor when their dinner was interrupted by d'Anglebert's phone call.)

Father Pitta was able to report that the letter addressed to Nicholas had been destroyed, in accordance with the instructions contained therein, shortly after his arrival in Tokyo; the letter addressed to Father Pitta himself, which contained a fairly lengthy précis of the two Pentagon studies that had furnished the basis for Project Arcade, was intact and in its original envelope, to which a few fragments of sealing wax still adhered. Two days later, Father d'Anglebert received two small parcels, one from Rome, containing a sample of the sealing wax that was normally used by the Vatican chancelleries, the other from Tokyo (which had been expedited on its journey by the U.S. diplomatic pouch).

One of Father d'Anglebert's classmates was a professor of physical chemistry at the Polytechnique, and he arranged for a complete laboratory analysis of the two samples of sealing wax to be carried out immediately. The proportions of gum lacquer and turpentine were different, and the crumbs of wax that had been recovered from Father Pitta's envelope contained additives that were unknown in Europe. It seemed likely that the sample had originated in the Soviet Union, in China, or in Japan. Shortly afterward, a ciphered message was sent to Cardinal Ratzinger from the office of the papal nuncio in Paris: "Have confirmation Irkutsk acquainted Project Arcade. Awaiting instructions. Michel."

The next day, Father d'Anglebert received a visit from one of the cardinal's secretaries, a pallid young man, clearly steeped in Vatican intrigue, who made a long speech detailing, with almost lascivious satisfaction, the strength and character of the opposition to Project Arcade that already existed within the Vatican. All that he could offer by way of instruction was a solemn and unnecessary caution to avoid saying anything about this to anyone (with the possible exception of Father Pitta) for fear of arousing the formidable array of sleeping dogs he had just described.

The young man went on to remind him, in an impressive speech that might have been memorized word for word, that the ultimate goal of the project was to restore true Christian values by creating a direct personal link between the Vatican and the masses of the faithful, of a kind that had not been seen in the world since Saint Peter preached in the catacombs of Rome. The fact that the project was essentially religious in its purpose and inspiration was never to be lost sight of, especially when dealing with the representatives of non-Catholic powers such as the United States and Japan. Certainly these two nations were valued and trusted allies of the Church, the secretary was quick to point out, but as far as the Vatican was concerned, neither politics nor technology could ever provide a substitute for salvation by the grace of God.

After the young man's departure, Father d'Anglebert was left to reflect on how remarkable it was that one could know so much and have so much to say and still miss the point. Now that the Russians were in the game, he and his colleagues—Nicholas Resaccio in particular—had a great deal more to worry about than the possible consequences of blundering into some old spider's web in the back corridors of the Vatican. Young Nicholas's path would undoubtedly have to be swept clear of a number of far more serious obstacles.

First, there was the question of Miss Wendy Keenes, about which his friend Pitta in Tokyo had been quite concerned. It was true that Miss Keenes had already received provisory clearance for the project and had come with the best possible recommendations—Ph.D. Oxon. and a pious protégée of the abbess of Faremoutiers. She was also, he suspected, a bit of what would have in his youth been called an adventuress, her life thus far having consisted of a rapid ascent of the academic ladder, culminating in a crisis of faith and now, as it seemed, an unabashedly careerist assault on one of the few desirable posts that the Church had to offer to an ambitious technocrat.

It was not so much that beauty, charm, and ambition were to be suspected on principle as that anyone who had so thoroughly succeeded in charming such very disparate beings as Mother Marie-Bernadette and young Nicholas Resaccio must have had some particular reason for doing so. It would be tragic for such a brilliant candidate to be needlessly sacrificed to the suspicions of fretful old men like himself and Pitta, much more so if she had performed this feat in the service of some power other than her own ambition.

D'Anglebert was pleased by the fact that Mother Marie-Bernadette conformed exactly to the mental picture he had had of her—a true *religieuse*, the epitome of kindness and dryness and humility and strength, small, lively, fluttering the folds of her outsize black robe with grand, almost theatrical gestures. The expression in her eyes told him everything that she was, inextinguishable faith and alert, ever-vigilant intelligence. It was quite cool, even cold, in her sparsely furnished office, and the abbess had perhaps also chosen to express her personality through the ascetic rigor of the decor.

"Sometimes," she was saying, "I even ask myself if we belong to the same Church. But if you want to know which one I belong to, it's the church of the poor in spirit, of the disinherited and the oppressed, of those who are hungry for God or hungry for love . . . or just hungry, for food."

"And is there another church as well?" asked d'Anglebert. "Did Christ want there to be another one?"

"Not Christ perhaps . . . but I have to ask myself all the same: When the Church develops its own appetites, for power and grandeur, then it is no longer Our Lord's Church, and the Church has given in more than once to such temptations, as you know, *mon père*. Popes have waged war to extend their territories or gain gold. Julius II wanted a tomb for himself that was even grander than the one that Michelangelo could create for him. What has all this to do with the true Church?"

"You might also say that the cathedrals—" he began, then broke off and began again. "You're perfectly right, of course. Yours is indeed the one true Church, the only one, and it's mine as well. Please believe me when I tell you this."

"Then I have a favor to ask you. Please spare us the gilded crosses and the weathercocks on the church spires. I believe that the Lord will be annoyed by the sight of all your antennas, and He'll send down His thunder to destroy them."

"I am quite convinced, *ma mère*, that the Lord must be quite used to such things by now. He may exist outside the stream of time, but I believe it's a serious error for us to believe that we can, or should, do the same. The Vatican has its own newspaper and radio station, its own printing press and, of course, for good or ill, its own bank. Radio Vaticano broadcasts in thirty-three languages; official documents are published in eighty-four languages. In the old days the Church never hesitated to express its message in sculpture and stained glass, and we're living in an age of electronic images. I can see no reason why the Vatican should not also make television broadcasts for the benefit of the world Catholic community. The first radio transmitter was set up in the gardens of the Vatican, with the full approval of Pius XI, and to my certain knowledge, it has yet to be struck by lightning."

"Perhaps not," said Mother Marie-Bernadette, "but shall I tell you what I think will happen? They say that now that everyone has a television set at home, no one goes to the theater, or even to the cinema. Why wouldn't it be the same way with these broadcasts of yours? Instead of going to mass, of taking communion together, of participating in the religious life of a real community, the congregation—if you can still call them that—will stay at home and switch on their television sets and be content that they've 'welcomed the Good Lord into their living rooms' or some such nonsense. They'll see the pope or a cardinal or a bishop, perhaps even their poor neglected parish priest from time to time, and that will be quite enough to convince them they've done their duty as Christians. Then, in ten years' time, in order to keep up, as you say, with the flow of progress, they'll want to insert a few commercial messages in between the sermon and the consecration of the Host. Now in France, I'll grant you, none of this would make much difference one way or the other, but there are places in the world, as in South America, I'm told, where the churches are still full of people every day. . . ."

D'Anglebert held up his hands in an appeasing gesture as if to say, That day may come, but we haven't reached it yet. Mother Marie-Bernadette's opinions were simple, even naive, but entirely sensible and, as far as they went, irrefutable. He could imagine that these very same objections, served with a great deal more subtlety and less sincerity, would do very well for the venomous old spiders in the Vatican that Ratzinger's secretary seemed to find so terrifying. "All I can say to that, *ma mère*," he finally replied, "is that in the years to come, when all these satellites and computers and sophisticated electronics have merely become the ordinary and accepted pathways of communication, if the Church refuses to adapt to this new environment, ours will most certainly be, as in the very beginning, the voice of one crying out in the wilderness and heeded by very few. If, for example, the Church had refused to make use of the printing press—"

"I know that you must think me terribly backward and old-fashioned," the mother superior broke in. "I can hear you saying to yourself, This is the sort of person who will have to be dragged along behind us, no doubt kicking and screaming in the most unseemly fashion, as the Church is propelled headlong into the modern age. You must find it very vexing that Our Lord Himself was so terribly patient with simple-minded persons and those who are as little children, since they can be nothing but a hindrance to the success of this wonderful enterprise."

She held up one hand, lost in the trembling fabric of her great wide sleeve, to keep Father d'Anglebert from interrupting her, as indeed he was about to do.

"You say that the Holy Father is in favor of this project," she went on, "and I certainly cannot permit myself to doubt your word. This must certainly be true, in any case, since the Vatican seems to concern itself with little else these days. Yet I still seem to recall a few words from a speech by the Holy Father a couple of months ago—I don't recall the occasion; it was just something I read in the newspapers. At any rate, he said that we should not yield to the temptation of continually expanding our knowledge while neglecting to exercise our intelligence. This, I believe, is something that deserves to be given a great deal of thought."

"Believe me, *ma mère*, that is one of our chief preoccupations at the moment."

"I'm very glad to hear it. And now I expect you'd like to talk about a more specific aspect of this vast subject, which is to say Wendy Keenes."

D'Anglebert crinkled up his eyes momentarily as a sign of assent. "Thank you, *ma mère*. I'd like to ask you for your candid opinion of Miss Keenes. I know it must be a good one, otherwise you wouldn't have given her such a strong recommendation for our project."

"A good opinion, yes." She paused for a moment. "Though it took some time to develop, I must say. This young woman intrigued me very much at first. She was so secretive—reserved and passionate at the same time. I was afraid that she might be lacking in humility. You might have thought that . . . that she was trying to dissemble, to let nothing of herself show through, at the same time that she did everything she could to make herself noticed . . . to distinguish herself."

"And what was it you particularly liked about her?"

"I don't know, perhaps that she seemed to be such a strange mixture of tough and brittle fibers. She was determined, even willful, and at the same time I felt that she could be hurt by the slightest thing. Also, she was very intelligent, brilliant I suspect . . . but in general, *mon père*, I don't usually find myself liking people on account of their intellectual qualities."

"And were you sorry to lose her? Wouldn't you rather have kept her here at Faremoutiers?"

"No." D'Anglebert was somewhat startled by the decisiveness of her reply. "No," she repeated, in a much softer voice. "I believed that there was some sort of combat going on inside her and that God would not profit from the outcome. She did not come here in search of faith or peace or the tranquillity of the contemplative life; she needed to be active, to be challenged . . . Tokyo, Rome. There was nothing for her here like that. And the contemplative life does not provide the sort of intellectual excitement that she clearly needed; she may make a first-rate scientist or a mathematician, but not a Benedictine. Her presence here made a number of the sisters uneasy, in spite of all her efforts to get along. It was obviously something of a strain on her. To be perfectly honest, although I had grown very fond of her, I was actually relieved to see her go."

"And Miss Keenes? Was she relieved to be going, do you think?"

Mother Marie-Bernadette laughed softly. "Oh, she was so careful not to let anything show. . . . I think she was quite delighted with this new prospect that had suddenly opened up for her, and she had been positively obsessed with the tournament in Tokyo for some time before that. She worked at it constantly. . . . That sort of passion for games and distractions is something quite foreign to most of us here, I'm afraid."

Father d'Anglebert smiled. "I believe that Pascal felt much the same way. But now, can you tell me something about your last meeting? What were the circumstances exactly?"

"Quite ordinary, I suppose. We were talking . . ." She bit her lip and seemed distracted for a moment. "We had been talking in the cloister, about her new post in Rome; then one of the novices came up with a note for Miss Keenes."

"And did she reveal the contents of this note?"

"She left immediately, almost without a word. . . . She seemed rather upset."

"Left the convent, you mean?" Mother Marie-Bernadette nodded. "Then she must have had an excellent reason for doing so. . . . Surely one doesn't just run off like that, even if one has already given up the intention of taking one's vows, or the Rule of Saint Benedict is no longer what it was."

"Am I obliged to answer all your questions, *mon père*?"

"I am respectfully *requesting* you to answer my questions."

"Respectfully but firmly."

"If you wish."

"Sister Doorkeeper came to tell me that a young man was waiting in the visitors' parlor. He spoke with an accent, a fellow countryman perhaps. Wendy—Miss Keenes I should say now—drove off with him in a white car." She smiled. "I'm told it was a Peugeot."

"And you haven't spoken to her since then? She made no attempt to explain her precipitous departure?"

"At the time she explained that the young man's father had died quite suddenly. He had asked her to accompany him to the funeral. It was the end of her stay with us, you understand, and we had no reason to detain her."

"Yet you still felt that this was not the true or complete explanation?" D'Anglebert was struck by how quickly their candid conversation had turned into the interrogation of a shrewd and evasive subject. Mother Marie-Bernadette was trembling all over, positively suffering with the necessity of having to answer all these questions. Miss Wendy Keenes must have some remarkable qualities indeed to make people want to love her so much; Nicholas Resaccio also had apparently formed a strong emotional bond with her almost immediately. D'Anglebert waited for the mother superior's reply, letting the silence accumulate between them rather than tempting the old nun to take some liberty with the truth in her answer.

"I made inquiries," she said finally. "There was no funeral that day at Coulommiers—she had told me it was to be in Coulommiers, but perhaps . . . I don't know. . . ."

He felt his heart go out to this severe and unyielding old woman who had suddenly been brought to the edge of tears. He pushed back his chair to get up, but the look of relief that appeared on her face was more than he could in good conscience ignore.

"You're not concealing anything from me, *n'est-ce pas, ma mère*? You realize of course that this would be a very serious error. Miss Keenes is in all probability going to be involved with the planning and execution of Project Arcade on the highest level. Whatever your personal opinion of the wisdom or the folly of this project might be, you should be aware that if Miss Keenes is anything less than . . . sincere in her commitment to it, it could mean a very serious setback for the Church."

"Please wait a moment," she replied in a voice that was barely audible. She pulled open a drawer in her desk and began riffling through the papers inside. "You see, I thought that something might come of this. . . ." She held out a scrap of paper, folded in quarters, in her trembling fingers. "This is the note he sent her. She let it fall—she seemed to be quite upset—and I picked it up. Then I let my curiosity get the better of me, may God forgive me."

D'Anglebert hesitated for a moment, then reached out and took the note.

> My father died yesterday aft. Don't know if I'll be coming back to the univ. or at all for that matter. What to do?
>
> M

"And is there anything else you can tell me about this young man, other than that he spoke with an accent?"

"He told Sister Doorkeeper that his name was Michael."

"A close friend, do you suppose? An ex-lover? Even a current lover perhaps?"

Mother Marie-Bernadette flared up at this. "You have no right—"

"Then why would you have allowed me to leave this room without showing me the note?"

"As I said, no one was buried in Coulommiers that day. And only one person in Compiègne—an old woman."

"An old woman," he repeated softly. But why lie about that, a lie that could be so easily found out, if they were really going to the boy's father's funeral? Unless the note was a lie as well. . . .

"And now, if you have no more questions for me," said Mother Marie-Bernadette, "I would very much like to be left alone."

After leaving the convent, d'Anglebert called an old friend and classmate from the Polytechnique, Pierre Jacson, now dean of the technical faculty at the University of Compiègne. It was 11:30 A.M. When d'Anglebert explained that he had a "small quasi-official matter" that he would like to take up with him as soon as possible, Jacson suggested lunch at a Chinese restaurant not far from the university science complex. In the manner of old college friends who have remained in academic life, they began by exchanging anecdotes illustrating the most recent inroads of intellectual faddishness and bureaucratic folly at their respective universities. Jacson was clearly curious to hear what the small quasi-official matter might be, but d'Anglebert found it difficult to broach the subject directly.

He was not really authorized to say anything about Project Arcade, even to a trusted friend like Jacson, but little by little he managed to convey the idea, in very general terms, that the Church was embarking on a serious effort to adapt the new technology, particularly in the realm of communications, to its own very special needs. He tried to be careful not to be too specific or, as he tended to do when discussing such matters, to get carried away by his own enthusiasm. Jacson, a nominal Catholic who had almost no interest in politics beyond the university level, seemed to think that "computerizing the village curé," as he put it, was a very promising idea.

"Well, I'm glad you approve," said d'Anglebert, "and the thing of it is, we've recruited a rather brilliant young woman to help us out with all this, but beyond the obvious fact of her brilliance, we really know very little else about her. . . . I can't say that this role of official snooper—"

"Quasi-official."

D'Anglebert nodded gravely. "I can't say that that particular role is one I find very congenial, and I'd much prefer to come up with something reassuring rather than the reverse."

"And how can I be of service?"

"I'm afraid all I have to go on is that she was involved with a student here at the university, and we thought if we could form some idea of his . . ."

"Of his moral character?"

D'Anglebert chuckled. "More or less."

"Well, I feel much the same way as you do, that it goes against the grain, but I'll try to find out what I can. You'd better tell me the name of this fortunate young man."

"That's part of the problem. All I can give you is his first name—Michael."

"Undergraduate or graduate?"

"I'm afraid I can't tell you that either."

Jacson raised his eyes toward the ceiling. "Color of eyes? Color of hair?"

"Nor either of those."

"It's just as well, you know. We've finally got most of our records into the computer, but I don't think they've been cross-indexed to that extent. . . ."

"He drives a white Peugeot."

"Ah, of course that makes all the difference!"

"Yes, and he speaks with an accent . . . probably Irish or English."

"That's what comes of his being called Michael. Probably a blue-eyed blond then, wouldn't you think? Would you like me to request a special assembly of all our male Anglo-Saxon students out by the parking lot? And then there you'll be, all dressed in your grand inquisitor's robes . . . and what's the Latin for 'Gentlemen, start your engines'?"

"That's very good of you, *mon vieux*, but I'm afraid it wouldn't help much. The young man in question would have left the university a couple of weeks ago, around October tenth. A day or so after his father's death, or so I'm told, though I'm not entirely sure about this last—"

"De Bonno!"

"What?"

"Michael de Bonno. . . . There's your man, I'm almost sure of it. He left us very suddenly, a couple of weeks ago, just after his father's death. Speaks with an English accent. But he wasn't a student; he was a visiting fellow, in biophysics, so perhaps he's not the one after all."

"No, no, I'm sure you're quite right. His father died about October tenth, you think? And he was buried somewhere here in the area? Compiègne, Coulommiers?"

"Not so much Coulommiers as Valletta, on the island of Malta, or thereabouts. Michael came from a well-known medical family on Malta—English-speaking, yes, but black-eyed Carthaginians rather than blue-eyed Anglo-Saxons. I'm quite sure that the funeral was going to be held on Malta."

"That's very interesting."

"You think he's the one?"

"It's very likely. What else can you tell me about him—his background, political views, personal life, that sort of thing? I know what you're going to say, but I assure you it's in a good cause."

"I *was* going to say that I don't think the role of junior inquisitor really suits me, but I can tell you that Michael de Bonno is a very presentable young man. He's done some very good work in neurology, they tell me, trained at University Hospital in London, did some graduate work at Oxford—I believe he may have been an undergraduate there as well. He never discussed his personal life or his politics with me, but I certainly know of nothing to his discredit. Will that do for a character reference, or would you like me to make inquiries?"

"Please. You'd be doing your old friend a big favor. First of all, to clinch the identification, I'd very much like you to find out about the white Peugeot, then basically anything you can about, as you say, his politics and his personal life, his background, academic or otherwise. And you needn't worry about this having any unfortunate repercussions for your Dr. de Bonno, since, from an official standpoint at least, the focus of our interest is on this young woman exclusively."

Two days later Father d'Anglebert was informed that Michael de Bonno had indeed been at Oxford at the same time as Wendy Keenes, had recently sold a new but battered Peugeot to a garage in Compiègne, had not been especially interested in politics, and had occasionally been seen driving around Compiègne Forest with an attractive redhead. *Thank God*, thought d'Anglebert, *for faculty gossip*. Four days later he had also learned that Dr. de Bonno had succeeded his father as director of a clinic on Malta, that his father had enjoyed close personal relations with both staunchly pro-Western and vaguely pro-Soviet factions in the Maltese House of Representatives, that Michael himself had recently been seen at a reception at the Soviet embassy (eyewitness testimony of the papal nuncio himself). Five days later he learned that Michael had been furnished with a complimentary ticket for a regularly scheduled flight to Tripoli aboard the Libyan national airline. He was not thought to have returned to Malta since.

6

Tokyo
November 13

There was still a great deal that remained to be done. Nicholas was certainly not without apprehension about the future; he knew very well what he was afraid of. He also knew how he would have liked things to turn out—that the months to come would be a logical and uneventful sequel to the weeks that had already passed. Nicholas was only really interested in two things, science and God. He vehemently rejected what he referred to as the Adam complex, namely, the belief that knowledge can only be gained by disobeying (or more probably, ignoring) God's law. On the contrary, he believed that his two great intellectual passions were not only compatible but actually equivalent, at least in the sense that the more he found out about the one, the more he felt he knew about the other.

He was naturally pleased when others seemed to share his beliefs but had never hoped to become the leader, or the symbol, of an identifiable movement, much less a "tendency" within the Church. Still, this had happened, beginning with the day that he had published a paper summarizing his work on a new programming language called PROLOG, originally developed at the University of Aix-Marseilles. His work on PROLOG had been of inestimable value to the Japanese designers of the new generation of computers, had in fact brought them one step closer to the creation of a true artificial-intelligence program. At the same time, Nicholas felt as if he had inadvertently caught his sleeve in the much more primitive mechanism of Vatican politics and was being dragged slowly and irresistibly into the heart of it.

The symptoms of the disorder that was soon to disrupt his entire life were initially very pleasant. It was thoroughly gratifying to be summoned to a special audience at the Vatican for the sole purpose of presenting his ideas to the pope. It was less gratifying to read in the Roman press of "the remarkable influence exercised over the Holy Father by this brilliant young Jesuit" and "the highly sympathetic reception afforded Father Resaccio's scintillating vision of things to come and of the role of the Catholic church in the Information Age." In fact, John Paul had listened attentively to what Nicholas had to say. The main point he felt he had to make was that, while not precisely "value-free," as many secular scientists have maintained, computer science was not inherently in conflict with the revealed truths of the Church, and, more important, computer technology might furnish the means by which the Catholics of the world could be safely shepherded across, as Nicholas put it, "the vast abyss that separates the nineteenth from the twenty-first century."

The pope had cautiously endorsed this viewpoint, pointing out that, in terms of Nicholas's own rhetoric, the other side of this abyss was in fact an unexplored country, quite possibly swarming with all sorts of modernist speculations, of the kind that had led even the most devout Catholics into lamentable error in the past and had thus posed a serious threat to the unity, harmony, even stability, of the world Catholic community. Nicholas was admirably firm in insisting that these computer applications would only provide a medium, an empty conduit through which the message of the Gospels could continue to be transmitted to the faithful in an increasingly bemused and fragmented world; the message itself would be neither altered nor distorted. Second, Nicholas pointed out, there was an entire generation growing up, in the developing countries at least, who might very well be relying on their computer terminals for most of the information they received about the world (aside from what television provided), and it was important for the Church not to lose contact with them altogether.

These arguments had won not only a respectful hearing from the Holy Father but also a certain measure of notoriety for Nicholas among the less progressive circles of the Vatican hierarchy. Shortly thereafter, the apprehension and disgruntlement of this group, always prone to sentiments of that kind, were crystallized into acute resentment by the pope's suggestion that Nicholas should be accepted into the ranks of the Pontifical Academy of Sciences. This was an assemblage of seventy distinguished scholars, essentially self-perpetuating (since nominations usually originated in the academy itself and were subsequently approved by the pope); most of its members had had to wait the better part of a lifetime for their appointments (their average age being exceeded only, it was said, by that of the Politburo in Moscow).

That an obscure young specialist—only thirty-five years old and a Jesuit—in a field that had been created (and out of whole cloth, some of them would have said) just forty years ago should have been elevated to this supreme scholarly dignity on the basis of a single, incomprehensible article and an informal lecture was naturally not much to their liking. Nicholas was surprised, abashed, and even a little saddened by all the fuss that seemed to have been stirred up by his appointment to the academy, as he was by his appointment to the much more substantial post of papal councillor on science and technology. He had even grown accustomed to being referred to in the press as "a papal favorite," a phrase that had made him feel more worthless and degraded than the unworthiest of the Borgia "nephews" of the Renaissance.

Now the preliminary work was all finished in Japan, though he felt that he would have preferred to stay indefinitely, to go on working at ICOT, surrounded by colleagues who shared his highly optimistic vision of technological progress and his profound indifference to its short-term political consequences. He would have preferred to go on learning and teaching, exchanging ideas, to forget all about the *combinazioni*, the cabals and self-important bureaucrats and palace intrigue, no matter whether the palace was called the Lateran, the Kremlin, or the Pentagon.

His meeting with Giuseppe Pitta and James Wilcox had been profoundly disturbing. He felt, first of all, that he had been a party to a second hijacking, that the entire project had been hijacked just as surely as AF-270 had been hijacked by the fanatic Mohammed Khomsi—and for essentially the same reasons. The two of them had as much as told him that they were taking over the management of the project and that in the future all other considerations would be subordinated to their political paranoia and mania for security. Since then, he assumed, he had never gone out without an escort of two or three of Wilcox's "people" from the embassy, though these, it had to be admitted, like Wilcox's terrorists and Red subversives, were customarily more apparent to the imagination than to the naked eye.

His next conversation with Father Pitta had pleased him even less.

At the outset, he had been very impressed by Wendy Keenes, by her evident intelligence and independent-mindedness, and it seemed only natural that she should be selected for the project team. Now things were slightly different. Wendy had become a sort of symbol of his personal struggle against certain prejudices on the part of his colleagues and against the out-and-out politicization of Project Arcade.

In light of the new investigation into Wendy's background, these prejudices had been promoted to the rank of "self-evident political realities"—serious constraints, in other words, on the logical evolution of the project—though Nicholas was convinced that these realities existed primarily as shadows in the minds of the mandarin policymakers in the Pentagon and in Rome. He was a priest, a scientist, a specialist in communications, and not about to be conscripted into either of these irrational political conflicts, between East and West in the one case, between the "conservatives" and the "progressives" in the other.

On the morning that Nicholas was due to fly back to Rome, Father Pitta had told him that they had received "some extremely troubling new information" about Wendy, whom he had not very gallantly referred to as "that redheaded plaster saint of yours." First of all, it turned out that she had had a lover, even after she had enrolled as a postulant at Faremoutiers; the man was a doctor who came from Malta and had recently flown to Tripoli as a guest of the Libyan government.

"And Miss Keenes?" asked Nicholas. "Where has she gone off to, do you suppose? What has she been doing since she left Tokyo?"

"I don't have that information," said Father Pitta. "She's expected to be in Rome in a day or two, just as you are."

The doctor's name was Michael de Bonno; he was the son of an eminent man, perhaps to be regarded as a member of Malta's ruling elite. It was well known that Malta was a nonaligned country, one which had enjoyed close political ties with Libya for a number of years. Moreover, it was not unusual for a small country like Malta to send such a person, even though officially unaccredited, on a political mission to a neighboring country.

It seemed unlikely that this Dr. de Bonno could be a terrorist or secret agent, or even if he were, that he'd be junketing off in such conspicuous fashion to the land of Qaddafi and secret terrorist training camps. This, at any rate, was Nicholas's analysis. He wanted Wendy Keenes working for him on the project, and he intended to have her. He was not about to change his mind merely on account of prejudice and speculation. On the other hand, it might be a good idea for him to have a private chat about all this with Wendy as soon as he could.

Now the decisive moment was at hand. Nicholas was seated in front of a terminal amid the well-ordered chaos of the ICOT laboratories in Tokyo. Professor Irushi Kanaka was about to begin his demonstration. Kanaka was as proud of his new program as if it had been the offspring of his own loins, and certainly it was a precocious infant, with a recognition vocabulary that exceeded a thousand English words, plus the remarkable abilities to translate those words, instantaneously, into three other languages—French, Spanish, and Italian—and to reproduce the exact pitch, timbre, and intonation pattern of the human voice that was speaking into the microphone.

Kanaka was certainly aware that this was just the first step. Today the program could only manage a very basic vocabulary in a limited number of closely related Indo-European languages. The professor was a thin, shock-haired man with ascetic features. Nicholas imagined that Lucifer, in his original career as the angelic bringer of light, must have looked very much like him. He was convinced that with the help of the best computer scientists, linguists, and acousticians in the world, his machine would eventually be able to speak all the languages of humankind, living, dead, or yet to be devised. The goal that Kanaka's team had set for itself was the creation of the prototype of a generation of computers that would relieve our brains of a number of basic tasks, just as the great inventions of earlier centuries had been designed to do the work of our muscles and in a more efficient manner than we would ever be capable of ourselves.

Kanaka and his young colleagues liked to say that their greatest achievement thus far had been to persuade the Japanese government and ten of the country's leading electronics firms to appropriate $850 million for basic research in linguistic philosophy. It seemed no less ironic, if not nearly as amusing, that though the sponsors' contribution to the cause of international understanding was undoubtedly generous, their motives were essentially nationalistic. The corporate sponsors thought of ICOT as the ultimate high-status showcase for innovative technology; the government considered it indisputable proof that Japan now led the world in the arts of peace.

Kanaka was uninterested in prestige politics, even less interested in marketing tactics, and he was still somewhat leery of the government's request that the institute sell one of the PSI-100 prototypes—identical to the machine that was to be donated to the Christians of the world on behalf of the Japanese people—to the government of Malta. He had an uneasy feeling about this. What use could they possibly have for it? It reminded him, somewhat, of the way the great powers were eager to provide missile launchers and jet fighters to Third World governments that had no one to use them on but their own citizens.

He and Nicholas had had many lengthy, late-night conversations about what the real aims of the ICOT project should be. Nicholas characteristically had suggested that their ultimate goal should be to release humankind from the constricting embrace of material necessity and thus to create one of the essential preconditions for the liberation of the human spirit. Kanaka was unconvinced that selling one of their machines to the government of Malta, a pauper state that had lived off the charity of the great powers—first Britain, then the Soviet Union—during most of its brief life, could possibly have much to do with the liberation of the human spirit.

Suddenly the machine began to speak. The voice synthesizer announced that it was ready, then provided its own translation: "*Prêt,*" "*Listo,*" "*Pronto.*" Professor Kanaka took the microphone and rose to his feet. His colleagues gathered around him, their faces expectant, their bare toes making fidgety furrows in the carpet—the Japanese custom of removing one's shoes indoors was observed even here in the basement caverns of ICOT. Nicholas got up from his chair and joined them. Kanaka walked slowly over to the machine, scowling fiercely like a man trying to dominate a bad-tempered dog, then counted to three into the microphone. An uncanny echo of his voice, electronically amplified, rattled from three different loudspeakers: "*Un, deux, trois.*" "*Une, due, tre.*" "*Uno, dos, tres.*"

Then the room was filled with applause. Kanaka beckoned to Nicholas to approach the microphone. "Professor Resaccio," he began, "it is a joy and an honor for all of us here at ICOT to offer this machine to the nations of the West on behalf of the people of Japan." Almost immediately, his voice was drowned out by an unintelligible babble as the machine provided reverberant Romance-language translations. Nicholas was a little taken aback by the effect of this; there was surely a Biblical precedent, but which was it? The Tower of Babel, perhaps, humanity's first great engineering feat, which had compelled the Lord to send down his angels to confound the human tongues. Or, more reassuringly, the New Testament account of the day of Pentecost, on which the Holy Ghost descended upon the Apostles in the form of cloven tongues of flame and inspired them "to speak with other tongues, as the Spirit gave them utterance."* But if the Lord ever intended to commute the penalty he had imposed on the builders of Babel, perhaps he would prefer to have it done through the intervention of the Holy Ghost rather than the ten largest electronics manufacturers in Japan. Nicholas glanced over at Kanaka, thinking he would be amused that his friend was beginning to have such curious misgivings at this late stage.

"These are the slaves of the future," Kanaka was saying, "the slaves that we hope will save all men and women from the drudgery of everyday life. It is our most cherished wish to set free the imagination of our fellow creatures, to allow them to devote themselves to creative pursuits, to culture and the arts. We wish for everyone to enjoy the leisurely existence of the aristocrats of Athens or the lords and ladies of the Renaissance. Our goal is to restore the honor and integrity of our species by abolishing class distinctions and by creating the necessary conditions for a new, just society. We are dreaming of a world in which there will be neither slaves nor slave masters."

Nicholas smiled to himself. The machine must have received some intensive vocabulary drill so it wouldn't be overtaxed by the rhetorical demands of this little ceremony. Certainly words such as *leisurely*, *aristocrats*, and *Renaissance* had not been included in its original thousand-word lexicon. He wondered if Professor Kanaka's gifted offspring had learned to say *mama*, *papa*, and *baby* yet.

"Dear Professor Resaccio, dear Nicholas, it was because of men like you that the government and the great corporate enterprises of Japan first decided to undertake this very ambitious program. We were confident that in the hands of a man like you, our ambitions would be magnificently realized. Most of all, you should recognize in our gift to you an expression of the tremendous debt of gratitude that we owe to the nations of the West. Most recently, we have benefited from the

*And when the day of Pentecost was fully come, they were all with one accord in one place.

And suddenly there came a sound from heaven as of a rushing mighty wind, and it filled all the house where they were sitting.

And there appeared unto them cloven tongues like as of fire, and it sat upon each of them.

And they were all filled with the Holy Ghost, and began to speak with other tongues, as the Spirit gave them utterance.

And there were dwelling at Jerusalem Jews, devout men, out of every nation under heaven.

Now when this was noised abroad, the multitude came together, and were confounded, because that every man heard them speak in his own language.

contributions of many greatly talented Western colleagues, without whom we never would have been able to set out on this exciting adventure. Through you, we hope to convey to all of them our most deeply respectful thanks."

Kanaka bowed to Nicholas, then handed him the microphone, which emitted a small spatter of feedback as it passed too close to one of the loudspeakers. Nicholas was slightly surprised by the grave and ceremonious tone of his friend's address, which seemed oddly out of place in this setting—a carpeted, white-walled room lined with metal and glass and plastic and full of barefoot men in their twenties, most of them badly in need of haircuts. The ideas he was very familiar with; they had discussed them many times—first, the possibility of a leisure-class culture, like that of ancient Athens or Renaissance Florence, that was egalitarian rather than aristocratic, supported by the incessant toil of supercomputers rather than of slaves or laborers, and second, the idea—very similar to something that Father Pitta had said to him during their first meeting—that Japan had gotten itself deeply into debt adopting the basic principles of Western science and industry and that the debt could only be repaid, and the national honor restored, when Japan had outstripped the West in technological achievements. This was undoubtedly one of the reasons Nicholas felt a certain kinship with Kanaka—because he saw himself as a kind of priest of science. Like many of his colleagues, he had given up a prestigious job in private industry to devote all his time to basic research at ICOT. Like Nicholas, he had taken his vows and now lived only for his faith.

Nicholas started to answer in Italian, with the English translation spilling out of one of the speakers, loud and clear, while the French and Spanish were reduced to a barely audible muttering in the interests of intelligibility. He was peripherally aware of the fact that while the quality of the voice reproduction was little short of incredible, the program's grasp of English idiom and word order was still a little shaky and the synthesized voice occasionally trailed off in midsentence, lit-

---

And they were all amazed and marvelled, saying one to another, Behold, are not all these which speak Galileans?

And how hear we every man in our own tongue, wherein we were born?

Parthians, and Medes, and Elamites, and in Judæa. . . . in Egypt, and in the parts of Libya about Cyrene, and strangers of Rome, Jews and proselytes.

Cretes and Arabians, we do hear them speak in our tongues the wonderful works of God.

Acts of the Apostles, 2:1–11

erally at a loss for words. Clearly there was a great deal of work left to be done.

"Professor Kanaka," he began, "it is with a sense of truly limitless gratitude that I accept this incredible gift on behalf of my colleagues . . . and my fellow Occidentals. I have learned an enormous amount while working with you all here at ICOT"—he pronounced it "eye-cot," in the English way, to keep the machine from getting confused—"and I can tell you that I'm very pleased to have this chance to prove myself worthy of your confidence, though I know that the debt of gratitude that I and all my colleagues owe to you and to everyone here at the institute is one that can never be repaid. My ambition is nothing more, and nothing less, than to keep working away at science and to serve the cause of peace. And I hope that today, with God's help, we have forged the first link in a chain that someday will encircle the whole of humankind not in the bonds of slavery but in the bonds of love."

Nicholas bowed his head and Kanaka stepped forward; they embraced warmly while the white room echoed with applause. Nicholas felt truly moved by the odd formality of this little ceremony. The few weeks he had spent in Japan had been wonderful, almost a sabbatical or vacation idyll, though his encounters with Father Pitta and James Wilcox had given him a foretaste of the sort of difficulties he was sure to encounter when he returned to Rome. He felt a little ashamed of himself, since while Kanaka's presentation speech had been heartfelt and thoroughly sincere, his reply had been somewhat less so.

On the other hand, he could hardly have told them the truth: "I expect to go on pretending to be a scientist while actually mutating into a kind of scheming politician, and I will try very hard to advance the cause of peace while conforming to someone else's idea of how to wage a kind of nonviolent warfare that saves you the mess and expense of the real thing." And it seemed to him at that moment that his real ambition was to take the seed that had grown and flourished here at ICOT and try to transplant it to the dry and stony ground of the Vatican, and perhaps elsewhere as well.

Tripoli

As usual, Michael had no idea where they were taking him. Since they were in Libya, however, he supposed that one place was very much like another, and in any case it hardly mattered now that he was with Wendy. It did matter that they were both with Abdul, whose company, beginning with his arrogant smirk and his air of insufferable condescension, Michael would willingly have dispensed with. He supposed that these were only some of the trials he would have to endure as the price of having her back again. The Fiat was rolling along now at a moderate speed, the side curtains lowered.

Abdul had told them that he had a surprise for them, but it appeared that this, whatever it was, was to remain a surprise until they had reached their destination. Now he seemed intent on striking up a conversation of some kind, though all he really had to say, to Michael at any rate, was, *I'm in total control, you have no power, I can do whatever I want with you.* Wendy sat back impassively; Michael, wedged between the two of them, reached out and took her hand. Abdul shook his head from side to side, a gesture that seemed to have affirmative rather than negative connotations.

"That's very good," he said. "Very good indeed. That's the reason that you're here, you know."

"What is? What's the reason?"

"Not because of your political convictions. You know as well as I do that you haven't got any to speak of and that we could never rely on you not to betray them for your personal convenience." He seemed to find this idea very amusing. "Politically, it seems that Malta must be a great deal closer to Europe than to Africa. You're a genuine European if there ever was one—terrified of the true religion, terrified of socialist revolution. I can feel your hatred for me, right down here." He tapped the pit of his stomach, then favored Michael with a broad, wolfish grin. "So why did we choose you? Because of your extraordinary technical competence? Because you were the only one clever enough to help us?"

Michael shrugged noncommittally, trying to pretend that he neither knew nor cared what the answer might be. No longer distant, Wendy seemed very tense.

"It was because of your past," Abdul went on gloatingly, "because of your emotional involvement with Wendy. That was why we chose you. We can be sure of you because of her, and we can be sure of her because of you. Neither of you has been chosen *primarily* because of your abilities. Miss Keenes is with us because of her . . . because of certain experiences, perhaps I should say, and it is because of those experiences that we can consider her to be our objective ally. It is because of them that we *know* that she will do what we expect of her, and one of those experiences, Dr. de Bonno, is you."

Wendy started to say something, but Abdul overrode her protest. "We do have complete faith in you, Wendy. You have been with us in our struggle too long for us to believe otherwise. But Dr. de Bonno has been imposed upon us by force of circumstance. The choice was made for us, do you understand? The choice was made for him as well, also by force of circumstance." He seemed to find this very funny, and Michael half-expected him to start talking about kismet or something of the sort.

"I came here voluntarily," said Michael sharply, "incredible as that might seem to me now. No one forced me to come to the embassy, and no one forced me to accept the proposition that was put to me there."

"And no man is permitted to foretell the future," said Abdul, "and yet the Colonel predicted that you would do so—*voluntarily*—many months ago. No one forced you, you see, because you had no choice."

Michael had nothing further to say to this. Wendy cleared her throat and made a partially successful attempt to say something in a normal voice. "What's this surprise you've been promising us then?"

"It's a present—a personal gift for you, Wendy, from the Chief of the Revolution. Because the two of you will have to spend some time working out the details of your collaboration, the Colonel has offered you the use of one of his summer residences for four entire days. As you know, the Colonel himself prefers to live in the utmost simplicity, but this place you are going to be staying is a villa built for the use of our late, unlamented King Idris. I trust you will find it . . . very comfortable."

Abdul seemed slightly embarrassed that such a description could apply to any of the Colonel's residences. "At the end of your stay there, you will be separated, perhaps for a fairly long period of time. You will not have any other opportunity to arrange some means of communicating between Rome and Valletta and the means by which the programs are to be transferred. We have also arranged a brief training program for you; you will be meeting several technical specialists. Wendy, you already have some experience of how these things must be done. Dr. de Bonno . . . Michael"—he smiled wickedly—"you of course have never operated as an underground freedom fighter, though your task will be by far the less difficult of the two."

The curtains were up again, and Michael was staring out the back window of the Fiat. The desert landscape, he had already decided, might have been beautiful if there had been a great deal less of it. Abdul's head was resting against the back of the seat, as if he had gone to sleep, but a vigilant glitter could still be seen behind his half-closed eyelids. Wendy seemed entirely preoccupied with her own apprehensions and anxieties.

He needed to think, and this was probably the only opportunity that he would have for some time. He was beginning to believe that revolutionary movements, like armies of every kind, preferred to keep their recruits in constant motion and a constant state of bewilderment. At times he felt that Wendy was the only thing in the world that mattered to him and that he was ready to give it all up for her sake—*all* including his human dignity, his cultural heritage, his most cherished values, just so he could be with her, just so long as she would let him keep on loving her.

Such reflections always left a slightly acrid and sickening aftertaste. He kept assuring himself that he was not the sort of person who could make such a devil's bargain, that he had no right to do such a thing. But it was difficult to say what the objection was exactly. His real cultural heritage was a hopeless muddle, though his immediate ancestors had worked very hard to turn themselves into imitation English gentlemen. He thought of himself as a Christian rather than a Muslim, but why was Christ necessarily to be preferred to Mohammed? Why liberal democracy rather than Marxism? Why the Atlantic rather than the Mediterranean?

While he was waiting to find the answers to all these questions, he could still not deny the impression, both rational and visceral, that what he proposed to do was not only an offense against reason and morality but also a betrayal of civilization as he knew it. The fact was that England and Rome and Christianity and perhaps even parliamentary democracy had all made him most of what he was. His father might have approved of this scheme in principle, but, as even the odious Henry Zubbieq had instantly admitted, they would never have sent his father to a terrorist training camp in Libya.

By finding Wendy again, by agreeing to be her partner in this grotesque adventure, Michael had thought he would achieve his heart's desire, albeit at an exorbitant price. But his happiness had not lasted more than a moment, and he felt deeply ashamed of the strange emotional amalgam that had replaced it, a mixture of simple relief that he had found her again and barely repressed terror. He did not wonder for a moment whether he would be able to carry on to the very end of the track that had been laid out for him. On the contrary, he wondered whether he would be cowardly enough to submit without a struggle, to perform a task that—though simple enough, as Abdul kept reminding him—was thoroughly repugnant to him. He was very much afraid that he would not hesitate when the moment actually came.

Suddenly the view had drastically altered, like a rapid cut in a movie. At least in a real movie, Michael thought to himself, the last twenty minutes of nondescript desert landscape would have been edited down to a five- or ten-second insert. Now, as before, they were confronted with a thick, whitewashed concrete wall pierced by a gateway that was protected by a movable barrier of concertina wire. Several dozen soldiers and a number of machine guns were in evidence. There was dust and noise and smoke, and, after a sufficient amount of shouting and scowling and fingering of weapons, the barrier was pushed aside for them.

To Michael's amazement, once they were inside the desert was transformed into a beautiful beach resort with the shaggy green crowns of palm trees in the distance, golden sand, and a white fringe of waves breaking on the shore. An offshore breeze had picked up—it was almost dusk—and the atmosphere was peaceful and relaxed. The Colonel's "summer residence"—a gold and white palace—rose up out of the desert like a mirage. At the foot of a broad staircase that led to the main entrance, four people were drawn up in a line. Michael almost expected them to be wearing tailcoats or little lace caps and aprons, but as the car approached it became apparent that they were all dressed in camouflage outfits, and of course all four were male. When they got out of the car, Abdul presented them, collectively, to Michael and Wendy as the instructors who would be responsible for their "revolutionary indoctrination."

They followed him up the stairs, past the elaborate portico with its azure tiles and gold and silver inlays, then past the slender columns of an interior courtyard with a splashing fountain in the Moorish style. They found the caretaker standing in the middle of a completely empty room whose walls and floors were made of slabs of gray and green marble. They followed him in silence, through many rooms, past corridors and staircases, until the caretaker opened a door and ushered them in. This was the entrance to a suite of rooms that might easily have been occupied by the unlamented king himself—Michael remembered having heard of him as a mildly disgraceful, Farouklike old party who had ended his life in exile on one of the Greek islands.

Wendy ran out to the terrace to admire the spectacle presented by the gulf, the bright blue water and the beaches that stretched as far as she could see in either direction. Michael advanced more cautiously, like a soldier picking his way through a mine field, eyeing the rugs and hangings, the enormous vases, reminiscent of the Forty Thieves, and great round silver trays. The disparity between these luxurious quarters and the austerity of the Colonel's residence of choice in Tripoli was striking but did not seem to suggest any particular conclusion. When he went back to the door, Abdul and the caretaker were gone. He was alone with Wendy for the first time in several weeks, and already the wicked old king's apartments, at first sight merely gloomy and overwrought, were beginning to seem almost hospitable.

Wendy had still not returned from the terrace, which probably meant, though the warm wind from the gulf and the sight of the breaking waves was enticing, that she was putting off the moment when she would have to meet him face to face. This time she would not get away with being offhand and mysterious; this time it would take more than a temperamental flare-up or an ultimatum or forbidding looks to keep him from trespassing on her secret territory, a territory on which—with the help of Abdul and Zubbieq and the Chief of the Revolution himself—he had already, so to speak, pitched his tent.

He remembered that this coastline had been identified with the Land of the Lotus-Eaters in the *Odyssey*; perhaps this accounted for the tremendous fascination of the view from the terrace. He had already stopped wondering if she still loved him and had begun to wonder if she would even pretend to love him now that her comrades had other means of ensuring his cooperation. Why would she bother to pretend? She had delivered her lover into the hands of Abdul and the Colonel, or rather she had furnished the revolution with a compliant dupe who would be useful in the furtherance of their schemes—because he was his father's son, primarily—and unlikely to betray them—because he was in love with Wendy, and because he had already shown himself to be susceptible to the mildest forms of blackmail and intimidation.

Then she appeared in the doorway, and he knew that, however much of the rest of it might be true, she still did love him. Her steps and her expression were uncertain, her lower lip seemed to be trembling. She stood still for a moment, watching him, and, with a feeling of inexpressible liberation, he broke away from his thoughts—they were all instantly, shamefully, joyously forgotten—and started to move toward her. *Welcome to Lotus Land.*

"The sun's going to set any minute now," she said. "Come and have a look?"

He drew her to him and savored this exquisite moment of contact, the feeling of her soft flesh. It was just as it had been in the cottage in the forest, as it had always been, but he had never felt her so passionate, so exuberant.

"Oh, Michael, I never meant to get you into any of this. I'm so sorry. I know you're never going to forgive me." This was said flatly, declaratively, as if she did not expect to be contradicted. He wanted to tell her that he would have done ten times, a hundred times as much, just to bring her back—betrayed his country, killed his mother and father, but he said nothing. Instead he kissed her for a very long time, and when they drew apart, she murmured, "Have you seen it?"

"Seen what?"

"Everything . . . all this. The silk rugs and tapestries and those little tables all covered with mother of pearl. Look at that water thing, what do you call it . . . *ewer* over there. Isn't that perfectly elegant? And look in here." She led him into the adjoining bathroom, with its marble floor, monumental bathtub, the fixtures in the shape of golden swans. "A chandelier!" she said delightedly. "Have you ever seen a chandelier in the loo before?"

They went in to explore the bedroom, which was hung with blue and silver draperies, and an immense canopy over the bed. The room was full of the sparkle of gems and crystal, like the eyes of so many tiny animals watching them. They walked almost reverently, as in a museum, trying not to stand in the way of the reflected points of light that flashed around the room, trying not to disturb the geometric pattern of the carpet.

"Just look at that now!" said Wendy. "Michael . . . please, I know you're going to think the very worst of me for saying this, but wouldn't it be a shame to waste all this on a *serious talk*, especially if we're going to end up tearing each other's heads off or something? We'll have a talk, and it will be very serious, I promise. I'll explain everything—at long last—and you'll understand. But not now, all right? Not tonight. We're not going to have very much time together, you know, not for quite a while and least of all in a place like this. Just let us have this one night. . . ."

He thought about what this meant—she had figured out another delaying trick, another way of keeping the upper hand. He thought about this for another fraction of a second, then grabbed both of her arms, threw her onto the bed, and threw himself after her. The massive canopy trembled, and in a moment or two the old king's—or the Colonel's—beautiful blue silk coverlet was badly rumpled. Suddenly, the setting did not seem very conducive to a free-form sexual roughhouse. They froze in position, convinced they had committed some sort of sacrilege, half expecting an indignant guard or curator to turn up at any moment. Michael quickly withdrew his hand from Wendy's breast.

"What if they're watching us?" he whispered. "Hidden cameras . . . concealed microphones."

Wendy opened her eyes very wide in a look of mock-alarm and sat up on the bed. Then, after stretching luxuriously, she unbuttoned the front of the sort of desert adventuress's outfit she had been wearing, a long white linen shift. She swiveled her torso from side to side, exposing her bare breasts to the scrutiny of the hidden cameras, then shrugged her shoulders and grinned. "I'm pretty sure it's all right," she said as she slipped out of her shift and tossed it to the floor. "A woman can generally tell about things like that, you know."

She kicked her legs in the air and catapulted a pair of leather sandals across the bedroom floor, then stood up to deal with her khaki slacks, cinched very tight with a broad leather belt. Michael admired the way she seemed to be able to compartmentalize her life—a quality he had not thought very highly of in the past—and to concentrate on the pleasures of the moment. Perhaps that was part of her revolutionary training, learning to take advantage of the odd minutes of respite from the struggle, and since he was there to learn the rudiments of the underground freedom fighter's trade, he would try valiantly to do the same. It felt like more than self-indulgence, amid surroundings of such richness and splendor, to shed his clothes in a sweaty ball on the floor—it was a genuine luxury.

Wendy gave him a wicked, expectant smile. Red-gold flames shone brightly in her close-cropped hair and in the triangular patch at her groin. Stray reflections of crystal and metal and colored glass flickered across her pale flesh, like the strands of beads worn by a sultan's favorite.

It seemed difficult to imagine her anywhere else but here, in the palace of a wicked Arabian king. The bed was a soft and vast expanse, but not nearly as big as the room itself. They filled it up with their cries and groans and murmurs; they fell upon each other on the precious silken carpets, under the chandeliers, in the mirrors.

Now, far from being concerned about hidden cameras and microphones, they seemed intent on providing a spectacle for whole battalions of eavesdroppers and voyeurs. Their bodies were in control; they could not be kept apart, and there seemed to be nothing, short of sheer physical exhaustion, that could satisfy the sharp animal hunger that they felt for each other. Trembling with ardor and excitement, they ran out onto the terrace and made love under the clear sky and the stars, on the smooth cold tiles in the bathroom, and of course in the great bird-headed bathtub.

It was very late now, and they were back in the king's big bed. Wendy was thinking about Scheherazade, the beautiful slave girl who had taught her sultan to prefer a good story even to the delights of endless sexual distraction. *The decor may be similar,* she thought, *but our positions are exactly reversed.* She, with considerable assistance from Michael, had done what she could to provide at least the promise of endless sexual distraction, and only partly in order to postpone the fateful moment when she would have to tell her story. Michael was lying beside her, a smile on his lips, but he was staring at her with a look of sleepy calculation that she knew very well. *Now he's going to try to get it out of me after all*, she thought. She was about to protest, to remind him of the bargain that he had subscribed to, implicitly, when he had picked her up and tossed her onto the bed. But then he reached out a hand, and she realized that she had completely misread his intentions. Not very long after that, Michael had fallen asleep, and Scheherazade had survived her first perilous night on the sultan's couch.

When she awoke, she found herself sprawled across the foot of the bed, on top of the covers, her skin covered with drops of cold sweat. Her thoughts were in disorder; she did not even seem to be able to see clearly. The room was nothing more than a cloud of discordant colors and incoherent shapes; then she remembered where she was. She wondered if a condemned man could feel so awful on the morning of his execution. Her arms and legs felt very heavy, and there seemed to be a terrible weight inside her chest. Michael's face, the face of her executioner, was just a few inches away, resting absurdly on an ornate silken pillow.

When he awoke, he thought he heard her talking to someone, her voice thin and unsteady. He opened his eyes, and there was no one else there. She had already started to tell her story, as a kind of last-minute rehearsal.

"What are you saying?"

Instead of answering right away, she snuggled up against his back, hooked one arm around his waist, and started to stroke his hair. "Michael, I wanted last night to last forever. . . ."

"But there'll be other nights, as many as you like."

"No, it will never be the same. Never like that again." She pulled away from him and sat up on the edge of the bed, with her back toward him and started speaking in the same soft, uncertain voice. "I was telling you about Brian. My brother Brian. I was hoping I could tell you the whole story while you were sleeping, and when you woke up, you'd know all about it."

"I remember you had plenty of brothers and sisters. I don't think I remember Brian."

"You never met him. He was killed, a while before I met you. A policeman came to the door . . . not the RUC, just a regular cop. I had to go down to the hospital to identify him, to identify the body. We wouldn't let my mother see him. It was horrible. More horrible than you can imagine. They had already packed him up in one of those awful sliding drawers, like a specimen in a box. The attendant yanked it out from the wall and lifted up the sheet so I could look at him. There was still blood on his face, and his eyes were open."

Michael thought of all the dead faces of strangers he had seen at the hospital, and he thought of his father, whose face he had not seen. "I assume it wasn't an accident."

"It was in a way, yes. There had been a demo, a riot if you like. An everyday thing in Belfast. Rocks and bottles, rubber bullets. They said there was also a gunman, a sniper; at any rate, a British soldier was shot and killed. They started in on a block search to find the killer; they'd switched over to real bullets by now, and my brother was shot while he was trying to run away."

"He wasn't the sniper."

"No, I'm sure he wasn't. I suppose it just wouldn't have been convenient for him to have been picked up at that particular moment. I didn't really know what was going on at the time. I was still a schoolgirl, and he'd already started at the university. He didn't come round to the house much anymore, but he was always the one I felt closest to. He *was* involved in . . . political work, I suppose you'd call it. His mates called him 'the Ambassador,' because he acted as a sort of liaison with a group of Libyan students at the university. Then a week later, I'd gone into a church of all places, and someone came up to me, and I found out all about it." She smiled as she wiped the tears from her cheeks.

"I had just gone in for a moment . . . to talk to God—I mean, quite literally, to tell him that He'd never hear from me again, that I hated Him because of what He'd done to Brian and because of what He'd done to me, making me hate everyone so much. I suppose I was having a sort of breakdown combined with an adolescent crisis of faith—I was just about as crazy as I've ever been. Then this fellow was kneeling right beside me at the altar rail. He set an envelope in front of me, looked over to let me know it was for me, then disappeared. It was like something out of a book by Graham Greene."

She smiled again, very faintly, and took a deep breath. "I tore it open and read it right there. I can still remember the light from all the candles flickering back and forth across the page. It was a letter from my brother, the sort of letter you write when you're pretty sure that something's going to happen to you. He said that because I was the cleverest one of the family—I'd already passed my entrance exams for Oxford—it was my responsibility to take his place in the liberation struggle in whatever way I thought would be most effective."

"At least he left that much up to you," said Michael, not troubling to hide the disgust in his voice.

"I wouldn't have done it if I hadn't felt much the same way about it, would I? I don't really suppose he was all that convinced I'd do it, but I was his only hope, as far as our family was concerned—the others are far too sensible and well behaved. He had ideas about the family honor, Brian did."

"Only instead of having a brother in the priesthood, he was content to have a sister in the IRA. . . . And I didn't realize that there were any Libyan students at the university in Belfast."

"Oh, yes, I suppose that's part of the reason they're there, really. And they've been very helpful. Sometimes they even deprive themselves of their scholarship allowances so they can contribute to the liberation struggle or to a strikers' fund or something of the sort."

"And they're very generous with their weapons too, I've heard."

Wendy stiffened at this but made no reply. She had swung her legs up onto the bed and crossed them, reaching to clutch her ankles with both hands and rocking gently back and forth. Michael was reminded that this was a very strange sort of discussion to be having with a beautiful naked woman. He tried to be a little more conciliatory. "And that was when you became involved in what you call the liberation struggle?"

"No, not till later, when I got over to England. While I was still at home, I didn't want to do anything to hurt my parents, in case I got into difficulties. But I came into contact with a more serious, much more structured group of Libyan students when I was at Oxford. They encouraged me to become involved in student politics, more as a sympathizer than as a real militant, not to do too much that would bring me to the attention of the college authorities, let alone the Special Branch.

"They kept trying to convince me that they were keeping me under wraps until I'd completed my education, both political and academic, and I could finally be of some use to them. At the time, I admit, I was convinced they didn't take me the least bit seriously. They thought I was just another noisy student radical. . . . I was used to that, to some extent. I'd always liked to play nice rough games with the boys, and they had always left me standing on the sidelines. This time, to my surprise, they decided to let me in the game."

"Precisely. *They* decided. They made up your mind for you . . . once again."

"And once again, they only made it possible for me to do what I knew I had to. Years and years later, when I was finishing up my doctorate, they suggested that I was ready to spend some time at a sort of training school here in Libya, so I could complete my political education as well, learn to become a real militant fighter. I hope you can understand what a difficult decision that was for me. I thought about you, naturally, and I read Brian's letter about a thousand times. I used to consult it like an oracle, and finally I suppose it said, Yes, go ahead."

Michael bit his lip and tried very hard not to look disgusted.

"I had hoped to go back to Belfast afterward, but they convinced me I could make a much more important contribution elsewhere—that there were plenty of people who were much better at that sort of thing than I was, and very few, believe it or not, with a genuine Catholic background and a Ph.D. in computational linguistics. It was only after many months of training, and just plain waiting, that I found out about Project Arcade. I know this all seems very unreal and theoretical to you, but from my perspective, I'm sure you can understand how I came to feel that a tactical alliance between the pope and Maggie Thatcher and the Pentagon, among others, wasn't going to do much to advance the cause of democratic socialism in Ireland."

Michael was no longer listening. He got out of bed and began pacing back and forth across the carpet. He wanted to talk to her, to convince her, to be brilliant, passionate, and persuasive, but somehow he found that his head was not full of words—to say nothing of geostrategic insights—but of images, not merely pictorial, but abstract, emotional. It had always made sense to imagine their love affair, from Oxford to Faremoutiers, as a series of dramatic episodes—passion, separation and reunion, desertion and despair, return and rediscovery, anxiety and uncertainty. Now he knew how to call these various episodes by their rightful names, beginning with recruitment, indoctrination, political action, practical education, reinfiltration . . . or rather, what was the jargon expression he had stumbled across in his father's correspondence? *Reinsertion.*

"You're mixing everything up!" he said finally. "You always used to say that the only real issue in Northern Ireland was civil rights. Nothing really to do with religion, and that was Protestant and Catholic you were talking about, so I can't really see how you could think that it has anything to do with Islam. And how much do you think your two precious colonels, Qaddafi and Akhmedov, care about civil rights?"

"That's all very well to say, Michael, but when it comes to trying to *do* something about it, you begin to realize that there are just two sides—the oppressors and the oppressed, justice and injustice, the ones who are trying to help people be free and the ones who want to keep them alienated and confused."

"And you think you'll be fighting for freedom and justice—side by side with Qaddafi and Gorbachev. Why not bring in the dear old ayatollah as well?"

"Here at least people believe in what they believe. They take their religion seriously. With us it's nothing but superstition for the women and the old people, and worshiping the golden calf for the ones who still want to get ahead. The Vatican is just money and politics and careerism and corruption like everything else. Look at the Vatican bank with all its scandals and embezzlers hanging themselves from bridges and things like that."

"So you think you're likely to become a Muslim then?"

"That doesn't have anything to do with it!"

"Maybe the Colonel doesn't think you're quite ready for that yet. But when the time comes, get ready to take the veil, or in this particular case, the chador."

"I don't think they call it a chador in this part of the world. And I wish you'd try to understand. You come from a country that's not a country, just like I do, a country that's always been a colony of someplace else, where people have never been trusted to rule themselves and where the so-called ruling classes are always selling out to whatever foreign power they think will have them. Look at Lebanon, for example, with the French and the Americans and the Syrians and the Israelis.

"The Russians, for all their faults, have always been sympathetic to liberation struggles waged outside their immediate sphere of influence. The Americans have not—they're hardly willing to admit that there *is* anyplace outside their immediate sphere of influence. The whole point of this Arcade business has nothing to do with religion. It's supposed to be like the U.S. cavalry in the movies, thundering to the rescue of all these embattled frontier outposts, the ones being threatened by the forces of 'Communist aggression.' And it has even less to do with 'liberalism' or 'democracy' or anything of that sort—it just means that the doddering old oppressive landlord is about to be replaced by a much more efficient multinational holding company, Ronald Reagan style. For us in Ireland, Maggie Thatcher doesn't even come into it. After a thousand years of faithful service, poor old England's about to be retired, and we'll all be under a brand-new management—IBM, Intelsat, AT&T."

Michael shrugged. "Far better the KGB than IBM, is that it? Have you heard about the Soviet pocket calculator, my dear Dr. Keenes? It only weighs twenty pounds and it comes with a two-hundred-foot extension cord. Is that the sort of future you're interested in?"

"The computer the Russians are going to be giving you, Michael, is the most advanced in the world."

"Yes, I know. They're very obliging, and *very* resourceful."

"Look, this isn't going to get us anywhere. I'd like nothing more than to convince you that what I'm doing . . . what we're doing is right. I think that would make things a lot easier, perhaps a bit less dangerous as well. But since that doesn't seem to be possible, I have only two things to say to you. One, I'm sorry I got you into this . . . but you didn't really do very much to avoid it. Two, I've loved you from the very first day I met you; I've never stopped loving you, and I never will."

"Three, we're in a hopeless fucking mess."

"Michael, I also have an important question to ask you. If you even think the answer might be yes, I want you to tell me about it now. Nothing's ever for certain in this life, and there's always a way. . . . At any rate, the question is, Do you have it in your mind to betray us? Do you think that it might even be possible that you could?"

Michael replied with a nervous bark of laughter. "You can tell our friend Abdul," he finally answered, "that the answer is no, on both counts."

Wendy's face turned white with rage, but she did not reply. *It had nothing to do with Abdul.*

At 8:15, the caretaker brought them their breakfast, which they decided to eat out on the terrace. They suddenly felt very happy and relaxed, as if nothing had come between last night's pleasures of the king's big bed and this morning's pleasures of toast and Turkish coffee. The sea was bright blue; the edge of the surf was ruffled with silvery breakers. This was, hedonistically enough, the same color scheme as their bedroom. It was going to be a beautiful day.

The hot needles of the shower, a separate installation from the swan-boat bathtub, revived them from this pleasantly languid state, more specifically, revived their memories of the night before. They were both surprised to discover that their conversation at dawn, so hurtful and hostile by turns, had actually served its purpose, and the thing itself could hardly have been much worse than the endless anticipation of it. There was no resentment, only a great relief and the reawakening of desire.

Michael found that Wendy was just as attractive in her desert adventuress outfit—looking something like a great woman traveler of some earlier century or the heroine of a silent film of the twenties—as she had been in any of her previous incarnations—as a fashionably unkempt science student at Oxford with her preposterous dyed-blond hair, as the refugee from the nunnery in her scratchy smock, or even, most recently, as herself, in the shower or the bathtub or the king's big bed. At 10:00 they pushed aside the sliding screen that gave access to the royal apartments and went out to look for Abdul. They wandered for many minutes through cool empty rooms before they came upon him, along with the four instructors, in the courtyard with the fountain.

They walked outside to the palm grove by the beach until they came to a sandy crater, its walls kept in place by a brittle netting of desert plants. At the bottom of this crater was the entrance to a buried red-brick structure like a cemetery vault. The words *underground command post* flashed impressively across Michael's brain, like a subtitle in a film. Inside, there was a large room equipped with chairs, maps, blackboards, and a powerful air-conditioning system; one of the instructors took the floor and began to describe, in English, the program of activities for the day.

The first was small-arms instruction. A pistol, rifle, submachine gun, and grenade were set before them; the appropriate pantomimes were performed, many times—inserting the clip, arming the grenade (which of course was a dummy), even breaking down the rifle into its numerous components. This was followed by a slide show with commentary, then by a hands-on run-through, first performed by Wendy, then by Michael. Then they walked down to the other end of the palm grove, where a firing range, above ground this time, had originally been set up for Colonel Qaddafi's personal use. The row of humanoid wooden figures, deployed like a ragged skirmish line just emerging from the shade of the palm trees, was still very far away when the instructor ordered them to halt. Michael assumed that the effect of four days' military training was intended to be psychological for the most part—to convince him that he was about to put his life on the line for the sake of the woman he loved and the Islamic revolution.

"You will be firing from two different stances," said the instructor. "First from a standing position, then from a prone position. You will begin at a range of one hundred meters, then you will move in to a range of fifty meters."

One of his colleagues trotted off and finally disappeared into a concealed trench behind the line of targets. Michael was handed a semi-automatic Soviet "assault rifle" and encouraged to do his worst. He was slightly relieved to discover that the targets were mechanized; like duelists, they stood with the long axis of their wooden bodies perpendicular to the line of fire, then, though for only three seconds, they swiveled around to expose the paper targets on their chests. His first two shots disappeared into the palm grove; he thought that one of them might have clipped off a luckless branch. On his third shot the flag went up behind his target; he had scored a hit. His arms felt stronger, his reflexes sharper. He saw that Wendy, cheered on enthusiastically by the Libyans, had done as well. She had had three years, after all, in which to perfect her technique.

He felt more comfortable shooting from a prone position, with a little rampart of sandbags to rest the barrel of his rifle on; sprawled on the warm sand, he found it much easier to control the nervous trembling of his muscles. After a few more shots, he suddenly realized that he was enjoying himself a great deal. It was impossible not to feel excited and triumphant after the flag went up over the target he had picked. He was starting to understand how they did it, how they managed to seduce vast numbers of women and children, peasants and university students, all over the world. After a few months of political indoctrination, a few sessions of "technical training" like this, you hardly noticed whether you were shooting at a wooden board or at human flesh. All that mattered was whether the flag went up. At the end of the session, after the Libyan had returned with their paper targets and Wendy was modestly contemplating the carnage she had wrought, the small-arms instructor came over to Michael and clapped him on the shoulder to congratulate him on his performance.

After that morning, Michael and Wendy had nothing more to say about politics, the question of individual versus collective responsibility, or the past or the future. They felt that by a tremendous effort of will they had situated themselves in the tranquil eye of a tremendous hurricane whose winds would start to rage again very soon. Somewhat uncharitably, they made no attempt to conceal their happiness and the delight that they felt in each other from Abdul; they invited him to share their lunch, but they paid very little attention to him or anything that he said. He had difficulty sharing in their talk and their jokes—his English vocabulary was not very well developed in that realm—and was soon left to conduct a lonely political monologue that wound down after twenty minutes or so, at which point he switched to his alternate conversational specialty, heavy-handed abusive banter.

"I strongly recommend that you perfect your skill at shooting, Dr. de Bonno. You know, you practically have a target painted on your chest, just like one of those wooden fellows out there. If the Americans find out what you're up to, they're not likely to miss with their first shot. If you see an American, you'd better turn quick, like this—" He swiveled his head and shoulders around to face Michael in imitation of the wooden figures on the target range. Michael and Wendy exchanged glances and then sputtered with laughter. Abdul was bewildered; he was not used to telling the sort of joke that ever amused anyone but himself. Michael and Wendy recognized that this new bond of complicity between them had made them idiotically complacent rather than anxious and fearful, but they could not bring themselves to imagine how this could possibly be explained to Abdul.

After he had left them to themselves, Wendy said to Michael, "You know, I think he's always been in love with me, poor fellow. And I'm sure he wouldn't mind pinning one of those targets to your chest himself." She said this in a flat, informational voice with no particular show of emotion.

"Did you ever go to bed with him?"

"He wouldn't have even dared suggest anything like that. He takes his job so seriously, very high ideals. And really, he's not supposed to become involved in my life in any way; he's supposed to invent my life outright. It'd be like a scientist interfering in one of his own experiments to make it come out right. It was his idea to send me to the abbey, for example—I certainly never would have thought of it on my own. It was also his idea to try and recruit you—otherwise I don't think they would have let me see you again, certainly not so soon. . . ."

"I'm getting the picture," Michael said. "I'm sure that somehow it was his idea for me to fall in love with you in the first place. And I'm quite certain that he was one of the people who ransacked the cottage in Compiègne and then tried to run me off the road." He stopped. Wendy had given him a very peculiar look. She was no longer amused.

"Shut up, Michael! And don't talk about that, now or ever. Because one thing I can tell you is that Abdul had nothing to do with that; nor do any of the other Libyans." She glanced around the terrace nervously, and then began to speak rapidly in French. "*Ce ne sont pas eux qui ont foullé la maison. . . .* They weren't the ones who searched the house. I don't know who it was, but they made off with quite a lot of stuff—letters, photographs, documents—that could be very damaging. And these people must never find out about it. They'd kill us if they did, I'm sure of it. First of all, because I let it happen, then because I didn't tell them about it immediately. It's what's known as being subject to revolutionary discipline, I'm afraid."

"But who would kill us? Abdul?"

"Precisely."

"And who's the other *they*? The ones who searched the house? Could it have been the Americans, someone from the West?"

"I told you, I don't know *who* it was! We might as well go back to speaking English, for all the good it does. We don't have any choice is what it means. We simply have to go through with it." She was silent for a few moments, then added in a much softer voice, "I have to find out who it was. I have to be the *first* to find out as well. It might have been the Russians, possibly the Iranians, some other interested party. People seem to feel safer when they can come up with these things for themselves."

That afternoon they had their first session of what Abdul referred to as "technical preparation." This consisted of a lecture on fifth-generation computers, with particular emphasis on the PSI-100, very abstruse and delivered in richly Slavic English by a guest instructor introduced by Abdul as Professor Vassiliev of Lomonosov University in Moscow. This reminded Michael of numerous graduate mathematics courses he had taken in which the instructor's accent was only slightly more comprehensible than the material itself. In the second part of the lecture, the instructor had wisely chosen not to deviate from a verbatim recitation of the documentation of the machine. Michael had heard of a special subsection of the KGB called the "X Line" that was largely concerned with the procurement of useful intellectual contraband of this kind.

It was, in any case, not the sort of information that was intended to be transmitted orally. He would have plenty of time to absorb all this later on, when he was back in Valletta. Michael allowed himself to drift off into a nostalgic lecture-room trance. He amused himself with the reflection that the Libyans had been able to find an Irish Catholic and a Maltese agnostic computer expert but not a Soviet Muslim one; apparently they had decided to draw the line at Colonel Akhmedov. He was called back to attention a few minutes later; Abdul was speaking to them, once more, in his harshest and most officious voice.

"The rest of the presentation is especially important," he said, looking pointedly at Michael. "I encourage you to give Professor Vassiliev your complete attention, since he is about to describe the means by which all communications are to be routed between Malta and Rome. You would do well to remember that if any contact between you is detected by our adversaries, all of our efforts will most probably have been in vain . . . and there will most certainly be reprisals, I need not specify on whose part. Accordingly, we have devised a means of communicating directly across the net that is quite ingenious and perfectly secure, but not entirely foolproof—you will have to observe the procedures that Professor Vassiliev is about to explain to you *most* conscientiously."

It took some time for the professor to cover all the details, but the gist of it was that he and Wendy could write messages to each other in secret files that no one other than themselves would have access to; these would automatically be erased as soon as they were read. Michael was compelled to admit that this system was in fact quite ingenious and would serve them very well. He doubted very much whether Abdul or any other Libyan had had much of a hand in its design. Abdul had of course claimed that *we* had devised it, but he had most likely been making use of the impersonal *we*, like a slick marketing executive taking credit for the latest inspiration of his company's R and D division. Undoubtedly, as he had remarked to Wendy, the Russians were very obliging and very resourceful.

The next morning, while they were sitting out on the beach, Wendy watched Michael's brooding expression for several minutes and then blurted out, "Christ, I should never have told you about any of this business. I wish you'd stop tormenting yourself, Michael. I know it's going to turn out all right. Don't you think that if the Americans knew we were up to something, they would have launched their masterful counterstroke by now? And Nicholas Resaccio seems to have been spending all his time trying to find me an apartment in Rome; I've had about ten different messages about it forwarded from Dublin. I'm really convinced they know nothing about it."

Michael smiled at her, but not because he was particularly convinced. "I was thinking about that picture, the one that fell out of the wood box in the cottage. Nicholas Resaccio. . . . You know, someone else sent me another paper with a picture of him—the one of the tournament in Tokyo—that finally made me realize that *you* were up to something, and what it was you were up to."

"Yes, that's the crux of it, of course. Our friend Abdul really does deserve full marks for that. He realized that Resaccio was the key to the whole thing, but apparently the others were very dubious. They were convinced that my convent background, and my turning up in Tokyo, and all would begin to seem like too much of a good thing. But Abdul was sure that it would turn out all right."

"He has tremendous confidence in you, obviously."

"Not so much in me as in Allah and in the revolution. He never has doubts, and, so far at least, he hasn't been disappointed."

"Our Abdul seems to relish the idea of you throwing yourself at other men. Sounds a bit perverted to me."

"You'd know all about that, I suppose."

"Well, this Resaccio really seems quite attractive, for a priest. . . . Do you suppose he's, you know, kept himself *pure* all this time? Do you suppose he's still *virgo intacta*?"

Instead of answering, Wendy gave out a savage cry and threw herself at Michael, who had already started to run toward the water. Their bare feet scratched deep furrows into the sand; by the time he had reached the shore, Wendy was right behind him, trying to bite his neck, pretending to scratch his face. Michael turned around and caught her by the wrists and pushed her away from him, a little more vigorously than he had intended. She fell back into the water with a shriek. The water was barely knee-deep, and she arose dripping and sputtering, her terry cloth robe clinging to her breasts and buttocks. She threw her arms around Michael's neck and pressed herself against him, soaking the front of his pants and shirt and laughing delightedly as she did so.

"Did he fall or was he *pushed*, you mean?" she said, accompanying each emphasized word with a shove that nearly knocked him off his feet. "Well, if you must know, it was neither one nor the other. I was recommended to him by the mother superior, a *most* respectable person I need hardly add, and my appointment was confirmed as the result of a lengthy personal interview, conducted in a public *restaurant*. So I hardly had to *throw* myself any distance at all."

After two more days it was no longer possible for them to ignore the fact that their time was almost at an end. Their last night together was as passionate and as nearly sleepless as the first, but there was something desperate in the way they clung to each other, as if to resist all efforts to pull them apart. The next morning the air was cool, there was mist hanging over the water, and the sky was overcast. Abdul led them out to the car in silence. Even he seemed subdued, if not actually sympathetic. There was a second car parked a few dozen yards away, on an unpaved track that led off from the road to the villa. It was a black Mercedes with four or five soldiers clustered around it.

"Colonel Qaddafi wanted to be here to witness your departure," said Abdul. "It is his way of assuring you of his support and his esteem."

Wendy and Michael stared in amazement at the other car; just as they were about to get into the back seat of the Fiat, they saw that the rear window of the Mercedes had been rolled down, but they could not make out the Colonel's face. Abdul spoke briefly with the driver; he was not coming with them.

"From now on," he told Michael and Wendy, "you belong to the revolution. This is something you must never forget. With the help of Allah and the forces of historical necessity, you will triumph over every obstacle that you encounter." He interlaced the fingers of both hands and pressed them together until the joints turned white. "You must also never forget that we are all joined together, like this, and this is the way it must continue to be."

Part 2

7

Rome
December 5

The weeklong conference on communication was not to begin for another three days, but the gravel walks that crisscrossed the Vatican gardens were already filled with shuffling scholarly figures, just as many, in fact, as if the pontifical academy was already meeting in plenary session. Father d'Anglebert paused for a moment to admire the Baroque assortment of fountains and ornamental basins, neatly trimmed hedges and archways; he cast a respectful eye on the dome of St. Peter's, and then headed off toward the Casina Pio IV, the seat of the academy, where he had arranged to meet James Wilcox.

They had to wait for some time in the lobby of this venerable building as the academicians and their guests filed slowly into the auditorium where the conference was to be held. Father d'Anglebert, at fifty-five, felt like a callow adolescent in such ancient and august company. He tried to imagine the feelings that Nicholas Resaccio, who was to give the principal address that day, might have about going up against such an audience. Resaccio, at thirty-five, was thought to be the youngest member ever appointed to the academy. The effect might be likened to that of a child prodigy performing before not a sympathetic public but a hostile crowd of elderly virtuosos. Or perhaps, thought Father d'Anglebert, if this young man was all his reputation made him out to be, it might be even more like the twelve-year-old Jesus about to confound the doctors in the temple.

D'Anglebert and Wilcox found seats in the last row of the auditorium. Most of the seventy academicians appeared to be in attendance, plus a somewhat livelier crowd of foreign observers in the first few rows. Carlos Chagas, the Brazilian biologist who was president of the academy, launched into his opening address. The mood was like that of an academic conference at which some remarkable disclosure was expected—not, admittedly, the sort of event that Father d'Anglebert had actually witnessed very often. At any rate, word had already gotten out that the Japanese had donated a powerful new computer to the academy and that this incredible machine was to be the mainstay of a very ambitious new project, under the direction of Academician Resaccio. What was still unknown to all but a few of them was that at the present moment they were virtually sitting on top of the powder keg itself, since the celebrated PSI-100 had already been installed in a chamber in the cellars that lay beneath the Vatican gardens.

"The battle of the ancients and moderns," said Father d'Anglebert in a low voice. "Are you familiar with the expression *bataille d'Hernani*?"

"Donnybrook Fair's more like it," replied the American evasively. He seemed to be slouching in his chair, as if trying to make himself as inconspicuous as possible, "keeping a low profile" as he himself would undoubtedly have put it. However much emphasis Father Resaccio chose to give to this aspect of the project, it would be difficult to conceal the fact that it had been originated, and would be largely subsidized, by the Americans. It was of course essential that the project *not* be characterized as a sort of ecumenical version of the Voice of America, designed purely to help the capitalist powers regain a few contested squares on the chessboard from the forces of international socialism. It was too bad, thought Father d'Anglebert, a little inconsequentially, that Resaccio had got such a reputation as a computer wizard and a master of go, which made him seem too much the cold and amoral strategist, not enough the naive and intelligent altruist that he really appeared to be.

The president had finished his introduction. Nicholas walked quickly across to the podium, clutching a sheaf of typewritten pages that had taken an enormous amount of trouble to prepare. As soon as he had typed out a fair copy he had submitted it to the Vatican for approval. There had been no reply, which Nicholas took to mean that while the pope's councillors had found nothing objectionable in his speech, they had convinced the Holy Father to withhold his categorical approval. In the language of the Church, he had received the *nihil obstat* but not the *imprimatur*.

Nicholas had heard that Southeast Asian peasants used their draft animals not only to plow their paddyfields but also to detonate any unexploded bombs or mines that might be lurking there. He felt, as the water buffalo undoubtedly did, that the part of the job that had to do with politics only made the rest of it more difficult. He was being asked to absorb the full impact of whatever controversy or criticism the announcement of the project aroused; the papal councillors had been less concerned with the fact that an explicit endorsement of his address to the academy might have stifled all such criticism at the outset. As he looked out over his audience, he recalled that this same learned body had taken no time at all to reach a consensus on nuclear disarmament three years before; who among them would want to contradict the Church's official position on the subject of peace on earth?

He began to read his address in a clear, controlled voice. "Christ came into this world in order to proclaim the Word of God. They were few who heard his message, a handful of the elect, and they in turn laid down their lives so that Our Lord's will and his love for us might become known to all mankind. Almost two thousand years have passed since those events took place that we read of in the Gospels, but in spite of persecution and human weakness, in spite of all temptation and all the vicissitudes of human history, the teachings of Jesus Christ have never ceased to prosper. Today there are more than a billion of us—including seven hundred million Catholics—who have heeded and revere them. Over the centuries, men and women have been impelled by the inextinguishable ardor of their faith to wander all over the world so that the numbers of God's people might be increased.

"True, their task has still not been completed; perhaps it will never be completed as long as this world lasts. But at this moment, we can imagine ourselves in the presence of an immense human family, diverse in their kinship, their manners and customs, and scattered throughout every nation of the world. But we can still only imagine them as one family, since we cannot talk to them or touch them or see them; we cannot even call them by name. I think that another task awaits us here in this twentieth century of the Christian era. It is the duty of all of us who have been called to God's service to set out as missionaries once again, though not into distant countries, for our work is here at the very heart of our One Holy and Apostolic Church."

The audience was hardly prepared for this; in the memory of the oldest academician, the maiden address of a newly elected member had always dealt with some aspect of science or philosophy; no one had ever had the presumption to preach a sermon.

"It is too late," Nicholas went on, "for us to take up the pilgrim staff and set out to win new lands for Christ. The time for such courageous deeds has passed. What is left to us is the humbler work of restoring the lines of communication between the hierarchy and the body of the faithful, and among the faithful themselves. In the world we live in there are men and women who are suffering because they are alone, because they are hungry—and, of course, their souls are frequently no less famished and denied than their bellies. In the more favored lands of the West, there are men and women who believe themselves to be lost, to have gone astray in a world that has been corrupted by materialism. They are all worthy of our concern. They all need our help in finding their way back to the Lord.

"It has been a number of years now since this question was addressed at Vatican II, at which time a decretal entitled *Inter Mirifica,* which dealt with the problems of social communication, was issued. I know that I have the honor to be addressing several members of the pontifical commission on the communications media that was subsequently created by His Holiness Paul VI. I have read all of their findings with great interest, and I have solicited their advice and greatly profited by it on a number of occasions.

"A number of those who are here with us today were also involved in the preparation of a pastoral letter entitled *Communion and Progress,* which emphasized the importance of the new communications media as a force for progress, for the advancement of culture, education, and religious faith. This document, which I have also gratefully consulted on a great many occasions over the past few months, was likewise concerned with defining the limits of progress, to use a phrase that has since come into fashion, and thus with striking the proper balance between experimentation on the one hand and circumspection on the other. The concluding sentence of this document refers to the future—which by now of course has become the present—as an 'age that is pregnant with possibilities, the age of social communication,' a characterization to which I for one would eagerly subscribe." He took a sip of water and went on again without looking up from the page.

"Thanks to the remarkably rapid pace of technological progress since 1971, when these words were written, there are many things within our grasp that would have been inconceivable then. For example, with the help of computers and telecommunications satellites, it is now possible for us to communicate directly and simultaneously with all of the world's seven hundred million Catholics."

D'Anglebert was trying to survey the reactions of the crowd. It would have been simpler, he thought, if the proponents and critics of the project could have taken their seats on different sides of the aisle, as in the Chamber of Deputies or the House of Commons. Those who had participated in the drafting of the two position papers on social communication were undoubtedly pleased at having their contributions recognized. The three other clerics who were also members of the academy, the only ones apart from d'Anglebert himself, were sitting in a little group several rows in front of him. Next to them was Archbishop Foley, the current president of the pontifical commission on social communication.

Since the archbishop, a former American journalist, was also responsible for the Vatican television station, CTV,* it was unlikely that he wished to associate himself with the three academicians' primordial views on social or technological change, more probable that he hoped to mitigate the force of their objections by having a private word with them as soon as Nicholas had concluded his address. (Project Arcade was so far beyond the scope of the normal programming activities of CTV that the project was to be supervised directly by Cardinal Casaroli, who, as far as everyday temporal affairs were concerned, was the real ruler of the Vatican City State.)

"We are no less concerned with individual freedom than ever before," Nicholas was saying, "perhaps even more so. Nevertheless, there are those who have taken it upon themselves to suggest that our mission is to enforce a more rigid standard of conformity upon the whole of the Christian community. But this community, by the mere fact of its diversity, is prey to many forces of divergence and disunity. It seems to me that it is our responsibility to restore some measure of coherence to the great mental and spiritual structure to which our seven hundred million brothers and sisters all contribute.

"It is in precisely this same spirit that, through the inspiration of

**Centrum Televisicum Vaticanum*: Established in 1983 with the purpose of providing televised news reports on the activities of the pope, of producing religious programs for broadcast on network, cable, or satellite TV, and of providing videotaped records of papal audiences for the benefit of private groups and individuals.

the Holy Father, it has been decided that the Vatican should be equipped with the most effective facilities for social communication that are currently available. This includes access to the television satellite channels that are maintained by a number of Western countries and—as I'm sure many of you are already aware—a remarkable new prototype of the PSI-100 computer, the very generous gift of the people of Japan. This in itself should prove, if such proof were needed, that this project may be perceived by the people of a non-Western, non-Christian nation as a force for progress and world harmony rather than as an act of cultural aggression or, indeed, as a threat of any kind.

"The nations of the Christian West have been no less generous in arranging for us to make television broadcasts, either directly or by satellite relay, to virtually every country on the globe. What is more, the simultaneous-translation capability of the PSI-100 computer will shortly be able to provide us with an audio track in the principal languages of virtually every one of these countries. The cost of providing the proper reception equipment for every Catholic household is likely to remain beyond our reach for some time to come, but our primary goal is to broadcast for two or three hours every day to every diocese—and very soon to every parish—in the world.

"We have been bold enough to imagine that every church of any importance might be equipped with a small parabolic antenna and a large-screen television, so that the congregation could assemble to watch a televised address by the Holy Father or a broadcast of any of the important observances in the ecclesiastical calendar—the papal benedictions in St. Peter's Square, the Stations of the Cross at Easter, the Feast of the Nativity. This is not to suggest that all of our broadcasts will emanate from Rome, of course, and at some future date it will even be possible for every parish that has been provided with this equipment to communicate with every *other* parish in the world.

"We see this as an opportunity to reaffirm the closeness of our ties with a common center as well as to celebrate the essential oneness of our vast community in harmony and in love. And in addition, I believe this arrangement may provide many Catholics with a chance to reexperience the living faith that inspires their formal ties to an institution that may sometimes seem cold and remote, even incomprehensible. I refer, unfortunately, to the Vatican. For the Church to live in harmony with its technological environment appears to me to be not only a duty but an absolute necessity.

"The generation that is growing up right now has learned to live in a world ruled by computers and computer-assisted communications. Whether we regard this development as admirable or deplorable, we have no choice but to admit it as a fact. If we expect to have anything to say to the children of tomorrow, we will have to master this new technology. Those who refuse to do so will find themselves imprisoned in the past. My colleagues and I regard this as our mission—to assist the Church in acclimating itself to this as yet unfamiliar world, so that the message of the Gospels will continue to speak, as loudly and as clearly as ever, to those who will be succeeding us as inhabitants of this planet.

"It is also my personal wish to be able to show those who are disturbed by the prospect of having to make some sort of accommodation with this new technology that these machines that have been invented by man can be used in the service of God and can contribute to the peace and happiness of ourselves and our fellow creatures. Our task, then, is to throw a bridge across the chasm that separates the present from the past and, in the spirit of the pastoral letter referred to earlier, to try to fulfill the promises held out by this new age of communication."

Nicholas paused to catch his breath; he was gathering up his strength for the final dash to the goal line. Apart from the usual coughing and squeaking of chairs, his audience still seemed highly attentive.

"In conclusion, I should point out that it is certainly possible for us to embark on such a quest without seeking to make ourselves as gods or going off in pursuit of knowledge that is God's alone. This would be a sacrilege, as well as an enterprise that was doomed to fail. I firmly believe that science and technology have only one thing to reveal to us, and that is the incommensurability of God and the impenetrability of His nature. Yet, if science alone will not permit us to look upon the face of God, it most assuredly will help us in loving and serving Him better.

"To my mind, this is the real and essential purpose of Project Arcade—that the people of God should be strengthened for the task of transmitting the message of hope and love and brotherhood that has been entrusted to us. For this reason, I would like respectfully to request that all of you who have honored me with your attention here today—I appeal to you as Christians, as men of science, as citizens of the world—do whatever lies within your power to ensure the success of our great enterprise, of our mission of peace and reconciliation among men."

Both d'Anglebert and Wilcox were disappointed in their predictions of a riotous confrontation between the ancients and the moderns. Part of the audience applauded lustily, others dutifully. After all, thought Father d'Anglebert, the Casina Pio IV was not the Parma opera house, and the learned gentlemen were hardly likely to burst out with a chorus of boos and catcalls. After Nicholas left the podium, the president of the academy returned to thank the speaker and, perhaps in the interest of peace and reconciliation among men, went on to review the Church's official position on satellite technology.

"Father Resaccio, you have given us a very clear picture of the complexity of the task that awaits you, and you must believe that all of us here appreciate the difficulties involved. Those of us who are accustomed to trying to navigate the two great rivers of science and faith know that the current does not always flow smoothly where they come together. I know that the Holy Father had hesitated for some time before giving the final approval for your project. In fact it was before this body, in October 1984, that he expressed his concerns about what he referred to as colonization by satellite, the possibility that space technology might be deployed in the service of cultural imperialism. On that occasion the Holy Father also acknowledged the more positive contributions that have already been made in the realm of communications, of meteorology, and of agriculture.

"Surely no one could reasonably suspect that the Vatican might intend to participate in the race for space, and it should be no less apparent that here on earth our concern is entirely with communication, rather than with persuasion or ideological coercion. We wish for nothing more than that those who share our faith should be able to join together in a way that has never before been possible. It is natural that men and women who share the same beliefs should seek one another out, should seek to communicate their shared experiences of the faith of Jesus Christ, to live together in a realm that if not geographically contiguous is still no less real. This is not to deny that this extraordinary technology could be transformed into an instrument of political, or even religious, propaganda, or used for the purpose of mass conversion or compulsion of any kind. But this does provide us with all the more reason to hope that the prudence and restraint with which we intend to proceed with our own program should serve as an example to all the world."

A stout, affable-looking man in the audience stood up and asked for permission to address the academy. The president recognized Viktor Afanasyev, a member of the Soviet Academy of Sciences and one of the many foreign observers who were not normally to be found on the premises of the pontifical academy but who had requested special permission to hear Father Resaccio's address.

"Mr. President, on behalf of the Soviet Academy of Sciences, I wish to express the gravest reservations with respect to the project that Father Resaccio has just outlined. It seems to me that in recognition of the dangers that you yourself, Mr. President, have just acknowledged, a far greater measure of prudence and restraint is clearly called for. From our perspective, this program seems not only audacious but adventurist in character, to say the least. When one wishes to be prudent in planning an enterprise of this kind, one naturally chooses the well-traveled path, the method that has been tried and tested. I am not questioning Father Resaccio's sincerity, but I would like to point out that he can offer us no assurances as to the manner in which this system will be operated once it is in place. There is no guarantee that the same prudence and restraint that have clearly been exercised throughout the planning stages will continue to be exercised once the system is operational.

"The fact that such a system could just as easily be used for the purpose of encouraging religious intolerance or political dissension in any country on earth is not one that can be readily denied. The fact that most of the technical and financial support for this project have been provided by the United States and its NATO allies offers us no reassurance as to the real purpose of Project Arcade. The argument that because this project is essentially of a religious character it could not subsequently be diverted to serve some other purpose is not one that we find compelling. On the other hand, we find it would be difficult to overestimate the risk to world peace and stability that would be involved. Consequently, I must respectfully suggest to the academy that this project should be abandoned here and now, before it is too late."

This time, the uproar in the hall was considerable. Father d'Anglebert and Wilcox exchanged meaningful glances—the Soviet observer's remarks certainly did not have the flavor of a spontaneous speech. The president of the academy called out for silence. "I would like to reply to Dr. Afanasyev on behalf of this body. Certainly your request will be taken into consideration. Nevertheless, I feel I must reiterate that the Holy Father has expressed the wish that these broadcasts be intended only for the world Catholic community, that the reaffirmation of the spiritual ties that bind this community together should in no way be regarded as a political act, least of all an aggressive one. In all other respects, it is our unalterable intention that this project should serve as a model that we can only hope will be imitated by all the world's cultures."

After a few formal words of thanks, the president adjourned the session. He had not hoped that the tension in the hall would be resolved by this brief exchange of diplomatic courtesies. Many of the academicians and their guests had remained in their seats and were talking excitedly among themselves. There were probably very few among them who would have condemned the project in quite such forthright terms as Dr. Afanasyev had, but there were undoubtedly a number who shared his suspicions to some extent. President Chagas could easily predict how many of his South American colleagues would analyze the situation—"Beware of Americans bearing gifts." It would be difficult to refute the argument that, as with several of the later Crusades, the essentially religious character of the project would not prevent its being diverted to rather sinister political purposes before long.

Father d'Anglebert caught up with Nicholas by the entrance to the casina and led him down one of the pathways through the gardens. His car was parked nearby, and he insisted on driving Nicholas back to his apartment. For several minutes they discussed Nicholas's performance and the reaction he had evoked in fairly general terms; as they reached the bridge over the Tiber, the sight of the frowning papal fortress of the Castel Sant'Angelo may have been what encouraged Father d'Anglebert to venture further with his analysis.

"I think it's already clear who the leaders of the opposition are going to be. There are only three other clerics, apart from myself, who are members of the academy. You'd do well to remember their names. . . . Pietro Scarpia, Franco Antonelli, David Kingsley. As far as they're concerned, you're the Antichrist, nothing less. They're all quite old now, but their prestige, in certain circles at least, is undiminished. They may have been a little surprised today to find themselves in agreement with Dr. Afanasyev—that was the Russian gentleman who spoke. They also feel that by agreeing to participate in the project, the Church is destined to become a sort of satellite, so to speak, of the Americans and to betray its apostolic mission. They believe in old-fashioned speculative science; they obviously don't care for technology as such. . . . Of the three, Kingsley is the one to watch. He's already started to organize a lobbying campaign against the project in the United States. Wilcox will tell you all about it. They've attracted a number of influential people, as well as financial backing from a number of fundamentalist groups. Quite a bit of it by all accounts."

"Protestant groups?"

"And Catholic. The ones who don't want to have anything to do with each other, essentially. What you might call an ad hoc tactical alliance. For all the purity of his motives, I suspect Kingsley's capable of being rather underhanded. At any rate, he appears to have been fishing in some rather murky political backwaters." D'Anglebert fell silent for a moment to concentrate on his driving as they turned off the Corso Vittorio Emanuele near the Piazza Navona. "They won't hesitate to attack you directly, you know . . . personally, I mean."

Nicholas smiled. "I take it that Father Pitta's been telling you that I was seen in a public restaurant with an attractive young woman."

"He has, and I'm sure that nothing further remains to be said on that subject. We'll take that lesson as read, shall we? And as a matter of fact, that wasn't what I was getting at. We mustn't lose sight of the fact that the project has enemies other than bigoted Texas millionaires and elderly priests. Dr. Afanasyev made his point very clearly today, I thought. The Soviet government is opposed in principle to any form of communication over which they don't exercise total control, plus they're painfully conscious of the fact that they're still five or ten years behind the West in computer technology and telecommunications. And this regime seems to be turning away from the cruder forms of propaganda they've relied on in the past; I'm sure they'd like nothing better than to go ahead with their own Project Arcade if they had the wherewithal. As it is, their main objection to the project is essentially the same as their objection to the American Strategic Defense Initiative—they refuse to believe that it won't be used as an offensive weapon once the system is effectively in place. Also, as I'm sure Father Pitta has told you, we believe that at least one of the more aggressive Islamic countries may be attempting to infiltrate the project."

"Yes, he did. He told me that Miss Keenes had an intimate friend who'd been to Libya."

"We still know nothing more than that, nothing definite, that is. You must understand that I'm *not* suggesting that Miss Keenes is a conscious agent of the Russians or the Libyans. The point is that she could be perfectly innocent in every respect—all save one, from what my information suggests—and still seriously compromise the future of the project. Thus far, the case against Michael de Bonno is purely circumstantial: De Bonno is linked, through his father, to the Labor Party regime on Malta, which has been thumbing its nose at the Western powers—not to mention the Church—for a number of years now. Malta is also a Libyan client state, or close to it, and Dr. de Bonno has recently flown to Tripoli.

"Our concern is obviously that there may be an attempt to extend the chain a little further, from Michael de Bonno, through Miss Keenes, to you." He took his left hand from the steering wheel and extracted an envelope from the inside pocket of his jacket. "The complete dossier on Dr. de Bonno, such as it is. I'll let you read it for yourself, and you can draw your own conclusions. My only advice at present is to be very cautious, particularly where Miss Keenes is concerned."

An hour later Nicholas was on his way to pick up his own car, an Alfetta that had been provided for his personal use and that so far had rarely left its garage. Wendy's apartment was on the sunny top floor of a nice old building on Via Frattina, complete with ivy-covered façade, a courtyard paved with cobblestones, and a fountain in the courtyard, now covered with moss and retired from active service since the installation of indoor plumbing not all that many years earlier.

Nicholas glanced at his watch as he ran up the old wooden staircase. It was already 7:30. He wasn't sure which one of them had first mentioned the opera, but it was he who had suggested that they might take in one of the first productions of the winter season. Personally, he preferred the honest theatricality of Verdi to the sentimental "realism" of *Cavalleria Rusticana* and *Pagliacci*, but *Cav-Pag* always brought out the best in the Roman operagoer, and Wendy had accepted his invitation with what seemed like genuine enthusiasm.

He was a little startled when she answered her door in her bathrobe, with her hair combed out in a kind of disheveled nimbus.

"I'm really not fit to be seen yet, so why don't you get yourself something to drink? . . . I think you'll find what you need in the kitchen cupboard. I swear I won't be more than another minute or two."

The musky fragrance of her perfume was quickly overwhelmed by the odor of turpentine as she disappeared into the bathroom; the room had been freshly painted, and, apart from a table, an armchair, and a deck chair, there was nothing in it but stacks of cardboard cartons. From behind the bathroom door came the sounds of running water and the vigorous strokes of a hairbrush. Ensuing sounds of drawers opening and closing, hissing aerosols, and rustling fabrics did nothing to relieve his impatience. He was about to shout through the bathroom door that they were already late when it swung open and Wendy appeared.

They still arrived too late to be seated before the orchestra had launched into the overture to *Cavalleria.* Wendy sat down on one of the carpeted steps to the balcony and gazed up at the ceiling while they waited for the applause that would be the ushers' signal to open the doors. She was very simply dressed, but she looked beautiful; he cast a critical eye over his tweed jacket and velvet trousers. Anyone seeing them would naturally assume they were a couple. Would they say to themselves, "What a handsome couple"?

They found their seats in time for Santuzza's entrance at the beginning of the first scene, followed shortly by Turiddu, her long-lost love. Right after the closing notes of every important aria and duet, the audience stamped and shouted and called out the singers' names.

"At Covent Garden," said Wendy, "they think it very daring to applaud when it's not the end of the act. I suppose the audience thinks it's bad form to make more noise than the paid performers on stage."

"In Rome," said Nicholas, "we don't make these invidious distinctions . . . and there are quite a few paid performers in the audience as well."

But the ovation had come to an end, and their neighbors hissed at them to be quiet.

Afterward they went to a little Sardinian restaurant for dinner. Wendy observed that the waiter who brought them their menus seemed to have been struck by tragedy. She suggested that like Canio in *Pagliacci* he had just found his wife in the arms of another, possibly back in the kitchen. Nicholas just managed a mournful smile.

"*Ridi, Pagliaccio!*" said Wendy, helping herself to a slice of roasted farmer cheese. "You seem a little preoccupied. Are you sorry this isn't a Japanese restaurant?"

"Not at all. . . . I suppose it's just the aftereffects of my own little performance, at the academy. It wasn't nearly as well received as *Cav* and *Pag*. Also, I had the impression that people were looking at us during the intermission. I think I've gotten to be too suggestible. People have been giving me too much good advice."

"How do you mean, people were looking at us? What sort of people?" She seemed genuinely alarmed.

Nicholas hesitated. He wasn't sure he had the right to take her into his confidence until he had the answers to a few questions of his own. On the other hand, he found it difficult to answer in generalities, especially since Wendy seemed unusually intent on what he was saying. "The project doesn't seem any too popular with its friends these days, to say nothing of its enemies . . . the Russians and so on. I think I'm getting impatient for the situation to sort itself out, so we'll know who we can count on and who we'll have to be careful of."

Wendy put her head to one side and looked at him curiously for a moment, then began to study the menu.

"I suppose it's difficult," he added, "for us to get used to the idea that some people in the world don't really like us."

Wendy looked up at him and gave him a smile so brilliant that at that moment he felt ashamed of himself for ever having suspected her of anything. Nevertheless, a few minutes later, while she was attacking a plate of *sebadas*, deep-fried batter glistening with honey, he decided the moment had come. "Is there anything you'd like to tell me about your friend Dr. de Bonno? I understand that you were at Oxford together and that while you were at the abbey, he was at the university at Compiègne, quite close by. You understand, there may be questions. . . ."

Wendy took a large bite of pastry and chewed thoughtfully for several moments before answering. "You're very well informed."

"It has nothing to do with me at all." He paused. "I wasn't being quite candid with you a moment ago. There have already *been* questions, about the nature of your relationship with this man, the nature of his current activities. I thought it was best to give you a chance to answer for yourself."

"I appreciate that," she said. "I was just caught a little off guard. Michael de Bonno is my truest friend in the world. And at one time he was more than that. But no longer. You're quite right that he was at Compiègne while I was at the abbey. On a research fellowship. He's a biophysicist—one of the best, they tell me. As for his current activities, he's gotten himself involved in what promises to be a lifelong project, computer mapping of higher cortical functions. Unlike you and me, he prefers real brains to electronic ones. . . . Oh, yes, and most currently, as of a couple of weeks ago, he runs a medical clinic on Malta, where his family comes from; the appointment sort of dropped in his lap when his father died last month. It's funny, but only the other day I was thinking how nice it would be if you two could meet. I'm sure you have a lot in common. And you'd realize right away that Michael is not the sort of person one ever has to *worry* about."

Nicholas was doing precisely that. That afternoon, he had been more amused than anything else by Father d'Anglebert's image of a chain of treachery and subversion stretching back through Wendy and Michael de Bonno to Colonel Qaddafi in Tripoli, perhaps even to Moscow. Was that her real purpose, to put him in contact with the sinister Dr. de Bonno, who would then proceed to sabotage the project in some unimaginable way? Did Wendy even realize what part she was really playing in this scheme? *If there was a scheme,* he dutifully reminded himself.

"But," she was saying, "that's not likely to happen for some time. Michael still has to get his clinic straightened out. Maybe later on, when we're all a little less busy." She gave him another brilliant smile, and a wave of relief swept over him. He still felt a little annoyed at Father d'Anglebert for having made so much out of so little evidence; the "dossier" he had given him consisted of just three short paragraphs. On the other hand, he was beginning to feel a little suspicious of himself for wanting things to turn out the way they had.

They began to discuss the project as they walked back toward Nicholas's car. Wendy was a specialist on artificial intelligence problems; she had already done some work on a simultaneous-translation program, which was the main reason even d'Anglebert and Pitta had been reluctant to recommend that her services be dispensed with. Now her task would be the very difficult one of improving and elaborating on the algorithms in the four-language program that Nicholas had brought back from Tokyo until it was capable of producing a simultaneous translation into twenty or so different languages, many of them completely unrelated and thus totally different in grammar and syntax.

"The pope speaks a great many languages already, of course," said Nicholas. "But we want him to speak *every* language, for his message to be received, in his own words and in his own voice, everywhere."

"I agree that his charisma, his incredible power as a speaker, is inseparable from his actual voice. It's not the same as hearing him through an interpreter, is it?"

"That's precisely the point. We of course want the translation to be perfectly accurate—not just word by word obviously, but phrase by phrase and sentence by sentence—but we also have to take into account that, as you say, the emotional impact is primarily conveyed by the rhythm, variations in pitch and intonation and so forth, by the music—or at least what the acousticians insist on calling the *prosody*—rather than the words themselves, like at the opera. We want all of our listeners to assume automatically that the pope is actually speaking to them in their own languages."

" 'Parthians and Medes and the dwellers in Mesopotamia' . . . like the Holy Ghost . . . Pentecost."

Nicholas smiled. "I see that you've been reading up on the technical literature already."

"And the hardware for all this already exists? I assumed it was still at the experimental stage."

"We have enough to start with. The Holy Father will record a certain number of phrases in all his various languages, enough to generate thousands and thousands of vocal spectrograms. Then the machine will get to work on those, assembling a virtually complete phonetic profile for the voice synthesizer, which I must admit is the most amazingly lifelike I've ever heard. Then, when the time is ripe, he'll be able to speak Finnish or Tamil or Japanese with his own inimitable accent, characteristic mistakes in pronunciation, and so forth."

"Sounds like we're all ready to go then."

"Yes, I think we are."

He stopped the car in front of Wendy's apartment, and she got out. "I hope you won't find it too boring if we talk more about this tomorrow," he called out through the open door. He waited until she had crossed the courtyard and reached the front door. When he glanced in the rearview mirror, he saw a white Fiat, just like the one that had been parked outside the restaurant a few minutes earlier. "You're too suggestible," he said to himself. "You're suffering from too much good advice."

Valletta
December 6

The ambassador and his staff had been banished to the upper story of the less agreeable of the two wings of the villa. Malta was not normally regarded as a very prestigious diplomatic posting, and Colonel Akhmedov was delighted to discover that the security arrangements had been allowed to become very lax. This was quickly put right. He had requisitioned a suite of rooms for his personal use since this was no mere inspection visit; he was likely to be there for some time, at least until the Libyans had carried out their operation on the mainland. The villa was well appointed and perfectly situated; he felt very appreciative of everything, from the plumbing fixtures to the delicious evening breezes on the broad veranda. It was like being the only guest in a five-star hotel, and the climate was even better than that on the Black Sea.

He felt in many ways that he had escaped from the cold shadow of Gaydar Aliev to the bright Mediterranean sun. Here he was a superior force. There had been no real need for him to go to Tripoli, except to remind the erratic Qaddafi who was really in control. The PSI-100 computer that the Japanese technicians were currently installing on the premises of the medical school had been paid for by the Soviet Union. Since there was no need to mention this explicitly, and the Colonel had barely addressed a single word to him, his visit to Tripoli had been very tedious.

In Baku he was regarded by his colleagues as an ascetic, or even a fanatic, because he did not get drunk and had very little to do with women. He was both respected and pitied, because he seemed to have no interest in life but the pleasures of command. Here on Malta, he had allowed himself to relax his normal standards in various ways; at the moment, for example, he was smoking an American filtered cigarette and reclining on a big soft bed, with one hand lazily stroking Leilah's smooth brown belly. Leilah was stark naked and very much at his disposal, though her manner was sometimes rather pert and disrespectful. Nevertheless, after so many years, he felt he had earned a few little treats like this.

"I've got you your accreditation," he said to her. "You're now the Maltese correspondent for the Egyptian Press Agency."

"Thanks. That's always been one of my ambitions."

"Your duties will not be very rigorous, I imagine. I can ask the embassy press officer to send in a few dispatches for you, if you wish. Your job is to get back in contact with Michael de Bonno. You shouldn't have any trouble doing that, I suppose. . . . What do you think of him by the way?"

"Quite charming, really. He has very nice manners."

"And he likes you as well, does he?"

"I think so, yes. He didn't act like he was just being polite."

"What sort of mood was he in, the other evening? Nervous?"

"A little. He seemed a little . . . overstimulated, a little out of control. He'd also had quite a bit to drink. I'm sure he would have told me the story of his life if I'd given him the slightest encouragement."

Akhmedov flicked his cigarette ash into the hollow of Leilah's navel. She pretended not to notice. "Don't flatter yourself. He's not going to be as easy to manage from here on in." He brought the tip of his cigarette closer and closer until he could see the faint orange glow reflected against her skin. "I want you to tell me about everything he says and does, down to the slightest detail. However, I don't want you to try to draw him out or encourage him to confide in you. Just be perfectly spontaneous—we know you're always capable of that. And you're not to call me or to initiate contact in any way. I'll be the one to get in touch with you."

She was yawning ostentatiously, and to punish her for this piece of insolence, he pretended to grind out his cigarette against her breast. She glanced down at her belly and saw with alarm that there was a glowing spark inside the little cylinder of ash that had fallen into her navel. She crushed it between thumb and forefinger.

"There may be others who will be taking an interest in this young man," said Akhmedov. "It shouldn't be too much of a strain on you to maintain your cover as a journalist. . . ."

"A glamorous lady journalist . . . a journalist in love. . . ."

"A journalist in heat, I would have thought. De Bonno will be receiving his instructions from Henry Zubbieq, the prime minister's chief of staff. Still, he won't have the opportunities that you will to make sure that everything's going according to plan. We want to know about any contact he has with anyone. We don't have very much confidence in your friend Michael de Bonno. The Japanese will be going home in a couple of days, and he may already be trying to find some way of releasing himself from our service. Sabotage, for example." He gave Leilah what he imagined to be a roguish look. "We can't have any of that now, can we?"

He reached over and stubbed out his cigarette in the ashtray on the bedside table and got up from the bed in a very deliberate manner. Leilah rolled over to his side of the mattress, then got up on her knees and elbows, as if she were about to engage in some sort of calisthenics. With a smile of triumph, Akhmedov reached out for her breasts with both hands and entered her from behind, as was the custom in his country.

Rome

The living-room window faced the courtyard, but from the bedroom she could look out over the red-tiled roofs of Rome toward the preposterous colonnade of the Vittorio Emanuele monument. It made it worthwhile to run up a couple of flights of stairs every day. Now it was dark, and the electric and neon lights of Rome were not very distinctive, but Wendy still liked to look out her bedroom window and think about being in Rome.

She had heard that even the poorest native Romans were supposed to have a kind of patrician dignity, and that, she felt, was certainly true of Nicholas. He had a great deal of energy and strength, but he was also very calm, almost serene. Over the last few days she had even begun to feel that to betray him would be almost the same as betraying Rome, not the Church or the Vatican but the city itself. Soon they would be working side by side, only he would be working to create and she would be working to destroy. Somehow she felt that knowing this in advance did not confer any particular advantage. She dreaded the moment when it would be true; she was not sure she would be strong enough, and she was trying not to think about it until it was absolutely necessary.

Instead, she tried to conjure up Michael's face, hovering outside her bedroom window, like Heathcliff's. Their four nights together in the old king's palace seemed like very distant memories. She very much wanted to hear his voice. Abdul had tried to teach her to control these "bourgeois individualist" impulses, which, she knew, were even more problematic in her case than they were with ordinary people. Tonight, however, she did not feel like denying herself this simple pleasure. Since they already seemed to know all about Michael, wouldn't it seem suspicious if she were to have nothing further to do with him? Perhaps, if her calls were being recorded, she might even be able to relieve them of some of their suspicions. She laughed to herself. When you really wanted to do something, it was remarkable how easy it was to convince yourself that it was the Right Thing to Do.

Michael picked up the phone on the second ring. He was in bed, he told her, but he was very glad that she had called just then, because he was having a pretty difficult time. He did not think it worth mentioning that he had the entire five pounds of documentation for the PSI-100 spread out all over the bedclothes, and he was not making very much headway. He seemed genuinely glad to hear her voice, but also a little apprehensive. She went on to explain that her new employers had been checking into her background and had come up with the name of Dr. Michael de Bonno, a citizen of a capriciously nonaligned country and himself of dubious political antecedents.

"I can't really explain why," she said, "because it's all very confidential. But I think your being from Malta has cost me a black mark or two. I'm sure it's nothing personal, and I know they'll change their minds as soon as they find out how boringly respectable you are. And you needn't worry, since I intend to go on taking my friends just as I find them."

There was a peculiar sort of fluttering sound on the line, and Wendy suddenly felt that this might have been taking things a little too far. She abruptly began to tell him about her impressions of Rome, the opera, the food, the good humor of the people, the elegance of the women, the attentiveness of the men, her apartment, the astonishing ugliness of the Vittorio Emanuele monument, and anything else she could think of. Michael, a little puzzled, countered with similar observations about life in Valletta. "I was just working really—when you called, I mean," he said. "My father was in the midst of a major reorganization, and he left most of the paperwork for future generations to catch up on."

Wendy gave him her address and telephone number, suggested that he might like to come to Rome for a couple of days to relax, admonished him not to work too hard, and then stopped short. She was on the verge of tears. If she couldn't say what she really wanted to say, then it was worse than not being able to talk at all. Still, there was really no one there to stop them . . .

"I miss you," said Michael suddenly.

Wendy couldn't help imagining the entire College of Cardinals, with headsets over their birettas, gathered around a tape machine in some musty basement. It was really too ridiculous, and much too sad for her to bear. "I do too," she said. "Let's write to each other, okay? Will you really do that?" She hung up.

She stretched out on her bed, and realized immediately that sleep would never come of its own accord. She set up her *go-ban*, just as she used to do at the abbey. She played a few mechanical opening moves, then realized that there was something a little odd about this game. It took her another moment before she realized what it was. This time, she wanted black to win.

Rome
December 17

Saint Peter himself and 157 (out of a possible 254) of his successors on the apostolic throne are buried in the crypt of St. Peter's, beneath the basilica. The level below is devoted to archeological excavations, first carried out in 1939 at the behest of Pius XII, since this is also the site of a Roman cemetery that was razed by Emperor Constantine to make room for the original basilica, as well as whatever remains of the Circus of Nero.

For several months a considerable portion of this sub-subbasement of the Vatican had been closed off to the public, on the pretext that there was some risk of a cave-in. One of the corridors that sloped down toward the Tiber had been walled up to prevent any members of the public from wandering in. On one side of the wall was the normal assortment of crypts, murky corridors, and dank, organic odors; on the other side was a stark and aseptic sequence of glass-partitioned cubicles and long, narrow rooms painted with antistatic paint and filled with the pale, wavering light of fluorescent bulbs.

The space beneath the floors was filled with miles of electric cables, instead of the bones of early Christians, the air with the continual thrumming of dehumidifiers and climate-control equipment. The walls were lined with the complex assemblages of metal and plastic and ceramic that represented the *ne plus ultra* of twentieth-century technology. Appearances to the contrary, as Nicholas might have pointed out, it was like a medieval abbey, whose resources would be dedicated entirely to the production of one enormous volume. This was to be the computer program that would permit a television transmitter on earth to gain access to the network of geostationary satellite channels that would be involved in Project Arcade.

Almost a hundred people altogether were going to be working on the project, which meant that more than the usual attention would have to be paid to the problems of security. There would be only a handful of terminals connected to the PSI-100, since only a small fraction of the project team would need direct access to the machine. Those who needed only a very small portion of the machine's enormous capabilities could work at terminals at home if they chose, though they could only work on the material stored in their own files. As Wendy liked to visualize it, you could write and cross out as much as you liked, but you had to keep your eyes on your copybook, and there was no way you could look over at the one on your neighbor's desk, still less sneak up to the front of the room and copy out the answers from the manual.

A still smaller fraction of the project team would be working at the systems consoles—the terminals in direct proximity to the PSI-100, and the only ones that provided access to all the programs stored in the machine, most notably the systems program, which instructed the machine to store and retrieve data in response to instructions issued by the user. The systems program could not only modify the basic means by which these tasks were to be performed but detect the presence of a material defect of any kind. Users were provided with passwords and access codes in the usual way, though these were expected to serve more than the usual purpose of protecting the sanctity of the programmers' files and preventing any of them from using up too much computer time.

After the systems programmer had presented his or her credentials at the console and had them recognized, in effect, by the central processor, all electronic barriers would be withdrawn and the programmer would be at liberty to roam at will, at least in theory. However, for the handful of honors students (Wendy among them) who were privileged to sit at the systems consoles, an additional precaution had been adopted, somewhat to the regret of Nicholas and at the insistence of Father d'Anglebert. Three of the programmers—"auditors" as they were called—were assigned the unlovable task of supervising their colleagues on the project team, running spot verifications to make sure that no one had strayed beyond the limits of his or her assigned territory and that none of the particularly critical or sensitive portions of the program had been consulted by unauthorized persons.

In spite of the auditors' every effort to be courteous, inconspicuous, and inoffensive, no one, least of all themselves, was very gratified by their hovering presence; the exercise of their function was not only irritating to their colleagues and damaging to their self-esteem but also very boring. The only aspect of this system that Wendy approved of was the fact that the auditors made no attempt to read what she had written in the files assigned to her but simply checked to make sure that she was writing in those files and had *not* attempted to open files she was not authorized to consult.

The day that she was issued the first set of passwords and access codes (which would be changed every week and were, instead of the cryptic or whimsical sort that programmers normally came up with, random sequences of numbers and letters), she stopped in a little café near the Pantheon, drank a cappuccino, and scribbled them all down on a paper napkin. Then she went into the ladies' room and pushed the napkin into the slot of the paper-towel dispenser by the sink. Another young woman was waiting by the door as she came out, and an hour later Michael would be able, by dialing a telephone number, to tap into the Vatican computer, more specifically into the portion of memory—the file—that had been assigned to Wendy. The only stipulation was that Wendy herself would have to be at one of the terminals at the same time and to have already opened her file—like the upstairs maid, as she liked to imagine it, who leaves the window open for her burglar lover. At this point, any data that was already in that file could be transferred directly to the duplicate machine in Valletta; they could also communicate directly "in clear" by typing on the keyboards of their respective terminals. Such a transfer would not be apparent to the auditors if they chose to run a spot verification on Wendy's terminal at that moment; they would see only that she had opened her own file to insert new material in the ordinary way.

At precisely 11:05 P.M., as arranged, Wendy sat down at one of the systems consoles and typed in the current sequence of access codes, followed by her password. Michael could send any messages he had for her, then erase them and break off the connection; the letters would linger on the screen just long enough for her to read them and then disappear. There would be no record of them anywhere in the machine. She could also send large chunks of the programs she was working on, which fortunately she did not have to retype; she could simply instruct the machine to duplicate them and transmit them over the phone lines. Michael, of course, was not subject to the same security constraints. He could keep a record of all their communications if he chose to, and, more important, the program material that Wendy relayed could be permanently stored in the machine on Malta.

All this system required of them was punctuality and a few simple precautions. She preferred for these sessions to be conducted at night, when there were fewer of her colleagues around, but the auditors were on duty at all times. They could hardly be blamed for enjoying the company of a fellow creature of any kind, let alone an attractive redhead, but though the actual risk of detection was probably very slight, Wendy wished they could have simply stopped by for a cup of coffee and a few minutes of pointless conversation without having to rely on the pretext of verification—*Hands in the air! Do* NOT *touch the keyboard! What are you doing now? What is the name of the file you are working on? What password did you use to gain access to that file?* After the answers were recorded in a little notebook, Styrofoam cups were produced and the auditor settled in for a short session of more or less diffident flirtation.

Wendy typed out a line of code instructing the machine to read the most recent entry in the part of her file that was used as a kind of notepad, for memos addressed to herself, brief messages, miscellaneous jottings of various kinds. Immediately, characters appeared on the screen:

```
Have rec'd further instructions re transmission of 3 days
ago . . .
```

At that moment, she saw one of the auditors, Renato Bertoni, walking slowly along the corridor on the other side of the glass partition. His lips were moving; he was probably singing to himself. He raised one hand in acknowledgment of her presence and disappeared down the corridor. Wendy felt her hands trembling. He was the most attentive of her suitors. Whenever he asked her to stop working and put her hands in the air, she noticed that he was staring at her chest instead of at the keyboard. He had probably gone into one of the other rooms to make sure that all the terminals had been shut down completely, but he would undoubtedly be back at any moment.

She stared at the screen; the message Michael had transmitted a full minute ago was just beginning to flicker and fade. He had not erased it nearly promptly enough to suit her, and a relatively lengthy block of text was likely to follow. Three days earlier she had sent him a few lines explaining about the simultaneous-translation program that she was going to be working on, that its purpose was to enable someone—the pope, for example—to express himself simultaneously in a number of languages and still give the impression that he was speaking naturally, spontaneously, *and in his own voice.* She had also duplicated and sent off the preliminary four-language programs developed at ICOT; the transmission itself had taken two hours, but once Michael had identified himself to the machine—had been substituted for Wendy, as far as it was concerned—Wendy was able to log out at the systems console to avoid attracting undue attention. The final version of the program, to be devised primarily by Wendy, would be ready in a very short time.

Nicholas had arranged for a public demonstration of the PSI-100's voice-synthesizing capability. Members of the press had been invited, and Nicholas seemed convinced that the audience, however skeptical initially, would walk away believing that Project Arcade was not just some sort of crackbrained futuristic fantasy but the technically perfect realization of an idea whose time had come. Nicholas was also convinced of the need for an aggressive campaign plan and a decisive early victory over his critics; he seemed to have boundless confidence in her ability to perform her share of this tactical miracle, but Wendy was beginning to think she might have been happier with less appreciation and much more time.

She felt as if she had been waiting for a very long time. *What was going on?* She tried to turn her chair so she could keep one eye on the screen of her console and one eye on the corridor—a physical impossibility. Finally, the cursor began to move, and the rest of the message appeared, one or two lines at a time:

```
Have passed on descr. of your mission to T. Now we know what Q
expects of you. Brace yourself. You will be instructed to sab-
otage the program in such a way that the P's broadcast can be
subtly distorted by the alteration of certain key words in the
sim. translation, so as to be more in keeping with what Q and
his friends would like to have him say. Phonetically (like dub-
bing new soundtrack for a film) and syntactically, alterations
cannot be substantial enough to cause discrepancies with the
TV image or to cause entire broadcast to lose coherence. Admit
this sounds diff. but not imposs. The command to substitute the
bogus program will originate either with you or here in M. Since
PSI will be the only intermediary between the speaker and his
audience, the nature of the substitution should not be imme-
diately apparent. P will be speaking at a rate of about 300 wds.
per minute. PSI can perform 1 billion ops. per second. Should
```

have plenty of time to figure out that a given sentence has 90% probability of finishing up one way rather than another (technique already used by human sim. translators). Will also have plenty of addtl. time in which to substitute equivalent words or phrase (from preselected glossary) which will have v. diff. impact on audience from that intended by speaker. It's all in the nuances, accdg. to Q. NOW HEAR THIS. Q wants subst. program to be ready in time for pub. demo. of real program for press and notables so that it can be tested (surreptitiously of course) under battlefield conditions.

Wendy smiled in spite of herself. The substitution of letters for proper names (*T* for Tripoli, *Q* for Qaddafi, *M* for Malta or Mdina, even *P* for Pope) would not survive very close scrutiny, but it made for a nice atmospheric touch—as if any were needed.

She almost leapt out of her chair as Bertoni's shadow flashed by on the white wall of the corridor. The message, notwithstanding Michael's ridiculous initials and abbreviations, had gone on for much too long, and he had still not erased the last few lines. He was in control of the file now, and there was nothing she could do. She would probably not even have time to load the program she was supposed to be working on in time for the verification. *Cut, for Christ's sake, Michael! Please, please cut!*

She imagined him comfortably ensconced at his little terminal in the de Bonno Clinic, or wherever it was, probably sitting on some sort of executive lounge chair and totally oblivious to the agony that he was putting her through. Bertoni had disappeared for a moment or two; when he reappeared at the door of the machine room, Wendy could only see his reflection in the pane of glass to her right. The glass was tinted, and the reflection was horribly clear; she could see that he was grinning broadly.

Finally, the last of the little green letters disappeared from the screen in front of her. *I love you, Michael,* she whispered to herself. *And I forgive you.*

Bertoni was already upon her. "Still hard at work, eh, Wendy? We should all chip in a few lire to get you a bed down here! Don't you ever get frightened, going home by yourself at night?" She had swiveled around in her chair and was about to formulate some kind of reply when, to her indescribable horror, a brand-new message appeared on the screen:

That's all for tonight. Till 3 days from now exactly. I'm counting the minutes.

This was inexcusable! He should have realized that sending her a message of fifteen or twenty lines would enormously increase the risk of detection, and now, for some unfathomable reason, he seemed to be intent on eking it out interminably, like a widow in Belfast chatting up the milkman. Two seconds passed, and the screen went blank. Bertoni was still driveling on about something or other. She cautiously advanced her index finger, in order to recall the program she was supposed to have been working on.

"Aren't we forgetting something?" said Bertoni. "Hands in the air? Do not, repeat do *not* touch the keyboard."

She was sure that she had pressed the key, but nothing had happened. "Whatever you say," she replied, a little distractedly. "Actually, I was just finishing up, so I suppose I won't be needing a bed down here after all, at least not tonight at any rate. . . ." She glanced desperately at the screen and saw the hideous flickering message, in bold capital letters.

I LOVE YOU

As usual, Bertoni was still savoring the preliminary stages of the spot verification. He was not looking at the screen. Wendy pulled back her arms, trying to make her breasts thrust outward, like the Italian girls she had seen on the Piazza Navona in their tight sweaters and retro uplift bras. Bertoni was sufficiently distracted; a moment later the letters had disappeared.

Her arms were aching. She could hardly believe that her ordeal was over, and it was with a sense of terrible, inevitable fulfillment that she watched the cursor start to move as a fresh line of text appeared on the screen:

I want to make love to you right now in the soft glimmery neon glow.

Now it was all over. Bertoni had looked at the screen. Her program would be coming up in a moment or two, but what good would that do now? *Shit, shit, shit, shit . . .*

"Well, I must say I'm very impressed," said Bertoni. "Just with a single keystroke, eh? Is that one of your ten most frequently used commands? Or did you have it timed to intercept me on my appointed rounds? Or is that what you say to all your gentlemen friends?" He had brought his face very close to hers; his breath touched her cheek, and she was sure that she was about to burst into tears. Her mind was racing, though it seemed to have taken her an incredibly long time to figure out what Bertoni was talking about.

He had apparently concluded that when she had surreptitiously touched the keyboard a few moments earlier she had caused this message to flash across the screen—a message that had clearly been prepared in advance and intended to coincide with his inspection visit. Whether he thought it was shyness or some sort of highly specialized depravity that had prompted her to put this invitation in writing was something she did not care to think about. Perhaps it represented the fulfillment, in graphic detail, of one of his most cherished fantasies.

Was there any way she could convince him that someone else had sent the message to her? She was not supposed to be communicating with anyone on the outside from the systems console, and there was no one else around at this hour. Besides, this would undoubtedly be an infraction that he would have to report to Nicholas, and that would mean the end of her mission. But he had reached the same conclusion ahead of her, sliding his hands up under her jersey, reaching around to cup her breasts, and moaning with anticipation. It was then that she realized that she had forgotten to put her arms down.

"Shh," he whispered to her, "don't be nervous. . . . We're going to have a wonderful time."

She supposed he must have been puzzled that she was turning out to be so stiff and uncooperative when she had proclaimed herself to be so willing. She decided that it would not be enough to submit; she was going to have to participate. She turned her head around and sought out his lips. He had taken one hand from her breast and was stroking the fringe of red hair at the base of her neck, which was still cut short, the way Michael liked it. She got up out of her chair with what she hoped was a low, passionate moan and pulled the jersey off over her head; she thought Bertoni might prefer to deal with her belt, her blue jeans, and panties, as indeed he appeared to do.

"Aren't you going to write me up in your notebook?" she asked him, as he started to take off his shirt; she somehow felt that she could not bring herself to go through with it until a formal bargain had been struck.

He looked at her curiously. "I wasn't going to mention it," he said, "as long as you never do it again."

The floor felt even colder and harder against her back than she had thought it would; she thought of all the wires and cables that were running along beneath it. The screen of the console was still glowing softly. She tried to make herself think about how furious she was at Michael. "In the soft glimmering neon glow" indeed. *To begin with, it makes your skin look all pale and sickly, like some sort of underground fish or fungus.* Bertoni seemed to be breathing in unison with the perpetual whirring of the machines and the climate-control equipment. She was praying for it all to disappear, like the message on the screen, which must surely have done so by now.

She thrust her pelvis forward and spread her legs, in the hope that this would hasten things to their conclusion. But Bertoni seemed to have interpreted this as an invitation to linger; she felt his lips moving from her breasts down to her belly. She was past pretending to be responsive, but Bertoni appeared to be well past noticing himself. She closed her eyes and tried to think of Michael, but it was no use; he would never have been so clumsy or so hurtful. She felt like crying out, like screaming or shouting for help. She tried to imagine Michael's face but she could not. Feeling curiously detached, she thought about how this was the way well-bred women were supposed to have felt about sex, even respectable, conjugal sex, in her great-grandmother's day. *Just lie back, my dear, and think of Ireland. . . .*

Afterward, she stayed under the shower for many minutes, perhaps several hours. She started out with water in a stinging stream, as hot as she could bear it. She tried to feel the water flowing over every part of her, to wash it all away. Then she turned off the hot water and stood in the cold cataract, soaping herself down and rinsing herself off a great many times, sometimes putting her head back to catch the cold water in her mouth and wash out the acrid taste. Her thoughts began to come back to her, the way the fragments of a dream sometimes did as she was stumbling around in the morning. She thought of Brian, who had sacrificed his life for the cause that she was fighting for, that she thought that she was fighting for.

She began to wonder, as she had heard that people generally did, if she had really done all she could to avoid what had happened. She had thought about many things . . . *1 billion ops. per second* . . . but she had done nothing, except try to pretend that she was enjoying it. She was horrified by her own passivity, and she fought hard against the conclusion that she had wanted it to be that way, that she had wanted to be punished and humiliated. *Because of what she had done.*

What had she done after all? Very little so far. But with her help the Russians and the Libyans might be successful in sabotaging the project; the Americans would be thwarted, the Church would be embarrassed, Nicholas and his Jesuit friends would be terribly disappointed, the Italian government would probably fall, and the Lord only knew what else. . . . But this was the first time she had been made to suffer, to be wounded in her flesh and in her dignity, for the choice she had made. Did it mean anything that this was also the first time that she had begun to experience doubt? To think that she might have made a wrong choice, so wrong that she deserved to be punished for it?

Wendy sighed impatiently. This seemed like a philosophical problem, which in her experience meant that it would probably go away of its own accord. There was another problem of a different kind, which was Renato Bertoni. It seemed to her that only someone who was primarily concerned with his private fantasies of conquest and possession would have taken very much pleasure in her bizarre performance. Perhaps it was gratifying to his vanity that he had reduced her to the state of a blurry-eyed accident victim.

The important point was that many reenactments of that scene would be expected; even leaving aside the more horrible implications, the fact remained that no matter how she behaved toward him from now on, she would never have a moment to herself while Bertoni was on duty, and there was surely nothing to stop him from spending all his free time in making her life unbearable. As it was, she hardly had time enough to devote to her real work, let alone what Michael would have called her bogus work; this was just enough to make it all seem quite impossible.

She turned the handle, but the hot water had long since run out. She did not feel entirely clean, and she was determined that this ordeal never be repeated. Then she remembered something else. When she had wanted to cry out for help, she had tried to imagine Michael coming to help her, running to her rescue. She actually saw a figure running toward her, but when it came close enough for her to see its face, she realized that it was not Michael at all, it was Nicholas, and, just for a moment, the terrible sensations of disgust and humiliation had almost turned to pleasure and relief. But why was it Nicholas? What did it mean? *Poor Michael,* she thought, *it looks like I might have betrayed you twice over.*

Rome
December 18

Wendy had been supplied with a list of five different cafés, along with specific days and times at which she was supposed to turn up in them. After several weeks of this routine, she was prepared to state that paper-towel dispensers were rarely replenished and bathrooms not very well maintained. The day after her encounter with Bertoni, she was supposed to go to Giolitti's.

She always tried to dress for these excursions like a Roman lady of leisure. Today she was wearing a white turtleneck and a suede skirt that came down as far as the tops of her leather boots. Since the weather was cool and damp, she carried a raincoat over one arm; she had put on a pair of sunglasses as well, on the theory that someone who looked as ravaged and fatigued as she did would probably not be eating chestnut ices in a café. She finished hers very quickly, feeling ridiculously conspicuous, and glanced around the room; she was almost the only customer, which made her feel a little better. She went into the ladies' room and deposited a red paper napkin in the towel dispenser, then paid her check and left the café.

An hour later she was standing in front of a souvenir shop on Via Barberini, huddled in her raincoat and waiting. A yellow Fiat taxi pulled up in front of her, and she got in. The taxi took off with a jolt, in the authentic Roman manner.

"Are there many women taxi drivers in Rome?" asked Wendy.

"I don't know . . . a few. You're supposed to put your hand up, by the way. Otherwise, how am I supposed to know you want me to stop? You're not running around all by yourself out there, you know. They're always watching. Where are we going, by the way?"

"The Vatican, the entrance to the museum."

"I'd rather not if it's all the same to you."

"Then where do you suggest?"

"The Baths of Caracalla. The traffic's not nearly so bad, and the baths are definitely worth seeing."

Wendy could not think how to begin. After a minute of silence, the driver glanced impatiently in the rearview mirror. That was the first time Wendy had seen her face. All she knew about her was her name, Suzanne, and the license number of the taxi. She seemed more Semitic than Italian—possibly Maltese, more probably Lebanese. Her face was hard-featured and pockmarked and not overly friendly.

"Something's happened," said Wendy. "I'm afraid it may have a very serious effect—"

"You'd better tell me the whole story, from the beginning."

Wendy had difficulty in doing so at first; then, after she had built up a certain momentum, she produced each additional detail with a kind of defiance, almost bravado. She told the story precisely as she remembered it, making no attempt to conceal the fact that it was Michael who was really to blame. The idea that she was implicating him, or that she might have done otherwise, had not really occurred to her. Suzanne kept her eyes on the traffic and did not say a word. They turned off in front of the Colosseum and headed out toward the Baths of Caracalla.

"Does this Renato suspect anything, do you think?" Suzanne asked finally.

"I'm sure he doesn't."

"Why did you come here, then? Because you needed somebody's shoulder to cry on?"

Wendy felt herself stiffening with rage. "You don't actually give a damn, do you? You don't care if I get a right old shagging from everyone at the institute, as long as none of them *suspects*, is that it?"

Suzanne did not reply. It was getting dark, and the windshield was suddenly flecked with raindrops. Wendy glanced out the window at the line of strangely dressed, large-breasted women who were clustered along the roadside, staring back at the cars with the bored, professional indolence of the waiters at Giolitti's. This was a little too much for Wendy.

"I suppose that's why you brought me out here," she said angrily. "I suppose that's what you wanted to show me. . . . Well, I'm telling you that my body's my own, and I'm not about to prostitute myself for the sake of the revolution. . . ."

"You're really being ridiculous," said Suzanne. She put her foot on the gas and turned off toward Viale di Porta Ardeatina.

"You can say what you like," Wendy said, "but I don't see how I can go on like this for very long."

"Why not?"

"I won't be able to do anything with him breathing down my neck all the time. I won't be able to send off any more programs, for one thing."

Suzanne pulled up to the curb, right across from the marble pyramid of Gaius Cestius. "Look at that," she said scornfully, "the absolute pinnacle of bourgeois exhibitionism."

"Sorry?"

"Gaius Cestius . . . not a pope or an emperor but a city magistrate, a rich nonentity who wanted to be remembered and could afford to build a pyramid." Wendy was amused by the peculiar brand of snobbery that was revealed by this remark. She was actually smiling when Suzanne reached back and handed her a scrap of paper.

"That's my address," she said. "Don't take it with you, just look at it and give it back."

"How do I get there?"

"It's near the EUR. That's where you're to go if they send for you. Take the subway. Get out at EUR Marconi. You'd better bring a camera. There'll be lots of tourists wandering around."

"Is it nice?"

"It's the ugliest place in Rome," said Suzanne complacently. "Courtesy of Il Duce. . . . The station where you get off is right over there, on the other side of the pyramid."

Wendy received the summons two days later. She left with plenty of time to spare, since she had become quite curious about the EUR district, the ideal Fascist city that had been built by Mussolini for the Rome world's fair of 1942, the *esposizione universale* that had never taken place. The architecture, of course, was Roman Revival and very impressive for its kind—a fascinating succession of sun-bleached marble façades, triumphal arches and porticos, and vast imperial plazas. Wendy was especially intrigued by the allegorical statues in the ground-level arcade of a grandiloquent structure called the Palace of the Civilization of Labor. She felt a little sorry for Suzanne, who was evidently incapable of appreciating such things. The Fascist city really *was* nice, like the pyramid of poor old Gaius Cestius, more or less in spite of itself.

At 7:00 P.M., she began to look for the address that Suzanne had given her, which was on a broad commercial street at the foot of the flight of steps that led up to the Church of SS. Pietro e Paolo. She felt apprehensive and had to pause for a moment for her heart to stop racing before she pushed the apartment buzzer. She had not been told who would be meeting her there, though she supposed it would be Abdul, who was perhaps the only person in the universe capable of making her feel worse than she already did. As a preliminary, she expected to be grilled by Suzanne on her impressions of the EUR complex, but when Suzanne opened the door, she seemed anxious and subdued. Wendy followed her down the hall to the living room without saying a word.

The man who was looking out the living-room windows, though he had his back turned and was dressed in civilian clothes, was immediately recognizable as Colonel Akhmedov. She had spent several hours in his company in Colonel Qaddafi's tent, though on that occasion she had not heard him speak a word.

"You'd better sit down," said the colonel. "Not here, though, in the other room." He directed her into a sad little parlor or dining room decorated with garish Botticelli prints that had probably been furnished by the landlady rather than the fastidious Suzanne. There was a Formica table but only two chairs; the colonel pointed a chubby finger at Suzanne. "Wait in the kitchen," he said. "I'll call you if I need anything." And Suzanne scuttled off obediently. Wendy was surprised. It had never occurred to her that Suzanne might have any connection with Colonel Akhmedov.

Thus far, Wendy had thought about the Russians in much the same way that an actor might think about the investors who had backed the play he was appearing in—as a set of remote, faintly ridiculous people with more money than they knew what to do with—in either of these cases, their direct personal intervention was to be regarded as a portent of impending disaster. Wendy admired and respected the Libyans because they were passionate in their commitments, sympathetic, and openhanded. The Russians were not known for being any of these things. She had expected that Colonel Akhmedov would remain on Malta for as long as necessary, since the Russians had a proprietary interest in the duplicate computer at Mdina. He began by addressing himself to her unspoken objections, though certainly not in a way that set her mind at rest.

"It was not my intention to leave my headquarters on Malta," he announced abruptly, "and certainly not to come here for a personal meeting with you. I would not have thought that either of those two things would be necessary or desirable." He sighed and peered at her through his wire-framed glasses in a schoolmasterly way. "Now, is there anything you wish to add to what Suzanne has already told me?"

"I don't exactly know what she's already—"

"*Exactly* what you told her three days ago."

"In that case, no. I mean there's nothing . . . except perhaps that Michael had no way of knowing what he was really getting me in for . . ."

"We'll be discussing that shortly. For the moment, I think it's best to confine ourselves to more fundamental notions, such as that you and your friend Dr. de Bonno are both subject to revolutionary discipline and that the success, or failure, of your collective mission is of literally incalculable importance for the entire socialist world. Balanced against these two considerations, we have the fact that your friend seems incapable of breaking himself of the childish habit of printing pornographic messages on your computer console." Wendy bowed her head, not because she felt particularly cowed or ashamed, but because she had had a prophetic vision of the colonel wiping a trickle of saliva off each of his wire-rimmed lenses, and she was afraid of what the consequences of this might be.

Perhaps the colonel had imagined something of a similar kind, since he went on in a much softer voice, and a tone that was almost conciliatory. "You came to us with an excellent record, and you have done very well so far. You mustn't think that I am holding you personally responsible for what has happened. It would be both unjust and imprudent to replace you at this point; in fact, I suspect it would not even be possible. This is not true, however, of your friend Dr. de Bonno. I was not originally in favor of his recruitment, and he seems to me to be a remarkably unstable young man. Our Libyan friends have a genuine flair for improvisation, I agree, but in this case I suspect they may have carried it too far. Mr. Henry Zubbieq of the prime minister's office has assured me that if Dr. de Bonno becomes incapable of fulfilling his responsibilities at the university, a substitute could easily be found."

Wendy looked back impassively at the colonel.

"I think we understand each other then," he said. "Either your friend learns to restrain these adolescent tendencies, or he does not. In the latter case, I suspect that his relations with the Maltese government will become very awkward. Now, there's one other matter that requires a more urgent and I suspect a more radical solution. . . . I believe you've already discussed this with Suzanne?"

"I don't know what you mean."

"But weren't you the one who suggested that this Renato Bertoni should be suppressed? Believe me, when we receive such a recommendation from one of our agents in place, we are inclined to take it very seriously indeed."

"But I never suggested anything of the kind. I was just trying to explain that—"

"That you would be unable to transmit as long as Bertoni was 'breathing down your neck,' as I believe you put it."

"Yes, perhaps I did put it that way, but I certainly didn't mean . . . I didn't mean it as a formal request for his assassination. Surely it would be enough if we could arrange for him to be sacked."

"It seems to me that the only way to arrange that would be for you to go to Nicholas Resaccio and accuse this man of subjecting you to some sort of sexual blackmail. Only the problem then would be, as it always *must* be when confronting a blackmailer, that you must be prepared to divulge what you were so desperately eager to conceal in the first place. And of course, if it comes to that, Bertoni will have a story of his own to tell . . . or are you also prepared to explain to Resaccio that you have gotten into the habit of using the console of the PSI-100 for the purpose of conducting an erotic correspondence with Michael de Bonno?"

"I think Nicholas would believe me rather than Bertoni. Obviously I have no intention of telling him about Michael."

"Very well. I must defer to your firsthand knowledge of the situation and the personalities involved. But let me ask one more question. Don't you feel that your standing with Resaccio, and thus your effectiveness as an agent, might be compromised by an incident of this kind?"

"No, I really don't think so." She stared back very hard at the colonel, and for the first time she could actually see his eyes, like colorless wet pebbles behind the glass.

"Then you're convinced that Resaccio will accept your story, that you will be absolved of all blame, that the unfortunate Bertoni will be dismissed, and life will go on as before." The colonel smiled and shook his head, as if it was Wendy who had just backed him into the corner and not the other way around. "Very well, Miss Keenes. As I say, we are always inclined to accept the recommendation of a capable agent in place, and if that is your recommendation . . ."

Wendy was trying very hard not to scream or burst into tears or fly at the colonel's throat. "You know perfectly well that it's not. You know that I could never hope to bring it off, and you know that something like that would *thoroughly* compromise my effectiveness as an agent. It's just that you're trying to get me to . . . when it's really you that's doing it."

"If you mean that I'm trying to get you to assume the responsibility for a course of action that will have lethal consequences for one of your colleagues, then I must emphatically disagree with you. First of all, I am willing to take full personal responsibility for *every* aspect of the operation, though it was my impression that it was you who first put forth the suggestion. Second, you have no reason to reproach yourself. By exercising the methods of dialectical reasoning, you and I together have arrived at what I believe to be the only practical solution to this problem. Third, I'm sure that on further reflection it will be clear to you that whatever sentimental notions of bourgeois morality you might have retained from your childhood should have no place in a discussion of this kind."

Wendy gripped the Formica-topped table to keep her hands from trembling. She had the feeling that Colonel Akhmedov was going to keep on talking—or rather, exercising the methods of dialectical reasoning—till he had sucked up all the air in the room. There was nothing she wanted more than to get up, to get out, to run.

But the colonel had still not quite finished with her. "Suzanne tells me she has had to remind you on several occasions that you are being kept under strict surveillance by both your employers, ourselves and the Americans. It may also interest you to know that agents of the Japanese government have been paying a great deal of attention to your project and to yourself in particular."

Wendy shrugged her shoulders, as if to say that she neither knew nor cared about that side of things (which of course would not have been strictly true).

"There are two of them here in Rome who have followed you from Tokyo, though we suspect that they may have made your acquaintance, unilaterally of course, at a much earlier date, perhaps in France or even in Great Britain . . ."

"I don't see how they could possibly have—"

"There are a number of ultraleft adventurist elements in Japan, the so-called Red Army and others, who have been in contact with the Libyans and the Palestinians. There are invariably defections."

Wendy was no longer listening. She was thinking about the cottage in the forest, the documents that had been taken from the wood box. She had suspected everyone else—the Americans, the Russians, the French, the Iranians, even the Jesuits, in the person of the inquisitive Father d'Anglebert—but never the Japanese. This, if true, was news with remarkable implications. She thought it had been very devious on someone's part, probably the Russians', to have tricked the Japanese into lending one of the PSI-100s for the purpose of sabotaging the work of the other one; she could imagine some rear-echelon version of Colonel Akhmedov congratulating himself on a job well done. Now it seemed that the Japanese had known not only about Project Arcade but about the Russo-Libyan counterplot from the very beginning. Out of all the murk and confusion of her previous theories on the subject, they had suddenly emerged as the real masters of the situation.

She saw that Colonel Akhmedov was looking at her in a curious, appraising way, but she was determined to say nothing. This was a piece of knowledge that belonged to her alone; just the thought of it made her feel exhilarated and frightened at the same time.

The colonel had risen heavily to his feet. "Remember," he said, "that Suzanne is the only person to whom you are authorized to speak in complete confidence. There is no one else—certainly not Michael de Bonno, for one. You would do well not to become overly dependent on the Libyans. I suspect that your instincts are not entirely sound where these matters are concerned. Nevertheless, Miss Keenes, you must learn to be more resourceful. Far better to avoid these situations than to waste time and energy in dealing with the problems that arise in their wake. To encourage you to do so, I should only have to tell you that if I am compelled to make another one of these little trips, you should not expect to be very happy with the consequences."

She walked, nearly ran, back to her apartment by a long, circuitous route. To her amusement and dismay, the Piazza di Spagna was full of Japanese tourists. In her present state it was not difficult for her to imagine an air-conditioned tour bus full of secret agents following her through the narrow back streets of Rome, nor to pick out at least a dozen faces she recalled from Tokyo—including that of the old man who had been so helpful at the go tournament, now outfitted with a polyester suit and an assortment of camera equipment—in the shops and cafés she passed.

When she got to her apartment, she immediately dialed Michael's number at the clinic. After a few of the usual self-conscious pleasantries, she announced, "Listen, I just called to tell you I hadn't forgotten about you, but I can't really talk now. I still have some work to do. I'm pretty desperately in arrears. I'll write to you, okay?"

"Okay. And in that case, you can be confident of a prompt reply."

It was almost midnight when she arrived at the computer center. She inserted her ID card in the two external security locks and tapped out her number on the keypad. There was no one in the machine room. She went out to inspect the corridors and make sure that Bertoni was not going to turn up. The auditor on duty lifted his eyebrows and gave her a sort of mock-pathetic look, as if to express the disappointment she must have been feeling at Bertoni's absence.

"I won't be long," she told him. "There're just one or two things I have to look at." *There's surely no need for that,* she said to herself. *I belong here. I don't have to explain myself. And as for Renato, if he's been talking to his mates, telling tales out of school . . .* Then she remembered that no matter how badly he might have been behaving, he could hardly deserve the punishment that awaited him.

She sat down at her console and typed the password to her personal file. Her fingers felt cold and awkward, and she could hardly take her eyes off the glass partition, for fear that the auditor might catch her unawares. Paolo was a very nice fellow, an ex-seminarian, now the father of six. She felt a ridiculous urge to run out in the corridor and strike up some sort of a conversation, then casually mention that a few critical lines of code she'd been working on had just appeared to her in a dream or she'd seen it all spelled out in a plate of linguine. *I hope this sort of thing gets easier as you go along,* she said to herself. *If you start showing the strain, I'm sure Colonel Akhmedov will want to have you put down for interrupting his vacation, assuming that Abdul doesn't get around to it first.*

She started to type something to be inserted onto the message pad in her file:

```
There's been some trouble with 1 of the auditors. A wants to get
rid of him. Watch out for God's sake. If he's not convinced that
you're cooperating, he'll want to get rid of you too. Please be
careful. Not much more I can tell you right now . . .
```

She glanced over her shoulder, then typed, `I love you.`

After a moment or two, the answer appeared on the screen:

```
Yours rec'd and contents noted. Promise to behave. I love you
too. Message ends.
```

That was all. This time, idiotically, she wanted to hear more; she wanted to hear about the glimmering neon lights. She sat and stared at the empty screen for several minutes, feeling disgusted with herself and very much like a coward. *Please be careful* was not likely to be of much help under the circumstances. She should have told him all about what had happened, with Bertoni and with Akhmedov. She should have told him to throw a few things in a suitcase, take a taxi to the airport, and get on the first plane to London or New York.

When Paolo finally came into the machine room, he found her slumped over the console, her head nestled in her crossed arms. He walked toward her very softly, but she awoke with a start when he was still three or four paces from her. Reflexively, she threw up her hands to cover the screen, which was flickering blankly, the words having long since disappeared.

8

Faremoutiers
December 22

When Nicholas had told her, "It's all arranged, Wendy, you're coming with me," he had been a little disappointed by her reaction. Just a few days earlier, she had seemed quite pleased by the prospect of returning to the abbey of Faremoutiers to attend the modest inaugural ceremonies that would accompany the installation of the first parabolic antenna and thus the symbolic launching of Project Arcade. The site had been selected by Father d'Anglebert, ostensibly on the grounds that he knew of no other religious edifice that was as close to Paris—for the convenience of the scientific observers and members of the press who had been invited—and also provided a setting that was less suggestive of the cold, oppressive modernity that many people, particularly those in the Church, still associated with advanced technology. He had also hinted to Nicholas that this was connected, in some obscure way, with the call he had paid on Mother Marie-Bernadette just a month or so earlier, but Nicholas had thought it best not to mention this to Wendy.

For the last few days, Wendy had struck Nicholas as moody and apathetic. At first he was inclined to attribute her emotional state to the pressures of work, which certainly weighed heavily enough on all of them. He had thought that an excursion of this kind, a return if only for a few hours to the shade and serenity of Faremoutiers, would be just the thing. Now he was beginning to think that she was not merely preoccupied about her work and that what he had taken for symptoms of fatigue were in fact those of deep depression.

When the wheels of the plane left the runway at Fiumicino, Wendy felt that she could really breathe properly for the first time in several days. Up until the very last moment, she had been expecting that the death or disappearance of Renato Bertoni would be announced and the demonstration, perhaps the entire project, would be canceled. A few minutes later she fell into a deep sleep and didn't wake up until just before they were due to land at Roissy II.

She felt very much better, and Nicholas also felt somewhat reassured (though more than a little guilty), concluding that she had simply been very tired, after all, and not necessarily nursing some secret anguish. They started to discuss the demonstration, for which Nicholas had great expectations, though only a small number of journalists had been invited, carefully selected to achieve a representative global sampling. The scheduling—which Nicholas had thought a trifle premature—as well as the site selection had been the work of Father d'Anglebert, who was convinced that only a small-scale run-through of this kind would convince the world that the sponsors of the project were fully capable of doing what they had set out to do—and that they intended to do nothing beyond that. He was convinced that this would at least counteract some of the more fantastic rumors about the project that had been bandied about, and Nicholas had since come around to this point of view. Since the perfected simultaneous-translation program would not be nearly ready, they had decided to confine themselves to a demonstration of the satellite relay system. For the time being, Wendy was off the hook.

Wendy glanced out the window from time to time while they discussed this. They seemed to be descending into the depths of a bottomless abyss that was filled with black smoke, like one of Doré's illustrations for the *Inferno*; the pilot had just informed them that the weather in Paris was cold and wet. As soon as they left the plane and passed the customs booth, Wendy caught sight of Father d'Anglebert, who had offered to drive them out to Faremoutiers. He seemed relaxed and was smiling, perhaps because he had just got word that the English manufacturers of the parabolic dish had delivered it precisely on schedule and all the other equipment appeared to be functioning perfectly.

The approach of winter had stripped the leaves from the trees of Seine-et-Marne, and Wendy was confronted with an unfamiliar landscape, blurred and smudged here and there with patches of fog, reworked with headlight beams like yellow streaks of chalk. In this setting, it was easy enough for her to imagine her inner being as fogbound and damp and desolate and to contrast her present state with the way she had felt when she had left the abbey, vital and young and full of passionate intensity. That, she recalled a little too late, was a line from Yeats, "The worst are full of passionate intensity," that Irish people were always having quoted at them when they started to get excited about politics. "The best lack all conviction" was how the first part went, and that was certainly what seemed to be happening to her. She had been trying to do so many things at once—to have a love affair and write an impossible program and give her life to things she believed in—with the result, so far, that she was about to attend a press conference and poor old Bertoni, back in Rome, was about to be done away with by a person or persons unknown. She had sometimes found herself in situations like this on the *go-ban*, when the only remedy seemed to be to wipe the position off the board and sort the stones back into their bowls.

Even the sight of the great iron gates of the abbey failed to evoke any kind of emotional reaction. Mother Marie-Bernadette was there on the steps to welcome them, seeming smaller and frailer than ever in the chilly evening air. Wendy had heard that she had tried very hard to dissuade Father d'Anglebert from choosing Faremoutiers as the site of the demonstration and had relented only when overruled by the bishop. Nevertheless, she seemed to be truly delighted as Wendy walked toward her and knelt to kiss her hand. The old nun plucked at her shoulders, brought her to her feet, then clasped her to her breast in an enthusiastic embrace.

"You're looking very pale," she said to Wendy. "You could do with a little of our good country air . . . though I'm not sure you can call this the country anymore. Have you seen what these gentlemen from Rome have got growing in my garden?" These words were uttered in a tone of querulous complaint, but Wendy could see that she was smiling; she had also been assured that Mother Marie-Bernadette's authority as mother superior would undoubtedly have been respected and that some other site would have been chosen if she had persisted in her opposition. Wendy turned to look where she was pointing. The parabolic antenna did look a bit like a hardy mutant survivor in a garden that had been killed by frost. The dish was almost four feet in diameter and equipped with a long metallic pistil that pointed up toward the heavens.

"At first I was afraid they'd want to put it on the chapel roof," said

Mother Marie-Bernadette in a loud-voiced aside to Wendy. "So it was almost a relief to have it out here instead."

They were invited to dine with the mother superior in a fair-sized room that smelled very strongly of beeswax and was normally used to store wax candles, jars of honey, and similar products that were offered for sale to visitors. The room's only decoration was a vase of flowers from the greenhouse, which had been placed in the center of the table. One wall was dominated by an enormous television screen, six meters on each side, almost twenty feet by twenty, which everyone seemed tactfully determined to ignore. In theory, the screen would be moved into one of the other rooms, where all the sisters could watch it, but only when the reverend mother had given her approval. At present, the reverend mother seemed more like an anchoress, dwelling in lonely solitude, than the abbess of a nunnery. The sisters had been instructed to remain in their cells for an interval of prayer and meditation "until all this commotion is over with." Two lay sisters had been exempted from this general order so they could serve at the table.

When the food arrived, Wendy deduced immediately that Mother Marie-Bernadette had instructed the kitchens to prepare a lesson in humility and frugality for their guests. The meat was even more leathery, the vegetables even more limp, than she remembered. She watched Father d'Anglebert taking the first sip from his wineglass and was not disappointed by his reaction. Reverend Mother had gone about as far as she dared in the direction of holy poverty while complying with her vow of obedience. Wendy was delighted by all this; Nicholas seemed oblivious. Only d'Anglebert needed to reproach himself for his attachment to worldly vanities.

"I suppose I don't even have to tell you that that thing will never be allowed into my refectory," remarked Mother Marie-Bernadette abruptly.

"What thing, *ma mère*?" asked d'Anglebert. "Oh, that thing!" He gestured with his fork at the gray-green surface of the television screen.

"Here at Faremoutiers," she went on, "we take our meals in silence, or we listen to a reading from the Scriptures. Perhaps you'd like us to have television sets in every one of our cells, and little kitchens too, so we could all cook our own meals. It wouldn't be the first time, you know. I've heard of abbeys that have been like that, and prisons too, I daresay. But not here at Faremoutiers, at least as long as I'm alive."

Nicholas seemed a little taken aback. He was still not accustomed to Mother Marie-Bernadette's forthright conversational style. D'Anglebert was fascinated. "Where would you put it, then?" he asked.

"Well, just think of it. Everyone eating dinner with their necks craned to look at the screen, gaping at all sorts of foolishness, I shouldn't wonder. With respect, *mon père*, it goes into the reading room and will never be turned on without good reason, which will doubtless be very rarely. As for the other one, I must tell you, I can't even bear to think of it."

"The other one?" asked Wendy.

"Another screen's been set up in the chapel," explained Nicholas.

"Oh!"

"Just as you say, my child."

"Forgive me, *ma mère*," said Nicholas, "but I suggest you're doing us a disservice in thinking of the screens as mere objects and rather unlovely ones to be sure."

"I know," said Mother Marie-Bernadette. "I'm surprised that Father d'Anglebert hasn't explained to you that I'm just an ignorant, backward old woman."

"I think that after tomorrow," said Nicholas with a smile, "you'll have a very different reputation to live up to."

"Well, it won't be any of my doing, I assure you. You gentlemen are our guests and Mlle Keenes too of course, but surely I needn't remind you that you and your apparatus are not precisely here at our invitation."

"Indeed not, *ma mère*. And it was precisely because it was painful to us that many good Christians should think so poorly of us that we felt obliged to be so rudely insistent. There are many who remain to be convinced that our intentions are no more than what we have said them to be and certainly no less. The choice of Faremoutiers as the site of this demonstration has tremendous symbolic value for us, underscoring that at a time such as this—when there are a great many far more critical choices to be made—we are determined to find our way back to the true sources of our religion rather than deluding ourselves with phantom visions of conquest and material reward. It is true, of course, that the abbey does not happen to be located at what I would call one of the crisis points of modern Catholicism. We are here in a Christian country, more or less, part of the developed world, with easy access to communications of every kind. France has been called the elder daughter of Mother Church, and, from a spiritual viewpoint, we are still in the suburbs of Rome. Our fellow Catholics are perfectly free to practice their religion; our bishops can still speak out as respected public figures, and we have no reason to believe that things might soon be otherwise. In other words, France has no great need of Project Arcade; yet France is one of the few countries that can furnish the personnel and resources the project is going to require.

"Tomorrow the eyes of the world, or at least of a great many people, will be watching us here in Faremoutiers. I'm sure you'll tell me that you could easily have dispensed with that sort of notoriety. Let us call it a sacrifice, and not a small one, that you are being asked to make for the Church. And if tomorrow, with your cooperation, we succeed in convincing the people who will be watching and the representatives of the press that our project does not represent a surrender but a genuine alternative to the uncertainty and materialism of the secular culture of the twentieth century, then I think we will have accomplished something very important."

The reverend mother, perhaps a little dazzled by this flight of impromptu oratory, simply pursed her lips and cast a doubtful glance in the direction of the giant screen.

"One of the things we're going to have to convince people of," suggested Father d'Anglebert, "is that that screen is not just a television set that's been put somewhere it doesn't belong."

"I suppose we'll just have to get used to it," said Mother Marie-Bernadette, "the way we've gotten used to little electric bells instead of big metal ones and electric votive lights instead of candles and microphones and loudspeakers and all the rest of it."

"What I meant to say," said d'Anglebert, "is that that screen is not just an unattractive piece of furniture, though it is all of that, I'll grant you. It's like the last, visible link in the chain that binds all the Christians of this world together—I might even venture to compare it to the silver cord we read of in Ecclesiastes, 'if ever it be loosed, then shall the dust return to the earth as it was and the spirit shall return into God who gave it.' You would not just be looking at television, *ma mère*, but listening to the words of the Holy Father, taking part in the exaltation of Holy Week in Rome or in the solemn deliberations of a council of the Church. And you will not only be listening, but speaking and being heard.

"I realize that many such opportunities might be willingly neglected by one who has chosen the contemplative life, but I also believe that the day may come when every Catholic believes himself to be alone, misunderstood, perhaps even abandoned. Nicholas is quite right in observing that we have gotten to be very spoiled here in France, but not all of our brothers and sisters are as privileged. They have to struggle with the hostile world they live in; they have to struggle with their doubts as well. When they think sometimes of that distant, legendary thing that is called the Vatican, they are no longer sure that there are *any* roads that still lead to Rome. They must be shown that Rome continues to exist; they must be shown the way. They need to be reminded that they are part of a great community—what those of us who take a special interest in such things like to refer to as a *logical state*. Without that, they will surely feel that they alone have been abandoned while all the others are being gathered together—the socialists, the Communists, the Jews, and the Arabs. The nations of the West still have their collective dreams of avarice, and the Chinese and the Japanese are absorbed in their dreams of a different future. It seems to me that if we fail to take advantage of this opportunity, we will face a future in which the Vatican will be no more than an ancient monument in a world that is shared between militant atheists and fanatical idolaters." D'Anglebert paused for a moment, aware that he was rapidly losing his audience.

"And if you'd rather not think of that screen in your chapel, *ma mère*, think of the satellite that transmits the actual messages, sitting motionless in the heavens, like the star in the East that brought the Magi, men of learning and of science, to the cradle of the infant Jesus."

"Amen," said Mother Marie-Bernadette, rising hurriedly from the table even though she had still not eaten her apple.

The next morning, Wendy felt that she was reliving what had been, at least in retrospect, a happy time for her. She got up very early, attended matins in the chapel, and had breakfast with the sisters in the refectory. Nicholas and d'Anglebert had left after dinner for a hotel in Compiègne. Wendy had spent the night at the abbey, though not in her former cell, and had lain awake for over an hour, thinking of all the things that had happened since she had left Faremoutiers. The only conclusion she had come to was that nothing had turned out the way she had expected, which did not provide her with very much guidance in pondering the future.

By midmorning the forty members of the press, representing the major Western press services plus a judicious sprinkling of exotics, had turned out in a light drizzle in the abbey garden, clearly anxious for the proceedings to begin. The much-discussed Project Arcade had been rechristened for the occasion, though Wendy was of the opinion that *Ouverture du premier espace confessionnel et social chrétien* seemed meaninglessly vague and cosmic whereas *Inauguration of the first international Christian congregation* was hopelessly boring and prosaic. Perhaps they had gotten it right in Arabic or Japanese. The objection had been that *Project Arcade* was too suggestive of a top-secret military operation, though she was quite sure the journalists would all call it that anyway. In their drab but expensive raincoats, with their wet hair plastered to their foreheads, the press looked disappointingly homogeneous. She had been hoping for at least a glimpse of turbans and saris and long flowing robes.

There were only five women among them, and only one of them looked the least bit interesting. This was an olive-skinned brunette, very nicely dressed, who arched her back like a cat to ward off the raindrops and was clearly not paying the least bit of attention to Nicholas's introductory remarks. Wendy glanced at the printed invitation list and decided that since she was neither Japanese nor Scandinavian, she was probably Leilah Zanoun, Medna News Agency. *Malta.* At that moment, she turned her head away as if aware that she was being watched. With the list folded damply in her raincoat pocket, Wendy moved in closer to observe the proceedings.

Nicholas was bareheaded, dressed in a pearl-gray suit, and he seemed to be far less miserable than anyone else. He was pointing an upraised index finger, seemingly at a large black rain cloud that was riding ominously low in the sky, actually at the fixed orbital position of telecommunications satellite TDF-1 at an altitude of 36,000 kilometers, or about 22,300 miles. At the same time a technician switched on the motor that focused the antenna, which was pointing south-southwest and tilted upward at an angle of 37°.

"Because the satellite's position is fixed with respect to the earth," said Nicholas, "the antenna will only have to be tuned in this once. What we are doing here could just as easily be done anywhere else on the planet, assuming you're within broadcast range of a satellite and you know the satellite's position in the sky. This greatly simplifies the technical problems at this end, and we should have no more difficulty in picking up a direct transmission from the Vatican than in receiving a broadcast from one of the local television stations."

A gust of wind blew across the lawn, and the raincoats all fluttered in unison. Nicholas was speaking with rapturous enthusiasm of an entire chain of satellites, spread like a vast concentric mirror across the sky, that would soon permit all the rest of the world to communicate with Rome, and vice versa, at any hour of the day or night. The technician gave Nicholas a signal to indicate that the antenna was focused perfectly. Nicholas looked up and seemed to notice for the first time that it was raining. The journalists had already begun to scurry for the shelter of the abbey porch, where Mother Marie-Bernadette was waiting to escort them to the storeroom in which the screen had been set up.

Wendy followed a little behind the crowd and found that the dark-haired woman reporter was waiting for her by the door.

"Miss Keenes?"

She nodded, a little warily.

"Leilah Zanoun, Medna News, Malta. You don't know me of course, but I have something to pass along to you, from a mutual friend, you know. . . . Hideous weather, isn't it? Too bad for Father Resaccio, he seems like such a charming man, though he seems to have taken it rather well."

"Our mutual friend—aren't you going to tell me who it is?"

"Oh, yes, of course. Michael. Michael de Bonno. Though I wouldn't have thought you knew that many people on Malta; it's a bit of a backwater of course—"

Wendy gestured helplessly in the direction of the departed crowd of journalists to indicate that they were going to be late for the demonstration. Leilah was rooting energetically in her purse, gradually divesting herself of various components of her Project Arcade press kit while maintaining a diversionary flow of conversation. "—though having just been reassigned from Cairo, one does appreciate the climate and the telephones working most of the time." She handed Wendy a sealed envelope. "When he found out they were sending me up for the day, you see. And of course, I'm going right back down again as well, so if there's any reply . . ."

"Thanks very much." Wendy hesitated for a moment. "Thanks, you're very kind, but why don't you just let me read this, and perhaps I could let you know. . . . If it won't be any trouble, I mean."

"Oh, absolutely no trouble whatever," said Leilah, and they trotted down the corridor toward the storeroom together.

The table had been removed, and the room was filled with straight-back wooden chairs; apart from the screen itself, the setting was hardly impressive; it resembled nothing more, it seemed to Wendy, than a rural primary school that had been fitted out for an election meeting or the celebration of some festivity of purely local significance. The aroma of beeswax and honey was quickly overwhelmed by that of wet journalists, and the puddles at everyone's feet had soon coalesced into a large shallow pool in the center of the room.

The screen itself was covered with a broad herringbone pattern of gray and white; suddenly there were a few vertical flutters, and the picture came into sharp focus—an aerial view of the Vatican, broadcast directly from Rome via Telespazio, the satellite relay station in the Abruzzi Mountains about ninety miles to the east. At exactly 10:30 A.M. the helicopter began to descend toward St. Peter's Square, providing a panoramic view of the Vatican gardens and the dome of the basilica, succeeded by the tip of the obelisk and the Bernini fountains in the square, seen from directly overhead. The pilot corrected his course to avoid these obstacles, and the helicopter touched down in the square, the image leaping briefly out of focus at the moment of impact. The legend *Roma 10:34 A.M.* appeared at the bottom of the screen.

Next, the camera lingered for several seconds on the steps of the basilica, then turned off to the right, toward Bernini's long, sweeping colonnade. It disappeared through a gateway and then through the shadows of the Pio Nono staircase and finally reemerged in the broad courtyard of San Damasio. There was a long, searching examination of the exterior detail of the loggias, and then, apparently with the help of a second video camera that had already been set up inside, the scene shifted to the fourth floor of the palace and the offices of the deputy of the papal secretary of state.

The liquid-crystal screen produced a very high-resolution image, so that the first sight of the cardinal's deputy, a little bit more than life size and with every line and wrinkle clearly defined, was a bit terrifying, like one of those portraits of glaring, wild-eyed ecclesiastics painted by Velázquez and El Greco. The cardinal's deputy was smiling, however, and he delivered a polite little speech, in French, then in English (most of the audience was so astounded by his appearance on the screen that they missed the first few sentences anyway). He expressed the wish that the next time he stood before the camera, he would be able to speak directly to Catholics all over the world, not merely through the skilled intervention of the audience of distinguished journalists that was assembled for this special occasion, but directly, wherever they might be, despite the immensity of the oceans and continents that separated them from one another and despite the infinite diversity of human society and culture.

The cardinal's deputy was replaced by a pointillist pattern of gray and white specks; several of the journalists applauded. Wendy knew that there would be a few minutes of shifting and stretching before the press conference that followed, and she decided to take advantage of this opportunity to open Michael's letter. She was sitting in the last row of chairs, next to Mother Marie-Bernadette. She had been interested to note that the reverend mother had watched the broadcast with rapt attention and not the slightest sign of annoyance or displeasure. If anything, she seemed rather proud that such a remarkable thing had happened at Faremoutiers.

Wendy tore open the flap of the envelope and sat fidgeting for several seconds, wondering what could have induced Michael to take such a risk. Leilah Zanoun had been a little dishonest in making herself out to be free and easy and empty-headed; what was to prevent her from being dishonest in other, more important respects? Also, it had not been clear at the time of Wendy's last transmission to Malta that she was going to Faremoutiers for the demonstration, so Michael had been willing to take the chance that his letter would not even reach her.

Mother Marie-Bernadette was staring straight ahead with a rather fixed expression. Nicholas and d'Anglebert were standing at the front of the room, about to take questions from the audience; this the mother superior clearly regarded as an anticlimax, like cold leftovers from last night's dinner. Once again, the spiritual and technical objectives of the project were examined in some detail. Nicholas was explaining that at first only those nations that had launched their own geostationary satellites would be involved—the United States, the countries of Western Europe, Brazil, Mexico, Indonesia—but that they expected this list to grow considerably longer over the next few years. A journalist from a French-speaking African nation asked Nicholas a long and rather aggressive question about cultural imperialism and "the colonization of outer space," and as he started to reply Wendy decided that she could not put off reading Michael's letter any longer.

It was handwritten, very hastily it seemed, with a scratchy ballpoint on one side of a sheet of stationery from the de Bonno Clinic.

"This young man seems quite persistent," said Mother Marie-Bernadette in an undertone.

Wendy simply stared at her.

"I recognized the handwriting immediately."

"But you've never seen it!"

"Only once, but that was on a memorable occasion. Do you remember, child, we were talking in the cloister?"

"In the cloister? The day I left . . ." Until that moment, she had forgotten about the note Michael had sent to her; it had simply ceased to exist.

"The young man's message. You dropped it on one of the flagstones. I picked it up and kept it in my desk; I'm still not entirely sure why. I didn't read it until some time later, you know, and only at Father d'Anglebert's insistence. But please, go on with your reading, child. I just thought it best that you should know. And if I might give you one last piece of advice—when you've finished with this one, please don't lose it. I have quite enough on my conscience as it is."

She returned her full attention to the two priests and the journalists, who were still discussing cultural imperialism, and Wendy began to decipher the letter.

Impossible for me to send word of this via PSI, for the simple reason that I think that somebody's got into the computer. Don't think it could be anyone over here, though it does seem like the kind of thing A would do if he could possibly arrange it. Someone over there? We may soon find out. The thing of it is, the programs you've sent me are full of little patches of meaningless code, sometimes whole lines of what appears to be gibberish. Is this some sort of security measure concocted by one of your padres? If so, I don't quite see the point. But clearly whoever's doing this must be aware that we're duplicating this material and sending it over the net, right?

Here's what we'll do when next we communicate via PSI: I'll send back all the stuff you've sent me thus far (I realize that will take forever) and you can run a comparison with the versions you originally sent out. Or it might be less cumbersome if I just send you a few choice specimens so you can verify that these were *not* included in the original program. Kindly state preference. Pending verification, think it's safe for you to assume that programs are crawling with bugs, and I mean the electronic surveillance kind, not the computer kind. Who, then, can the bugger be? If not Rs or Ls even RCs, perhaps an outsider will beat the favorites to the finish line.

I love you,

M

P.S. I suppose you can trust Leilah Zanoun, up to a point. She doesn't seem any worthier of your trust than anyone really, but it's hard to see what difference it can make at this point.

Wendy put the letter back in the envelope and leaned her head against the wooden crosspiece of her chair. She felt as if someone had been hitting her over the head with a hammer at regular intervals for the past few months. At first, it had been very painful, but now she had almost stopped noticing. In the front of the room, Father d'Anglebert was discussing the thorny question of the project's finances; he spoke of the "generosity of the nations of the Christian West" as well as the "disinterested contribution of the people of Japan." Wendy gave out with an inaudible snort of derision. Currently she did not think it at all likely that anyone had approached this project with generous or disinterested motives. The reporters seemed to be of much the same mind; soon there were questions being raised about "government-subsidized cartels" and "Japanese penetration of Western markets," "the objective interest of the United States in the political pacification of Third World countries," "the inevitability of the Soviet backlash," and so on.

Nicholas was quickly drawn into the fray. The real political issue, he announced, was one of basic human rights. Human beings were guaranteed freedom of conscience, hence the right to determine their cultural and spiritual affiliations on an individual or on an *international* level. There was no plot, this was not propaganda; these coherent cultural territories already existed, like unmapped constellations, it was just a question of providing the appropriate technology so each of these points of light would shine more brightly and the connecting lines between them could finally be drawn. The emergence of nation-states in the early modern period, he went on to say, had brought with it the conviction that there was really no such thing as Christendom, as an international Catholic community, but as mankind was about to move up to a more advanced level of technology . . .

The reporters were left to fill in the rest of this assertion for themselves; one of the technicians had suddenly appeared at Nicholas's elbow to inform him that an extremely urgent call had just come in for him on the radiotelephone in the service van. Nicholas excused himself and strode out of the room. Father d'Anglebert took the next question. A few minutes later Nicholas returned, looking pale and distraught. Wendy knew immediately what had happened. D'Anglebert took one or two more questions, but Nicholas said almost nothing during the few minutes that remained of the press conference. By this point even the most disputatious of the journalists were beginning to think about the buffet that had been arranged for them at a nearby *auberge*. It had not been thought prudent to tax the resources of the abbey kitchens to that extent.

"What is it?" asked d'Anglebert after the audience had risen and started toward the door.

Nicholas waited until he was certain that no one was within earshot; he saw that Wendy was still standing by her chair, as pale and stiff as a marble statue. Mother Marie-Bernadette was no longer in evidence. "One of the auditors at the center has been murdered," he finally said. "This morning at seven o'clock, while he was on his way to work. He was driving down one of those narrow little streets off Via Giulia. A van was blocking the intersection; he got out of his car, and a motor scooter with two men came up behind him. It was the pillion rider who fired the shots, five of them. Killed almost instantly. The motive was undoubtedly political—a classic case, according to the carabinieri, only of course the victim is generally not an ordinary officeworker who takes home nine hundred thousand lire per month."

"And you're sure he wasn't up to something?"

"Bertoni? Good Lord, no. I'm sure it was nothing like that."

"And has anyone taken credit for the attack?"

"A Japanese extremist group, oddly enough . . . the Nihon Red Star Brigade or something of the sort. Since it's the first time anyone's ever heard of them, at least in Rome, and since Bertoni worked for the Vatican, the investigators are assuming that the real assassins came from a slightly more conventional background—Turkish Muslim fanatics backed by the Bulgarian intelligence service."

"Perhaps this is farfetched, but the business about Japan may be a sort of confidential message for *us*. . . . To let us know what their motive was, that they weren't just striking at the Vatican but at the project itself."

"But why Bertoni?" asked Nicholas. "I know it seems rather heartless to mention it, but he can be replaced easily enough. Why not one of us?"

Wendy had come up to the front of the room. She had heard Bertoni's name and did not need to hear any more, but d'Anglebert rapidly explained to her what had happened.

"There's a flight at one o'clock," said Nicholas. "We have to get back right away. The rumor mills in Rome are already grinding, of course, and Michel and I will have to have some sort of statement ready by this afternoon. I've just been told that three of my eminent colleagues in the pontifical academy—Kingsley, Antonelli, and Scarpia—have been camped out in the editorial offices of *L'Osservatore Romano* since this morning. It seems they've written an editorial piece entitled 'Project Arcade Claims Its First Victim,' and they intend to have it appear in tomorrow's early edition."

Part 3

9

Valletta
April 11, 1988

Father d'Anglebert never forgot a face, and he had even given himself a special dispensation to retain the afterimages of all the beautiful women he had ever met somewhere in his capacious memory. But every talent, however useful, has its limits. Unlike the casino bouncer with a more practical kind of photographic memory, who could have immediately classified her as a card counter or a countess or whatever she might happen to be, all that Father d'Anglebert could say about this beautiful young woman was that he had seen her somewhere before. She was tall, dark-haired, with a very good figure, and was carrying an expensive-looking camera; she seemed to have recognized Father d'Anglebert as well, or perhaps she merely had a special penchant for the clergy, since she clicked off a rapid-fire sequence of shots in a highly professional manner as soon as d'Anglebert had been cleared through customs at Luqa Airport.

He was a little annoyed by this, since no one on Malta was supposed to be aware of his arrival except Ettore Ghinzani, the papal nuncio, and a few members of his staff. Ghinzani himself did not turn up until several minutes later, when the young woman with the camera was no longer in evidence, and d'Anglebert decided not to mention the incident.

"I trust you'll forgive me if I take you to your hotel in an ordinary taxi," said Ghinzani. "A little less conspicuous that way, and no one takes any notice of me around here, I can assure you."

"Just as you say."

"You'll be staying at the Phoenicia Hotel. Overlooks the old Valletta harbor; it's the nicest on the island. And the tourist season is already well under way, so I don't suppose anyone will be taking any notice of you either."

The airport was in the interior of the island, though still only five or six miles from the coast; the rather violent gusts of wind that met them at the entrance to the terminal still tasted of the sea, and the sun was not hot, although it was shining brightly. As soon as d'Anglebert's suitcase was stowed in the trunk, Ghinzani turned to him with a smile and said, "You may say whatever you like in front of the driver, you know. He's one of my secretaries. The taxi's borrowed for the afternoon."

Ghinzani seemed to enjoy playing the role of Vatican spy master, but he hardly looked right for the part, or much like a diplomat either, though he was a graduate of the pontifical academy on the Piazza Minerva and would certainly be a bishop and most probably a cardinal someday. He was short and chubby, dressed in a simple black soutane; he reminded d'Anglebert of one of those intellectual abbés, fond of good food, good wine, and good talk, who were always turning up in eighteenth-century novels.

D'Anglebert had never expected to become a bishop, and Nicholas liked to tell him that it was a pity that the papal military forces had been disbanded during the last century, causing him to miss his true vocation. It was true that he did look more like the commander of a tank or paratroop battalion than a priest. For over thirty years he had spent all his excess energy in hauling himself up sheer rock faces in the Alps. He kept his white hair cut short, his jaw was slightly prominent, and his eyes were the cold blue-gray color of the interior of a glacier. It had also been many years since he had stopped wearing what he referred to as "the uniform"; the little cross stitched into the lapel of his coat was the only vestige that remained.

"Things seem to be getting along a little better now," he remarked to Ghinzani. "For a time it appeared that this wretched murder was going to get the best of us. There's certainly no shortage of suspects, starting out with the ones who have already confessed—first this imaginary Red Star Brigade, then the Sword of Saladin, the same Muslim group that was responsible for the hijacking of AF-270. I suppose it's possible that we'll never really know the truth of it."

"Frankly, I've been more concerned by our own people's reaction.

I seem to recall that a serious political attack on the Church was always taken as the signal for all of us to close ranks. This time it seems to have been taken as the signal for an all-out insurrection in the Vatican."

"An insurrection in which the rebel chieftains have been trying to pass themselves off as the voices of respectable conservatism. Now they claim that they'd known from the beginning that some sort of terrible catastrophe was waiting for 'those who have preferred to heed the siren song of modernism rather than the Word of God.' That last phrase is verbatim, by the way, Your Excellency. I read it just the other day."

Ghinzani chuckled appreciatively. "Yes, I believe I did too. It makes it much more difficult to counteract that sort of irresponsible agitation when the agitators in question are not wild-eyed seminarians or renegade priests from Holland or South America but worshipful old gentlemen like the Reverend Father Kingsley."

"We had hoped that the demonstration of the satellite relay at Faremoutiers would convince everyone, even Father Kingsley, that there was nothing the least bit sinister or dangerous about the project—some of our more enthusiastic supporters criticized us for going out of our way to make the whole thing seem rather dull and innocuous. But, as it turned out, we couldn't have been more wrong."

"I hope you're not suggesting that Father Kingsley and his associates are implicated in any way."

"No, Your Excellency, I admit I'm not quite prepared to conclude on the basis of the coincidence that Father Kingsley is a secret member of the Sword of Saladin. But I am prepared to criticize him for trying to turn poor Bertoni's death into a political windfall and for introducing a tone of real hostility, even viciousness, into the public controversy that's grown up around the project. And I must admit I mainly envy him for the success he's had in mobilizing support for his position, among both laypeople and the clergy, in America and in Italy especially, but also in Spain and Africa, Canada and Brazil. Several cardinals from the people's republics have lent their names to their governments' official protests against the project . . . in response to the usual sorts of pressure, I suppose. All I can really tell you is that the ones who wanted to come to Rome to take this up with the Holy Father had no difficulty at all in getting their visas."

"And the Holy Father himself?"

"He continues to lend his support to the project, of course, but in these last few months Father Resaccio and I have seen him fall prey to doubts and reservations, although, to be perfectly honest, we have also seen very little of him. I suspect there have been several occasions when our requests for an audience have been denied without his ever having been informed. Obviously, he has other matters to concern himself with. Unfortunately, however, that is not the case with us, Your Excellency. We need to make a breakthrough, to force a conclusion of some kind before Kingsley has his way. I hear he's called for a special synod, even an ecumenical council, to resolve this question by sheer weight of numbers."

"They want to read you out of the Church altogether, with bell, book, and candle."

"They want us to *leave* the Church in any case, all the reformers and modernists and all who have heeded the siren song. They want to make the air too poisonous for us to breathe, so we'll have no choice in the matter. Or to speak a little less metaphorically, they're waiting for us to do something so reckless and foolish that they'll be able to go to the Holy Father and say, 'You see, you see what they're capable of? That's what it's been leading up to all this time.' " D'Anglebert shifted in his seat, embarrassed by this outburst. He was also a little wary of speaking so candidly to a man whom he knew to be a friend and an ally, but only by reputation.

"I think there's somebody following us, *eccellenza.*" The driver had spoken up suddenly. "The white Fiat's been following us since we left the airport."

D'Anglebert swiveled to look at the white car about fifty yards behind them. He thought the driver was the woman who had photographed him at the airport, and then he remembered and felt very foolish, as he generally did on these occasions. *Faremoutiers.* She had been one of the journalists at the demonstration, an Algerian or an Egyptian or something of the kind. He shook his head and again decided to say nothing.

"The Holy Father is still with us," he said, returning automatically to his earlier preoccupations, "but his position is not unalterable by any means. And I don't need to tell you, I'm sure, that there are a number of people in his entourage whose positions have begun to alter quite perceptibly, on account of this Bertoni business. They were all for it as long as the Japanese and the NATO powers were prepared to foot the bill and it would bring a lot of prestige and reflected glory for the Church. Also, I think there was a certain amount of local boosterism, and even chauvinism, involved—the idea that the Vatican was going to have its own space program, if only in a very small way.

"And I think that most of them sincerely believed that the project was going to address itself to a critical problem—that despite the papal visits and all the rest of it, the center doesn't really have all that much contact with the periphery. . . . But now it's beginning to seem that this may involve us with far more serious problems—that in addition to having a space program, the Vatican is going to have to conduct its own independent foreign policy, and there is some risk that we may be ground to dust between the upper and nether millstones of superpower politics. There are some who remember—though not, I trust, from personal experience—what it was like when the popes waged war and defied the great powers of their day. And it's perfectly true, as one of them said to me the other week, 'Our business here is to proclaim the peace of Christ throughout the world, not to promote a third world war.' "

They had reached an intersection on the outskirts of Valletta, and the driver stepped down brutally on the gas pedal. Both his passengers were thrown back against their seats for a moment before he slowed down to a more conventional speed, glancing once or twice at the rearview mirror with a satisfied expression. "I beg your pardon, *eccellenza*, Father. I should have said something beforehand. It's just that the light was about to change, and I thought it might be better if we left our escort behind us."

Leilah stopped at the first telephone booth she came to, even though this meant leaving the car in a no-parking zone. She dialed Akhmedov on his private line.

"Well?"

"They lost me in the suburbs, at a traffic light, boringly enough. I'm quite sure they did it on purpose. I suppose he must have recognized me from before."

"Who must have? D'Anglebert?"

"Yes, and I have the pictures to prove it. I'll show you tomorrow. Ghinzani came to meet him, in a taxi of all things, but the driver didn't look much like an ordinary taxi driver. Probably a bishop, at the very least."

Akhmedov gave a grunt of satisfaction. The fact that they were taking these precautions, even in such an amateurish way, suggested that his assessment of the situation had been accurate. "Where were they going?"

"I have no idea. They just kept on heading into town. Damn! There's a cop sniffing around my car. I left it right beside a no-parking sign."

"Don't worry," said Akhmedov indulgently. "I'll pay the ticket. That means that d'Anglebert will not be an official guest of the nuncio. They'll put him up at a hotel, and there aren't all that many hotels. I want you to get back to Michael's at once. I'm sure d'Anglebert is going to contact him tonight. Perhaps even turn up in person."

"But if he already knows about Michael . . . I thought the whole point . . ."

"I believe that our Dr. de Bonno has been *burned*—I believe that's the technical term—and by the Inquisition as well, which seems no more than fitting. Why else would d'Anglebert be here on Malta? Just keep a close watch on your friend Michael. I want you to be there when d'Anglebert calls."

"I have no idea what you're talking about. But don't bother to explain. I'm going over there right now."

When they reached the Phoenicia Hotel, Ghinzani asked the driver to keep going for a few more minutes, since it was safer for them to talk in the car than just about anywhere else on Malta.

"I must confess," d'Anglebert was saying, "that the more reliable of our allies seem to be found outside the Church these days. I would have much preferred it if the Vatican could have remained the real driving force behind this project, but most of our support is currently coming from the NATO countries. Since Bertoni was killed, the project has taken on a more clearly political coloration. Those who are sincerely convinced of the existence of a group calling itself the Sword of Saladin have interpreted it as a warning on behalf of the Islamic world. Those who are a little more tough-minded about such things detect the hand of the KGB or their Bulgarian bully boys."

The taxi drove past the ramparts of Fort St. Elmo for the third or fourth time and headed back up Merchants Street.

"Such people are also not uncommon on Malta," prompted the nuncio, who still had no very clear idea of why d'Anglebert was on the island.

"The Americans are convinced that Nicholas Resaccio's computer center has been penetrated, as they put it, by a Soviet agent. I've had suspicions along those lines myself for several months now—you'll recall I made inquiries about a Dr. Michael de Bonno who had flown to Libya back in November—but no firm evidence to base them on. As you may have heard, the university medical school at Msida has acquired a Japanese PSI-100 computer that's identical to the machine being used by Resaccio."

"Not really my area of expertise, I'm afraid . . ."

"The Americans are convinced that information has been passed from the machine in Rome to the one on Malta. Needless to say, that is not supposed to be happening. The Americans have also been rather slow in providing evidence to back all this up. Still, I'm basically inclined to agree with them."

"And you believe this evidence is to be found on Malta?"

"I'm looking forward to a talk with Dr. de Bonno. He seems to be at the intersection of several different lines of inquiry. He is intimately acquainted with Wendy Keenes, one of Resaccio's most trusted collaborators in Rome, also a young woman whose political affiliations have been called into question in the past. He has some connection with the medical faculty at Msida that entitles him to privileged access to the computer, and, as I'm sure you know, he's very well connected in a political way as well."

"He was seen at that reception at the Soviet embassy, but of course I was there myself. I've seen him once or twice since then, I knew his father slightly, and I've always heard the de Bonnos spoken of as a fine old Catholic family. I'm sure you're aware, Father d'Anglebert, that it's difficult to take any interest at all in politics on Malta without getting mixed up with all sorts of curious people."

"I am indeed, Your Excellency, and I have a strong suspicion that it's something of that sort that has put Michael de Bonno in his present . . . rather equivocal position. Of course, if I suspected him to be a conscious agent of the Soviets or the Libyans, there wouldn't be much point in discussing it, but as it is . . . I wonder if I could beg the favor of an introduction. Emanating from a source of such unimpeachable probity as the office of the papal nuncio, that seems like something that even the most wayward son of a fine old Catholic family could not resist."

Ghinzani chuckled. "Since you put it that way, I'm sure it could be arranged."

The taxi rolled past the canopy in front of the Phoenicia Hotel. The driver glanced over his shoulder and then turned back down toward the harbor.

"The first real test of the technical rather than the political side of the project is going to take place in five days," d'Anglebert was saying. "The Holy Father will make a televised address that will be transmitted—via the Telespazio relay station in the Abruzzi and an entire fleet of satellites in permanent orbit around the earth—to some forty different countries. The broadcast will be seen in churches that have been equipped with suitable antennas, and I'm sure it will be picked up by the national television networks in the usual way. The PSI-100 computer in Rome will be charged with coordinating the satellite relay, and instantaneously translating the words of the Holy Father into some fifteen different languages, making use of a remarkable computer-synthesized reconstruction of his prerecorded voice patterns."

"To reduce it to laymen's terms then, you're trying to tell me that it's All Rather Important?"

"Either way, it's going to be a historic moment. A success will put us over the top, and if there's some sort of a problem, a failure will undoubtedly put us over the edge. The Soviets and the Libyans—not to mention the likes of Father Kingsley—have already made such a fuss about Project Arcade, have already attracted so much attention to it, that they're unlikely to arrange another assassination or any of that bully-boy stuff. In any case, whatever precautions we're able to take against that sort of thing have already been taken. Sabotage or infiltration, some kind of burrowing from within, seems much more likely."

"And if Michael de Bonno is really the guilty party, you think that merely confronting him with the knowledge of his crime is going to make all his deep-laid schemes come to nothing?"

"I'm not sure they're really as deep as all that. From what I've been able to learn of him from talking to some of his former students and colleagues in London and Compiègne, he never seems to have had much interest in politics. They describe him as being reserved, preoccupied with his work, even a little naive and complacent. Perhaps his father's death has affected him in some way, but it seems doubtful that it would take the form of sudden conversion to the cause of Islam. Nor is it likely that he had the feeling of being touched by grace the first time that Mikhail Gorbachev appeared on his television screen."

Rather than attempt another tour of the harbor, the driver had pulled up in front of the hotel at last.

"So you think," said Ghinzani, "that if you offer the proper inducements, he could be persuaded to abandon his mission—and his allegiance to Islam or Gorbachev, as the case might be, is only what you might call circumstantial?"

"Precisely, Your Excellency. And since his life is going to be in serious danger if I can persuade him to abandon his mission, I will also have to provide equally serious guarantees of his safety. We've already been in touch with the American embassy, and they're prepared to help us in any way they can. I think that after I've had a chance to meet with him and discuss this, he'll agree that he has no choice but to leave the island immediately."

"So the circumstances of your meeting with this young man will also have to be rather special?"

"Yes, and since I don't really know my way around, I thought I'd leave it to you to arrange the time and place, or to make a suggestion at any rate. It would be helpful if there was a place where a helicopter might land in the immediate vicinity."

"My, my," said Ghinzani appreciatively. He looked up the street toward the old British barracks and Great Siege Road, which leads out to the ramparts. "I'll have to give that some thought. You'd better call me at the *nunziatura* this evening."

"I will, Your Excellency. And thanks for the lift."

The driver retrieved his suitcase from the trunk, and d'Anglebert slipped him a couple of shillings, thinking that the nuncio would want appearances to be maintained at all costs.

Rome

At night the EUR looked even more like a phantom city, the capital of some vanished, arrogant race of giants, and its alternate name, E42, seemed even more deserved, as designating a vacant spot on the grid, the site of an event that had never taken place.

Abdul was looking out the window of Suzanne's little apartment at the empty street below. Suzanne had already gone out and was sitting behind the wheel of a van parked across the street, in front of the apartment building where the Iranians had been preparing for their mission for the last four days. Mohammed Khomsi got into the van beside her; his four comrades were to ride in a second van that was parked behind them. The substantial amount of matériel and munitions that they would need had already been loaded into the two vans. Abdul would not leave the apartment until he had seen them set off on the drive to Avezzano in the Abruzzi Mountains.

Half an hour later, he was knocking on Wendy's door. She was surprised and not overly pleased to see him. She was getting ready to go out and would probably have to spend a good part of the night at the computer center.

"Has it been called off for tonight then?" This was the only reason she could think of for Abdul to have turned up like this.

"Not at all." He sat down on a pile of cushions and lit a cigarette, his eyes darting around the room with insolent curiosity.

"You realize that I'm in a hurry? I'd imagine you of all people should realize that. Or would you rather just sit there sneering at my furniture for a little while longer?" She shook her head incredulously. This was the night that she too had been preparing for. She was going to transfer the entire memory contents of the Vatican computer into its counterpart on Malta, not only the prototypes for the translation program that Nicholas had brought back from Japan and her subsequent modifications, but also every scrap of information concerning Project Arcade that had been generated by the entire project team over the past several months.

This meant that the entire satellite relay network, in addition to the simultaneous-translation capability of the machine itself, could be just as easily controlled from Malta as from Rome and that the pope's broadcast, scheduled to take place in five days, could simply be blacked out or tampered with in any number of ingenious ways. For example, his speech might be broadcast in Dutch to the Catholics of Indonesia, in English to the Catholics of Mexico; but it was much more likely that the Colonel's scheme would be carried out—the language of the pope's address would be suitably distorted in translation so that the doubts and suspicions expressed by the detractors of the project would appear to be confirmed rather than dispelled.

As instructed, Wendy had spent a great deal of her time devising a kind of pirate modification of the basic translation program that could take advantage of the enormous disparity between the speed at which the human brain and vocal tract could generate speech and the speed at which the PSI-100 could process information. She had dutifully sent this off to Malta, but the tremendous task of compiling the glossaries of near-synonyms and ambiguous alternative phrasings in each of fifteen different languages she had had to leave to the Soviets and the Libyans. She was not really convinced that they could bring this off in any very subtle or plausible way, but even the most unskillful performance on their part would proclaim to the world that Nicholas Resaccio and his Vatican technocrats had been pathetically incapable of carrying out the task they had set for themselves. A reasonably skillful performance, on the other hand, would most probably detonate a serious political crisis in the Church and perhaps the rest of the Western world as well, as the colonels Qaddafi and Akhmedov had predicted.

"Khomsi and the others won't be in position until a little less than two hours from now," Abdul was saying, "so you see, you have plenty of time to get to work." This was the first time that Wendy had heard the name of the leader of the commando team; before that it had just been "the Iranians." Before the hijacking of AF-270, she had been told on various occasions that an important operation was to be carried out by "the Iranian engineer" in conjunction with the Soviets, but after she had left the abbey, she had read every word of the extensive press coverage of the event. Thus, it was impossible for her not to recall that the real name, or the *nom de guerre*, of the Iranian engineer was Mohammed Khomsi.

"I don't suppose you mean Mohammed Khomsi? I thought he'd been sent to Siberia for thirty years—or kept there rather, since he was already there when they caught him."

Abdul answered with one of his superior smiles. "Since, as you say, he was already in Siberia, I think they decided to send him to a villa in the Crimea for a couple of months instead."

"Doesn't that seem a little risky? I mean, he was a kind of international celebrity for a couple of days at least. What if he's recognized? What if he gets picked up here in Rome, or at Avezzano? It won't take them long to figure out what he's been up to, and then Colonel Akhmedov won't have the Sword of Saladin or the Bulgarians or anyone else to hide behind anymore. Really, I thought he was cleverer than that."

"Akhmedov doesn't even come into it. Gaydar Aliev is the man in charge, and he happens to be very clever. Hijacking is a capital crime in the Soviet Union, so Khomsi was officially under sentence of death. One month ago, he was exchanged for three Iranian Communists, officials of the Tudeh party, who had been imprisoned in Tabriz and were also about to be executed. Also, celebrity he may have been, but I don't think that a recognizable photograph of Mohammed Khomsi has ever been published in the West."

"So if anyone has to take the blame, it will be the Iranians."

"I suppose so, but that's their job, after all. To take the blame, to risk their necks, to get caught, and to get killed. In any case, it's really the Sword of Saladin and not the Iranians as such. And as soon as we've heard the last of Project Arcade, I suspect we'll have heard the last of the Sword of Saladin as well. I've never cared much for the name myself, since the real Saladin was a Kurd, and the Kurds have always hated the Iranians."

"Who are the other four—Khomsi's comrades in arms, I mean?"

"Just what the job requires—technicians who have had commando training. The Iranians are just as determined to destroy the project as we are, perhaps more so, but their contribution . . . perhaps you might say that it's according to their means. And of course we mustn't forget that Aliev and Akhmedov are Iranians too, of a sort. Suzanne is the only contact between Khomsi and the rest of us in Italy. There's no need for us to meet face to face. I'm sure it's just as well."

Abdul glanced at his watch. The two vans were headed for Telespazio, the satellite relay station outside Avezzano, less than a hundred miles from Rome. When they had occupied the control block of the station, Wendy would receive a coded message at the computer center in Rome. A small antenna had been installed on the roof of the Casina Pio IV, the seat of the Pontifical Academy of Sciences. This had been one of the first concrete achievements of Project Arcade, since the antenna was aimed in the direction of Telespazio and could thus pick up direct data transmissions from all over Europe, so that the project team and the PSI-100 itself could be continually kept informed of the progress of the satellite relay system and the installation of the screens and antennas in churches in participating countries. The information gathered in this way was expected to develop eventually into an enormous data base to which every Catholic diocese would contribute.

The primary goal was to compile a kind of demographic register of the members of all the Catholic congregations in the world—name, age, address, occupation, and so forth. The secondary goal was to encourage the international Catholic community to become accustomed to communicating in this way and thus to draw closer together in the manner so often evoked by the oratory of Nicholas and d'Anglebert. At the same time, it was hoped that the personnel at the center would have learned to manage this data base effectively, since it would undoubtedly turn out to be the largest ever assembled—a kind of golden bowl, filled with almost infinite quantities of useful but very minutely detailed information, to go along with Father d'Anglebert's silver cord.

Once Wendy had received the signal, her task for the evening would be very simple. All she had to do was hook up all the modems—short for "modulator-demodulators," the helpful black boxes that allowed the computer to communicate electronically with the outside world—to the antenna and then instruct the computer to read and transmit everything in its auxiliary memory banks, simultaneously. This represented an enormous amount of work for the machine, but very little for Wendy; all of its memory contents would be relayed to Telespazio for transmission to a third party via satellite. The rest of it would be up to the Iranians.

Wendy was growing impatient. She was anxious for it to be over with. The transfer itself did not pose any problem—"A monkey could do it," in the programmers' favorite catchphrase—but the strategic importance of this easy night's work was truly enormous. In the same way, she thought, you might consider the purely mechanical task of pushing a button somewhat easier if it was going to open the door of an elevator rather than, say, touch off a nuclear Armageddon. She could not quite believe that it could be that simple, that Nicholas and d'Anglebert and the others could let her get away with it; she was afraid of them, and she was afraid of her own weakness.

"I'm going now," she announced.

Abdul stubbed out his cigarette and got to his feet. "I'll join you there later."

"What?"

"You don't expect me to let you go through with this by yourself, do you? It's rather important, or didn't you know that?"

"All right," said Wendy. "Then why don't you just go in my place? Would you like your own set of keys, or are you just going to blast your way in?"

"You don't have to have a doctorate in, what is it?—*computational linguistics*—to know that there are ways of getting into such places that don't require a set of keys or a gun or a magnetized card. I didn't mean to alarm you. Perhaps I should have said that I'll be with you in *spirit*."

Wendy walked over and looked out the window, the one without the view. "Meaning what exactly?"

"You have a terminal here in the apartment, correct? I'll get on it, and that way I'll be able to keep track of everything that's happening. Otherwise, how will we know if something goes wrong?"

Wendy suddenly realized that Abdul was perfectly serious. Somehow the idea of his staying in her apartment was only slightly less horrifying than the idea of his trying to fight his way into the center with machine guns blazing. "Then perhaps I'd better show you how to switch it on before I go. . . . Look, it took me ten years to learn how to do what I'm going to be doing tonight, and you've got about ten minutes to catch up." Abdul was lounging on the stack of cushions again, and she went over and knelt down beside him.

"Father Resaccio's waiting for me. That was your idea, I know, and a very good one. The thing is, though, if I wasn't still here fucking about with you, I'd already *be there*!" Abdul had suggested that Wendy invite Nicholas to join her for a game of go at the computer center, explaining that she had a long and tedious compilation to get through that would probably take most of the night; the idea was, of course, that the auditors were unlikely to come bursting in shouting "Hands in the air! Don't touch the keyboard!" with Nicholas sitting right beside her.

"I'll be perfectly all right on my own," said Abdul. "I've spent a week on Malta, where, as you may have heard, there's another system very much like the one you're working on. I don't claim to have learned all about it, but I think I learned enough to be able to get into your file from the terminal so I'll know that everything's going as it should."

"Except it doesn't work that way. The transfer that takes place tonight is going to involve the entire memory contents of the machine, and it's not all going to be funneling out through my little patch of memory—God forbid."

Abdul shrugged, as if to imply that these subtleties were of no great importance. "There's something else I have to tell you. The Iranians are going to take control of Telespazio, whereupon Mohammed Khomsi will send a signal directly to Malta. There must not be any direct contact between Telespazio and the Vatican. Michael de Bonno will relay a coded message to you, in the way that you've been doing all along. You will not recognize the code words, but I will."

"And will Michael, since he'll be sending it to me?"

"No. He will not be sending it to you. One of our people will be with him at all times during the next five days, and she"—Abdul paused for a moment to emphasize the feminine pronoun—"will be the one who types in the recognition code on his keyboard. It will appear on the screen of your terminal at the center, of course, and I will be able to see it here as well. That will tell me that we're all ready for the transfer to begin. The code will be followed by the words *Go ahead*, just like that, in clear. This will be your signal to begin the transmission to Telespazio. Obviously, if I see the words *Go ahead* without the proper code words, I'll know immediately that all is *not* as it should be and that either you or Michael or someone else using the system is trying to deceive us. You understand that we are obliged to take these precautions."

"Of course. I'm not offended if that's what you mean." She realized that for the last several minutes she had been picking stray bits of wool off the sweater she was about to put on.

"We estimate," Abdul was saying, "that it will take approximately one hour for the entire memory contents of the computer to be transmitted by means of the antenna on the roof of the papal academy to the satellite relay station at Avezzano. As we discussed before, you will tell Resaccio that the machine is compiling a newly revised version of your simultaneous-translation program; that will give you an opportunity to get up occasionally and make sure that everything is going according to plan. And here's something quite interesting that we've never discussed before. The Iranians are going to relay your radio transmission from the Vatican to Malta via Arabsat, the Arab communications satellite. That way, no one else will be aware of the ultimate destination of all this fascinating material that's pouring out of the Vatican."

"Assuming that Mohammed Khomsi is clever enough to reorient the transmitter in the direction of Arabsat."

"The others will take care of that. Naturally, none of the usual personnel at Telespazio will be permitted to observe any of these proceedings. After the data transfer is completed, the transmitter will be returned to its original position. No one will suspect the real reason that Khomsi and his friends have come up to Avezzano."

"What do you mean the real reason? Are people supposed to think that it's just pointless mischief making, or that they've come to look for work in the potato fields?"

"Not exactly. They will be making certain demands on behalf of the Sword of Saladin. The telecommunications facilities at Telespazio would seem to have a natural appeal for a militant group with a well-known fondness for the conspicuous gesture."

"What sort of demands are they going to be making?"

"Principally the release of Mehmet Ali Agca."

"The loony who shot the pope. The one who thinks he's Jesus."

"The same. Naturally, their demands will not be met, most certainly not within the time it will take to set things up for the data transfer. As I say, these fellows are qualified electronics specialists, but they should have no trouble passing themselves off as a pack of desperate fanatics. They're close enough to the genuine article as it is—militant Shiites, so many Ali Agcas with a couple of years at technical school. The personnel in the control block will be taken hostage, of course—"

"What about security? I seem to remember hearing that Telespazio is surrounded by a military camp with a couple of hundred troops with dogs and barbed wire and machine guns. Very like Tripoli in fact."

"Once they've got into the control room, none of that will make any difference. As soon as they've made their demands, they'll threaten to shoot one of their hostages every hour."

"And will they do it?"

"Certainly, if they find it necessary to maintain their credibility, though I suspect they'll be quite credible enough without that."

"And then?"

"Then they'll just have to stay on the air for a couple of hours. They'll tell the whole story of AF-270 and the death of Renato Bertoni all over again, they'll recite suras from the Holy Koran, and they'll keep on demanding the release of Ali Agca. The Italian government will refuse to negotiate, of course; perhaps the pope himself will attempt to intervene. Then, along about dawn, the commandos will offer to forget all their demands in return for a helicopter and safe passage over Italian territory, taking one or two hostages with them, I suppose. So you see, Wendy, you can simply concentrate on doing your job and winning your game of go, and you won't have to worry at all about Mohammed Khomsi."

"At the moment, I can't really say that I'm the least bit worried about anyone except myself—"

"And Michael? As I told you, he's going to be very well looked after for the next five days. I believe you've already made the acquaintance of the comrade in question. An Egyptian woman about our age, very attractive, a journalist. . . . Her name is Leilah."

Wendy nodded wearily. *Poor Nicholas. Poor Father d'Anglebert.* After all their fussing about Libya and Malta, at least they might have invited one North African journalist who was based on Malta and who was *not* in the pay of the Colonel. She remembered Leilah saying that she had only recently been transferred from Cairo to Valletta, perhaps especially for the occasion.

"When the data transfer has been completed," Abdul was saying, "Leilah will send a second recognition code that will appear on both our terminals. Once again, she and I will be the only ones who will know the code words in advance. They will be followed by the message *All OK.* At that point, you can tell Father Resaccio that you've finished compiling your program. And, naturally, you will actually have been compiling such a program on another processor, in case Father Resaccio should express some interest in what you're doing, and it will be this material that appears on your screen—"

"We already discussed that," Wendy said exasperatedly. "I can see you picked up quite a bit during your wonderful week on Malta. But you mustn't forget that I started doing this ten years ago, while you were still tending your father's goats or whatever it was. . . ."

For a moment she thought Abdul was going to hit her, but he merely smiled. "Ten years ago, I was already a student, and I was obliged to make my living as an ordinary worker. I was not yet computer-ready, as you might say."

"Ten years ago," said Wendy, "I don't think anyone in Libya was computer-ready. I think you were still perfecting the abacus, or had you even got past the finger-and-toe stage yet?"

She had said this with deliberate malice—not just to hurt him, but because she wanted there to be an end to it all. She wanted him to knock her down or to leap up and strangle her, or for there to be a terrible quarrel that would end with him telling her that she was not worthy of the great task that awaited her. She wanted anything to happen that would mean she did not have to go through with it. She believed there was going to be a great deal of blood spilled at Avezzano that night; the Iranians *were* going to shoot their hostages, she was convinced of it. People like that cared nothing for Allah or the revolution or Khomeini, except as an excuse for shedding blood.

"It's true," said Abdul finally, "that I'm an ignorant, uneducated fellow, but there's one thing I know for sure. If anything goes wrong this evening—and I mean, for example, if one of the recognition codes does not show up on that screen—there are going to be two less doctors of philosophy in the world tomorrow. One of them will just disappear, as simple as that. The other will be sent back to Tripoli for her *re*education, so she can learn to be happy tending her goats by the shores of the Gulf of Sidra."

He took a deep breath and continued, in a very different tone, "Go on then, if you're so damned eager to go. Your handsome priest is waiting for you. But before you go—write down all your codes and passwords and dial the number to connect your terminal." Wendy scribbled down the access codes for the week and the password for her own individual file, dialed the number, and waited till she heard a sound like a dog whistle, then pressed the key labeled CONNECT on her terminal. Abdul sat down at the terminal, and the sight of him there, staring at the screen, made her so uneasy that she left the apartment without another word.

Valletta

When he heard the doorbell ring, Michael was tempted not to answer, since there was no one he could imagine he would be glad to see at the moment. Surprisingly, it was Leilah, wearing a dark-blue dress of some shiny, filmy material dotted with sequins that made her look even more attractive than usual. She was also wearing a curious expression, half-apologetic and half the sort of sultry sexpot look he remembered very well from the first night he had met her. Normally, he would have been delighted, but at the moment, he had to admit, his initial prediction still held. He had not had very much time to spend with her these last few weeks, but Leilah had been remarkably . . . *attentive* was the word that occurred to him. He had tried to encourage these attentions as much as possible, but it still seemed like her persistence was somewhat above and beyond the call of whatever attraction she might have felt for him. Crudely put, she did not seem like the type to go chasing around after men.

"Are you just going to leave me standing here?" she asked.

"What's the occasion?"

She flicked back a tendril of dark-brown hair that had fallen over her face, threw two dark-blue spangled arms around his neck, and pressed two dark-blue spangled breasts against his chest, while propelling herself across the threshold at the same time. "No special occasion. I just wanted to see you . . . very much."

"I'm sorry. Really sorry. But tonight's not a very good . . ."

She tightened her grip and raised her lips toward his. "What's wrong with it? Seems perfectly all right to me."

"Seriously, I was just about to go out. I have to drive over to Msida in about an hour."

She brought her arms down to her sides and drew away from him slightly. "So late? I suppose you're going to tell me it's one of your *sleep experiments* again."

"Yes, it is, though you needn't talk about it like it was some kind of sexual perversion. We're doing an experiment on stage four brain functions—since you asked—and delta waves of a frequency of less than one cycle per second. I've got all my data stored in the PSI-100 computer at the medical school, and tonight I'm supposed to present my findings to a group of Soviet colleagues." He watched Leilah's reaction for a hint of some guilty awareness on her part but was disappointed. Her expression was basically unchanged, partly seduction, partly pity for anyone who could resist her powers of seduction.

"We used to see a lot of them in Cairo, you know—Russians. Frankly, I never found them as fascinating as you seem to. The smart ones aren't even allowed to leave the country, because then they'd never come back."

Michael laughed. "I'll be sure to ask them if that's true. . . . But now, I think you'd better go. I've only got an hour to get things ready."

"All right," she said, walking past him into the living room, "then I'll only stay for an hour." This was a large room filled with evidence of his father's taste for Neolithic figurines, Catalan primitive paintings, and other expensive but not very attractive art objects. Michael's resistance was beginning to crumble. After all, what was the point of kicking her out?—unless he was determined to make the first part of the evening as devoid of pleasurable sensations, not to say unbearable, as the rest was going to be. He sat down opposite Leilah on the arm of an enormous leather chair.

"I didn't exactly mean that I've nothing else to do till then," he said. "I have to get back to work in a couple of minutes, but if you'd be just as happy sitting there . . ."

"Perfectly happy. I just didn't feel like being alone at the moment—I feel a little depressed if you must know. I'll just fix myself a drink and sit down somewhere, and you can get ready for your Soviet colleagues."

Before Michael had a chance to analyze the hidden implications of this remark, if any, the telephone on the hall table rang. As he walked over to answer, he noted with some surprise that Leilah, who had been draped informally over a squashy leather sofa, was sitting up very straight, as if she had expected to have to get up and answer it herself.

"Dr. de Bonno?" said the soft Italian-accented voice at the other end of the wire.

"Speaking."

"I'm calling to discuss a confidential matter of great importance. Can you speak freely?"

"I suppose so, but what's it about? Who are you?"

"I'm calling on behalf of His Excellency Monsignor Ettore Ghinzani, the papal nuncio in Valletta."

"Good Lord, you'd better hold on a moment." He glanced over at the sofa. Leilah was slouched back against the soft leather cushions; she appeared to have succumbed to her depression and to be quite oblivious. "Yes, sorry, please go ahead."

"His Excellency wishes to arrange a personal meeting with you as soon as possible. He has something very important to say to you. I think you can guess what it's about. Naturally, His Excellency would prefer it if this meeting were held in a . . . privileged place. You understand that this is primarily to ensure your own safety. Please be ready at eight forty-five tomorrow morning. We will call again at that time to provide further details."

"But what—"

"I should perhaps mention that not only your safety but that of a great many others, including one who is very dear to you, is also involved. I hope that we can count on your cooperation?"

"Yes, certainly, of course."

"Thank you very much, Dr. de Bonno. Remember, at eight forty-five tomorrow morning." The line went dead.

He came back into the living room; he had been too astonished by the origin and content of this phone call to notice whether Leilah was listening or not. She was still sitting on the couch in the same position, though whether her torpor was genuine or simulated he could not say. He went over and collected a glass, a bottle of scotch, and his father's antique soda-water siphon from the sideboard—in what he suspected to be an unnaturally hearty and deliberate manner—and set them down in front of Leilah, then switched on the television. "I'll be right next door if you want anything," he said. "But you have to promise not to get up from that couch until it's time to leave."

"Promise."

He left the door of the study ajar, just enough so he could see the back of Leilah's head reflected on the screen of his terminal. He switched on the modem and dialed a number that would connect him with the PSI-100 at Msida, then typed a few lines on the keyboard, requesting the computer to patch him through to its counterpart in the Vatican. As requested, he typed in the string of codes and passwords that would give access to Wendy's file, then—contrary to his usual practice over the past few months—he asked the machine to create a brand-new file somewhere in its capacious memory, specifically in the region that hereafter was to be designated by the "address" NC22. He lit a cigarette and began to type.

> Wendy my love, if you ever read this it will be because I haven't had a chance to erase it, which will be because I'll undoubtedly have left Malta, in one way or another. That will also mean that, for one reason or another, my part in all this business will be finished. But before, or rather after, I go I'd like to tell you something interesting that I've found out, something that I don't think any of your friends know about, either the ones in Rome or in Tripoli.

Michael glanced over at Leilah. She appeared to be watching television comfortably enough, since her head had subsided below the back of the leather couch; in its place there was a long bare leg, ticking slowly back and forth like a metronome. Depression seemed to have given way to anxiety, or merely boredom.

> I've also taken the liberty of recording my observations from day to day in a secret file in the depths of your machine. Address is BB34. Hope you have a chance to read it, and I trust you'll agree with my conclusions, even though I'd be the 1st to admit that they're really rather incredible.

When he glanced away from the screen, he saw that Leilah was standing in the doorway, looking pouty and impatient. "I thought you were going to behave," he said. "Please . . . just another few minutes and I'll be done."

He wrote for another twenty minutes, first with a kind of sublime unconsciousness of any other thoughts but those he was bent on recording, then more slowly and haltingly as a dull fatigue that was born of anxiety took hold of his brain and his fingers. When he could not write any longer, he instructed the machine to save the text and store it at the address he had selected, NC22, closed the file, and switched off his terminal. Leilah was stretched on the couch, smoking a long, pale-blue cigarette with a gold-colored filter; she had not bothered to turn off the television set, though the station had already gone off the air.

"All right, you can do whatever you like," said Michael, "but I have to go now, okay?"

Leilah looked up at him with a strange, dreamy expression. "All right. In that case, I'm coming with you." She got to her feet and picked up her purse, then slipped the strap over her arm, as if to confirm her stated intention. Michael tried to remember why he had thought that an hour spent with Leilah would turn out any less badly than anything else that had happened that evening.

He finally decided to take no notice of this and went to the study to get his jacket. When he came back, she was holding a revolver in her right hand. It was a very small revolver. *A woman's weapon*, he remarked, idiotically, to himself.

"Leilah?"

"As you see, I'm all ready to go."

"What the hell's going on? Where did you get that thing?" he said, struck by the incomprehensible notion that she had not brought it with her deliberately but had picked it up around the house somehow.

"It was a present, from someone we both know."

"What are you talking about, for Christ's sake?"

"I expect he's got quite a few of them. He's a military man, you know, almost a general . . ."

He smiled weakly. "Don't tell me, let me guess." He stepped across the room to turn off the television, since he could think of nothing better to do.

"It's time for us to go now, Michael. You've got work to do, at the university, some very important work, and I've got to go with you to make sure you do it properly." She lowered the barrel of the revolver. "We shouldn't have to be enemies, Michael. We both want the same thing; we both want it to go off all right, so the colonel won't be angry with us. I know you'll agree that it's best for the colonel not to be angry at us."

"You know what I really want?" said Michael. "I want to find somebody who has absolutely nothing to do with Project Arcade, who's not working for it or against it, who doesn't give a fuck whether it lives or dies, or better than that, who's never heard of it in the first place. I'd be willing to pay any price you'd care to name just to go off and spend the rest of tonight with somebody like that. . . ."

"We'd better hurry now, or your *colleagues* are going to start worrying about you. Just a few more hours, Michael, and then everything will be all right. And afterward, you can go off with whoever you want."

They drove over to the university in silence. The underground computer complex was swarming with Soviet technicians and engineers. Generally at this hour Michael had the place to himself. Now he felt like they were all there to keep watch over him, as if he were some exotic animal that was too dangerous and valuable to be left on its own. He sat down at a console, and Leilah wandered off to talk to one of the Russians. After a few minutes she walked over and picked up the telephone in the adjoining cubicle; he watched her through the glass partition. She was calling Colonel Akhmedov. He realized that he had forgotten all about the telephone call from the papal nuncio's office. He wondered if he was going to be back in his father's house by 8:45 the next morning. According to Leilah, at any rate, it would all be over by tomorrow.

Avezzano

Mohammed Khomsi had been looking forward to this mission for some time. The diversion of AF-270 had been the first really important operation entrusted to him. Before that he had served the imam for many years, in Paris, London, and Beirut, but only by performing the lowliest and bloodiest of tasks, like a butcher rather than a soldier—blowing up cars in front of supermarkets and disposing of poor deluded apostates and émigrés, the littlest of the little satans in the Shiite demonology. Now he was very proud that his superiors had finally called upon him to make some use of his real capacities, instead of just his courage and his convictions.

The greatest of these was that there was no god but God and that the Ayatollah Khomeini was truly the twelfth imam, who would redeem the world for all the people of God. It disturbed Khomsi very much to see the world of Islam torn apart by sectarian violence, since he believed all Muslims to be his brothers. This made it only slightly less painful to be fighting under the direction of heretics like Colonel Qaddafi, who refused to acknowledge the transcendent authority of the imam, and

Communist renegades like Colonel Akhmedov, but this was merely a sign that it was still an imperfect world, and it was better to be striking a blow against the *mustakberin*, the imperialists and exploiters, than against fellow Muslims.

The last time, on flight AF-270, he had depended solely on his own courage and ingenuity to carry out a plan that was almost entirely of his own devising. This time, he had been put in command of a curious little squad of four radio engineers, selected by himself and hastily provided with a few months' military training, and a skinny Lebanese woman, very Westernized but not very friendly and as silent and dull as a stone. At the moment he wished very much that he was riding with his comrades in the other truck, so he could have joined in the jokes and prayers and songs that there always were before battle. It was a dark night, and they had been on the road for an hour and a half. They were well into the mountains by now, and the road ahead of them looked very steep and narrow in the beam of the headlights. He kept craning to see into the rearview mirror and make sure that the others were still behind them.

After a time, he did not feel like being silent anymore, and began to recite, inwardly, a long string of verses from the Koran, a great many of which were particularly suited to this occasion, since the Prophet himself had had much experience preparing for battle. After a few minutes, though he hardly realized it, he was declaiming, practically shouting them, out loud in a kind of exaltation. Suzanne's knuckles were white as she gripped the steering wheel, but he had almost forgotten that she was present, and it came as a great surprise when she finally spoke.

"We'll be there in ten minutes."

He nodded absently and began to review his plan for the night, which was basically a simple one. Far outnumbered in men and matériel, they enjoyed only the tactical advantage of the extreme improbability of their appearance on the field of battle. Telespazio was guarded by between one and two hundred troops, but this silent, neglected spot in the middle of the Abruzzi had probably not been a serious military objective for anyone since the days of Hannibal and his elephants.

A few miles from the town of Avezzano, the vans turned off onto an unpaved country road, bordered on both sides by vast potato fields, that led them to a large barnlike building with an assortment of agricultural vehicles and a small car parked alongside it. Suzanne got out of the van; the keys were in the ignition of the car. She started it up and was driving back toward the highway a few moments later. When she reached the intersection, she stopped the car and waited, her lips pressed against the mouthpiece of a walkie-talkie. A few minutes after that, a tractor emerged from the building pulling a trailer covered with a large tarpaulin and chugged off slowly in the direction of the highway.

Rome

Her footsteps echoed off the concrete floor of the long sloping corridor that led to the entrance to the computer center. This was the first time, Wendy realized, that she had really thought of herself as walking down a genuine catacomb—though admittedly it was a sanitized, air-freshened, and fluorescent-lit one—with the dust of ancient Romans and Christian martyrs commingled with the earth around her. She felt overwhelmed, truly alone, with neither friends to love her nor allies to protect her. She was the champion of Abdul, whom she despised, about to enter into a contest with Nicholas Resaccio, whom she admired, on his own home ground, the outcome of which would be decided by Michael, whom she loved.

Over the last several weeks, Michael had almost become a stranger to her. He sent back a batch of programs to her, after highlighting the anomalies that he had brought to her attention in the letter delivered by Leilah, and since then all their communications had been as cold and courteous as if the two machines had simply been talking to each other. From his side there were no more pedantic jokes or endearments or messages of hope or despair, and Wendy had instinctively followed his lead. She had no idea whether Colonel Akhmedov had ever told him the true story of Renato Bertoni, but Michael had become convinced that a much more formidable figure, an omniscient and unknown stranger, had been intercepting all their communications.

It was obvious enough that he was right, or at least that the programs that had been transmitted to Malta had indeed been tampered with, *vandalized* might have been the better word, since the numerous patches of code that had been added seemed as impertinent, omnipresent, and incomprehensible as the graffiti that ruined the walls outside her apartment building. Unfortunately, the idea of vandalism also reminded her of what had happened to Michael's cottage at Compiègne and what had happened to Bertoni and Colonel Akhmedov's story about the two

Japanese agents who had been following her around in Rome, and that was another line of inquiry that she did not quite dare to follow up on just yet.

Another image came into her mind, of a film or a drawing she had seen, of a fishing rod lying by the shore and an enormous fish with a line in his mouth waiting patiently in the shallows to pull somebody in. She thought of Jonah and the whale, and she thought of herself being pulled in and swallowed and then vomited up alive on the Libyan shore. . . .

Nicholas was waiting for her at the first security lock, smiling and relaxed. He greeted her with a chaste brotherly embrace, in which their cheeks brushed each other but their lips did not touch. As they walked to the machine room, Nicholas asked a few questions about her work, which she answered in a perfunctory way. As they approached the console, she asked impulsively, "Is it true that a whale's throat is really too small to swallow a man, like Jonah?"

Nicholas laughed. "Or Pinocchio. But I understand that's only true of some of the larger ones, like the blue whale, the ones that live on plankton. Why do you ask?"

"And those are the ones that no one's allowed to catch because they're almost extinct?"

"I think so. Except for the Russians, of course."

"And the Japanese."

"That's right."

Wendy nodded, as if an important point had just been clarified.

"You seem to be in a very odd mood tonight," said Nicholas. "Not quite your usual self. Are you thinking about your compilation, or about our game, or are you still thinking about whales?"

"A little of each, I expect. . . . The work and the whales are all right, but I'm worried I'm going to take a pretty bad beating at the other thing." She caught sight of the little table that Nicholas had set up by the console. "Oh, couldn't we play over there? . . . I'd hate to have to sit right by the screen like that. There's too much noise, and it makes it hard to concentrate, don't you think?"

"Whatever you like, but this way you'll have to be getting up all the time to run in and watch the screen."

"Perhaps I'll really be running a go-playing program in here that will render me invincible." This seemed like an extremely foolish and dangerous bit of banter, since the last thing she wanted was to excite

Nicholas's suspicions at this point. Still, having said it, she did not particularly regret it.

He smiled. "I trust you, plus I don't think you'll have much trouble winning with the means already at your disposal." He picked up the table and the go set and carried them around into the adjoining room, on the other side of the glass partition.

"You still prefer white?"

"Black," she said. "Or we can choose at random if you prefer."

"And I'll give you nine stones, as before?"

She made a face. "Very well. I'm sure I haven't improved since then." A nine-stone handicap plus black to play first was about as powerful an opening advantage as she could have, but she knew that Nicholas was hardly about to let her win deliberately. He wanted to concede as much as possible at the outset and still win in the end.

She went in to start running her compilation while he set up the board. At the same time she switched on a second screen and consulted her own message file. It was empty. Michael had still not gotten the signal from Avezzano. In the other room Nicholas was waiting. He had set a small sandglass by the board so they could time their moves. Wendy added a tenth black stone to the nine that were already in place, a little too close to the edge to be considered an orthodox opening move. It seemed to him that she was being a trifle overscrupulous in trying to offset a handicap that she must have decided was excessive. Still, she looked very pale and preoccupied and seemed to be having trouble keeping her hands from trembling. Just as Nicholas was deciding that she was much too proud and that this time he would do nothing to spare her pride, Wendy had almost persuaded herself that her opponent had already seen through her and knew exactly what to expect.

The stones clicked against the wooden board while the air purifiers snuffled softly in the background. Dotted lines were drawn, sketching out territories. Wendy felt herself being thwarted and driven back; Nicholas was playing very aggressively. She was not given a chance to develop a position or to organize a defense, but required simply to defend herself, stone by stone, with a sequence of forced and inefficient moves. It seemed that Nicholas wanted revenge for what had happened in Tokyo, not just to beat her but to humiliate her as well. But when their glances met over the board, apart from the look of intense concentration, his face seemed just as always, humorous and solicitous. Her few small counterattacks appeared crude and overelaborate, all of them blocked or pinched off easily enough, and most of them seemed to fit in all too well with his plans for further aggression and conquest. *It seems like I can't keep the smallest thing from him tonight,* she said to herself. *And it doesn't look so good for the great big things.*

The next time she checked the screen, her file was still empty. It was eleven o'clock, and things should already have started by now. *Abdul must be tearing his hair out,* she thought, and the idea of that, though not especially encouraging in itself, still made her feel a little better.

Avezzano

Twice a week Leonardo Magni took the late engineering shift at Telespazio, beginning at 10:30 P.M., and since at that hour the narrow, winding road to the station was rarely encumbered with tractors and potato trucks, he was glad of the chance to take his BMW out for a brief high-performance run. Tonight, however, he was more than disappointed to find himself stuck behind a tractor pulling a cart heaped high with potatoes beneath a flapping tarpaulin. Except for a lantern on the tailgate of the cart, the tractor had no lights and was picking its way along the center line of the road on this very dark night. Magni blew several blasts on the horn and revved his engine impatiently; a van had come up behind him and was flashing its headlights. He noted with some concern that the lashings of the tarpaulin were very loose; conditions were ripe for an avalanche all along the north face of this great mountain of potatoes.

Then the avalanche actually occurred, just as the tractor was trying to settle into its proper lane and allow him to pass. Potatoes were rebounding from the windshield and the hood; others were squashed beneath his wheels like fat brown bugs. When he got out to remonstrate with the driver of the tractor, the latter anticipated him with an abundance of gestures and angry words in some unknown language warning him not to add insult to the injuries already suffered by his precious cargo. The man was probably a Turk or a Yugoslav or something of the sort, sadly unacquainted with modern methods of agriculture.

Feeling far from satisfied with the results of this encounter, Magni was about to get back in his car when he noticed that the occupants of the van had got out of the cab to survey the damage. One of them was crouched down between the two vehicles; the other appeared for some reason to be hanging back in the shadows. "Everything all right?" Magni called out, but there was no reply. He got back behind the wheel and started his engine, crunched ahead over the dense, unsteady carpet of potatoes that covered the road for another ten yards, his windshield wipers alternately squirting and slashing through the layer of fine brown dust on his windshield until it no longer looked like he had been speeding across the African veld for several days. He had to keep this up for all of the last three kilometers of the route to Telespazio.

When he had almost reached the gate at the perimeter, he realized that the van was still following him. He slowed down for a moment or two, but the driver of the van, presumably lost, had come to a halt at the edge of the expanse of bare black earth, two hundred meters wide, that surrounded the station. Reassured by this, Magni regained speed and drove up to the checkpoint. The perimeter was secured by a tall wire fence, with watchtowers at intervals equipped with powerful floodlights that swept across the barren zone beyond the wire. Inside there was an inner enclosure of wire, the space between patrolled by soldiers in pairs, each accompanied by a guard dog.

The antennas atop the control block glimmered faintly in the reflected light, like a colony of monstrous, phosphorescent beings from some other world; the low cinder-block buildings that comprised the guardhouses and the control block were hidden in shadow. The soldiers who were not required to man the checkpoint or the watchtowers drowsed or played cards in their barracks; only a handful of technicians was on duty at this hour, and the transmitters largely looked after themselves. The outer barrier was raised, and the BMW drove up to a second checkpoint secured by a heavy electric gate. One of the guards waved a greeting to Magni and gestured in the direction of the van, still perched on the edge of the forbidden zone, to let him know that they would open the barrier for him as soon as the intruder had been driven off.

At 10:46 P.M., Mohammed Khomsi pressed his thumb down on the switch of the radio-controlled detonator that he held in his right hand. The BMW exploded in a sheet of white light, then was engulfed in a ball of flame. One panel of the electric gate flew open, torn clean off its hinges. A long section of the outer wire was flattened by the shock wave; one of the towers was tilted at a crazy angle, and a whole string of searchlights had gone out. A half-dozen bodies were lying on the hard black earth just inside the perimeter.

The splinters and metallic debris continued to fall for several seconds; the ball of flame flared up and then subsided to reveal a blackened shell of metal that had come to rest in a shallow crater just beyond the electric gate. The final echoes of the blast died away, to be replaced by wailing sirens and the frenzied barking of the guard dogs. The soldiers who were scrambling out of the guardhouse had not seen the van before the explosion, and it was hidden from sight for a few moments longer; a tall barrier of flame secured the narrow gap between the single leaf of the electric gate that had survived the blast and the still-burning wreckage of the BMW.

There was a tremendous crash, a shriek of metal, and a shower of sparks. The van came hurtling toward them, its windshield shattered, its rear tires burning, then spun around on two wheels, straightened out, and accelerated furiously, making for the center of the compound. The guards just had time to let off a few rounds in the wake of the intruder before the second van crashed through the barrier of flame and was upon them, bounding along at top speed on four blown-out tires. Two of them were knocked off their feet and narrowly escaped being crushed beneath its wheels; the rest stood their ground and fired, but this second fusillade was no more effective than the first. In less than two minutes the vans had drawn up outside the control block. Three of the Iranians had thrown open the outer door, stormed inside with weapons drawn, and ordered the ten startled occupants of the control room to lie face down on the concrete floor.

Rome

The group of black stones in the upper-right-hand corner appeared to be finished. Nicholas had launched two devastating attacks, one right after the other, though he had given Wendy the chance to make half an eye at the edge of the board, which might ultimately frustrate his chance of wiping out the entire group. He had tried too hard to press his advantage, which made him vulnerable to a stunning counterattack. With just three moves, she had saved her group and was now in an excellent position to wreak havoc among the attacking force.

"That's what's called 'being left in possession of the field,' " said Nicholas. "But," he added, putting down a white stone, "we can still encircle the whole lot of you if you're not careful."

Wendy looked at her watch, then looked back to admire the breach she had made in the enemy lines. She tried to imagine how Mohammed Khomsi, with a troop of four at his command, could have done as much against so many. "I'll just be a minute," she said, and she had to restrain herself from getting up and running into the machine room. When she opened her message file, she found that the much-discussed secret recognition code had been entered by Leilah Zanoun on Malta:

```
The hour draws nigh, the moon is split in twain (S54, V1)
```

The next line was the signal she had been waiting for:

```
Go ahead (NC22)
```

The purpose of the letters and numbers in parentheses was not immediately clear. Possibly they were part of Abdul's recognition code. She typed *S54, V1* on the keyboard. Nothing happened. Then she remembered that she had actually heard Abdul speak those words, many months before. It was a verse from the Koran, one that he seemed to find full of recondite significance with respect to Project Arcade. *S54* was undoubtedly Sura 54, Chapter 54 of the Koran, and *V1* was the first verse. *So much for that then. NC22* seemed a little more difficult, until she remembered that this too was a scriptural quotation, of sorts, from the programmer's manual for the PSI-100. Copies of this useful volume were strewn all over the machine room; she picked one up and flipped rapidly to the glossary of programmer's code.

NC22 was listed as "Section of memory not currently accessible to user. Consult supervisor to obtain proper access codes." *NC* presumably stood for "not in circuit." This was a message that would normally be displayed on the screen if she tried, metaphorically speaking, to set foot in such a protected zone. But since no one had done that, it had clearly not been displayed by the machine, but typed by Leilah, which seemed unlikely, or by Michael. *Perhaps he's left a message for me, somewhere else; perhaps he's telling me where to find it.* She tried typing *NC22* on her own keyboard. She expected to get the usual friendly admonition from the computer, telling her not to stick her nose in where it wasn't wanted, at least without the proper access codes. Instead, to her surprise, she discovered that she had brought up something from someone else's memory files, the text of which began to materialize on the screen:

```
Wendy my love, if you ever read this it will be because I haven't
had a chance to erase it, which will be because I'll undoubtedly
have left Malta, in one way or another. That will also mean that,
for one reason or another, my part in all this business will be
finished. But before, or rather after, I go I'd like to tell you
something interesting that I've found out . . .
```

She had gotten no further than this when Nicholas suddenly appeared in the doorway.

"Having problems?"

She clutched the edge of the console with both hands, tried to keep her heart from pounding and her hands from trembling. Then, astonished to discover that she still had full control of her motor functions, she reached out quite calmly and pressed the ERASE key.

"Is everything okay?" asked Nicholas, starting to walk toward her.

"Everything's fine. I'm just making sure the compiler's doing its job properly, and I've got test programs running simultaneously on another processor."

"You're playing a simultaneous exhibition match, in other words. Three opponents at once, possibly more, or in a word—multitasking. I think you'll agree with me that it's a lot easier for the machines than for flesh-and-blood creatures like ourselves. However, if you'd care to join me next door, I think you'll also have to agree that you completed your primary task, which is to free yourself from my clutches by any means you can."

He seemed to be in an excellent humor, which, she hoped, was simply because of the way the game was going. She didn't much care for the implications of some of his phrases, like that business about "three opponents at once" and "freeing herself from his clutches," and she was sure that he was about to come right out and start talking about "playing a triple game" or something even worse. The more she thought about it, the more she was convinced that he knew all about it, that he was only waiting for *what*? Waiting to play his last stone, waiting to finish the game?

But when she got back to the board, she suddenly saw another opening. To escape from the threatened *hasami*, the scissors stroke, she would have to play *there*, near the center. Nicholas was unprepared for this; she thought he actually gave a start. She felt better, reassured. It meant that the game would not be over for a little while longer.

She managed to keep concentrating for a few more minutes, then started thinking about Michael. She was burning with curiosity about the second, longer message that he had left for her inside the machine.

She was also curious to know how he had gotten into this forbidden inner sanctum of memory, though it was typical that he would think of using the world's most powerful computer like a tenpenny composition book to record his "day-to-day observations" in. She pictured him standing on a beach in Malta, with a message in a bottle that he hoped the seas would float to his beloved Wendy, who would perhaps be tending her goats on the Libyan shore. . . .

Idiot! She had forgotten all about Abdul and Khomsi and the rest of them. She had been so proud of herself for the way she had picked herself up from the console, walked so coolly out of the machine room, and then played an exceptionally good move besides. She had allowed herself to be so distracted by Michael and Nicholas that she had forgotten to do the one really essential thing. . . . Abdul was probably foaming at the mouth by now, though the image of Abdul as a rabid dog somehow did not afford much pleasure at the moment. She got up and excused herself, but Nicholas hardly appeared to notice that she had left the room.

Avezzano

The control block had no windows, but the ten men inside had certainly heard the explosion and all the cacophony that followed; the closed-circuit TV monitors showed scenes of confused and distant battle, with clouds of smoke, running men, and careening vehicles. Two of them had got up and opened the door—which was not exactly in accordance with security regulations—to see what was going on. They were met by three armed men with smoke-blackened clothes, ugly-looking automatic weapons held in their trembling hands, and knitted black masks pulled down over their faces.

The order to stretch out on the floor, face down, was obeyed with alacrity, since it was obvious that the intruders were no less terrified than their captives. They soon discovered that, strictly speaking, it is not humanly possible to lie still and to lie face down on a cold concrete floor, though "Lie still!" and "Face down!" appeared to be the only Italian phrases that their captors had taken the trouble to learn. They kept putting their heads to one side and craning their necks to try to find out what was going on.

One of the terrorists remained on guard while the others ran out the door, then came staggering back with heavy crates that they set on the floor. Then two more of them appeared, one shouted out an order, and they all threw themselves to the floor, their arms crossed over their heads. The Iranians had not had time to get all the explosives out of the second truck. There was a second explosion, much louder than the first, as the truck was enveloped first in a mounting pillar of fire, then in a descending, spreading cloud of smoke and soot, dirt and debris. The heavy steel door of the control block blew open, and they could see the glare of the flames outside. The sound was so loud that they could feel it vibrating through the earth, throbbing painfully in their eardrums, for a long time after that.

Then, a little dazedly, the Iranians got to their feet and began to break open the crates. The little bundles of plastic explosive were distributed around the control block and strung together with electrical wire. Khomsi stood in the doorway, raised the bullhorn to his mouth, and shouted through the dense clouds of rolling smoke that still surrounded the control block: "No more shooting! If you try to take us, this building goes up as well, and these ten men are dead!"

The technicians were nudged to their feet and herded into a little room on the upper floor of the control block that was furnished with cots and posters and an old armchair where those who had worked extra shifts sometimes slept until dawn rather than attempt the mountain roads at night. This was where they would stay, bound hand and foot with electric cable and with one of the Iranians to guard them, until the operation was over. Khomsi's task was simply to pick up a phone and call the guardhouse. In a moment he was talking to the camp commander, and he went on talking for some time, first invoking the names of the Supreme Being and his Prophet and the Imam Khomeini to let them know—as he thought to himself and not without some amusement—that he was a dangerous fanatic not to be trifled with. Then he explained that one of the hostages would be executed for every hour that elapsed before their demands had been met. The precise nature of these demands would be announced very shortly, and at that point they would begin counting.

For a moment the other two Iranians stood hesitantly in the flickering bluish light of the innumerable monitor screens, computer displays, and consoles that filled the control room. In a few minutes they had established radio contact with Malta, transmitting the same set of prearranged code words to indicate that Telespazio would be able to relay that data transmission from the Vatican in a matter of minutes. Outside the building, unseen by its occupants (the closed-circuit monitors had been filled with wavering static since the explosion that destroyed the truck), there was a graded tract of several acres inside the wire enclosure. Twenty-five parabolic reflectors, each almost a hundred feet in diameter, were mounted atop tall pylons, their great metal corollas turned up like a field of sunflowers to face the sky. When the two Iranians had located the control panel for one of these antennas and typed in a new set of coordinates, corresponding to the position of Arabsat, almost 23,000 miles above the surface of the earth, the reflector shifted slowly, almost imperceptibly, on its reinforced-concrete stalk.

Khomsi hung up the phone. He took his bullhorn and walked over to the doorway. Several hundred yards from the control block, helmeted figures were piling sandbags into a low palisade; he could hear military vehicles circling the perimeter of the station, and there was a helicopter almost directly overhead. Then he could see nothing; the station was plunged into darkness. He began shouting into the bullhorn, demanding that the floodlights be turned on again, that all the lights in the watchtowers be trained on the ground outside the building. He glanced back into the control room; one of the Iranians signaled to him that the reorientation of the antenna had been completed. He stepped back inside and picked up the phone; it was then that he announced that he was speaking on behalf of the Sword of Saladin and that the first of the hostages would be executed in exactly sixty minutes if the Italian government had not agreed to the release of Mehmet Ali Agca.

Rome

After Wendy had switched on all the modems, an operation that was accomplished not by hand, of course, but by means of a short sequence of keystrokes at her console, she instructed the PSI-100 to read its entire memory contents, and less than a second later the first of these vagrant bits of information was being received at Msida, a couple of hundred miles away (notwithstanding a detour of almost fifty thousand miles, from the antenna atop the casina in Rome to the reflector at Avezzano and then via Arabsat to Malta). After checking to make sure

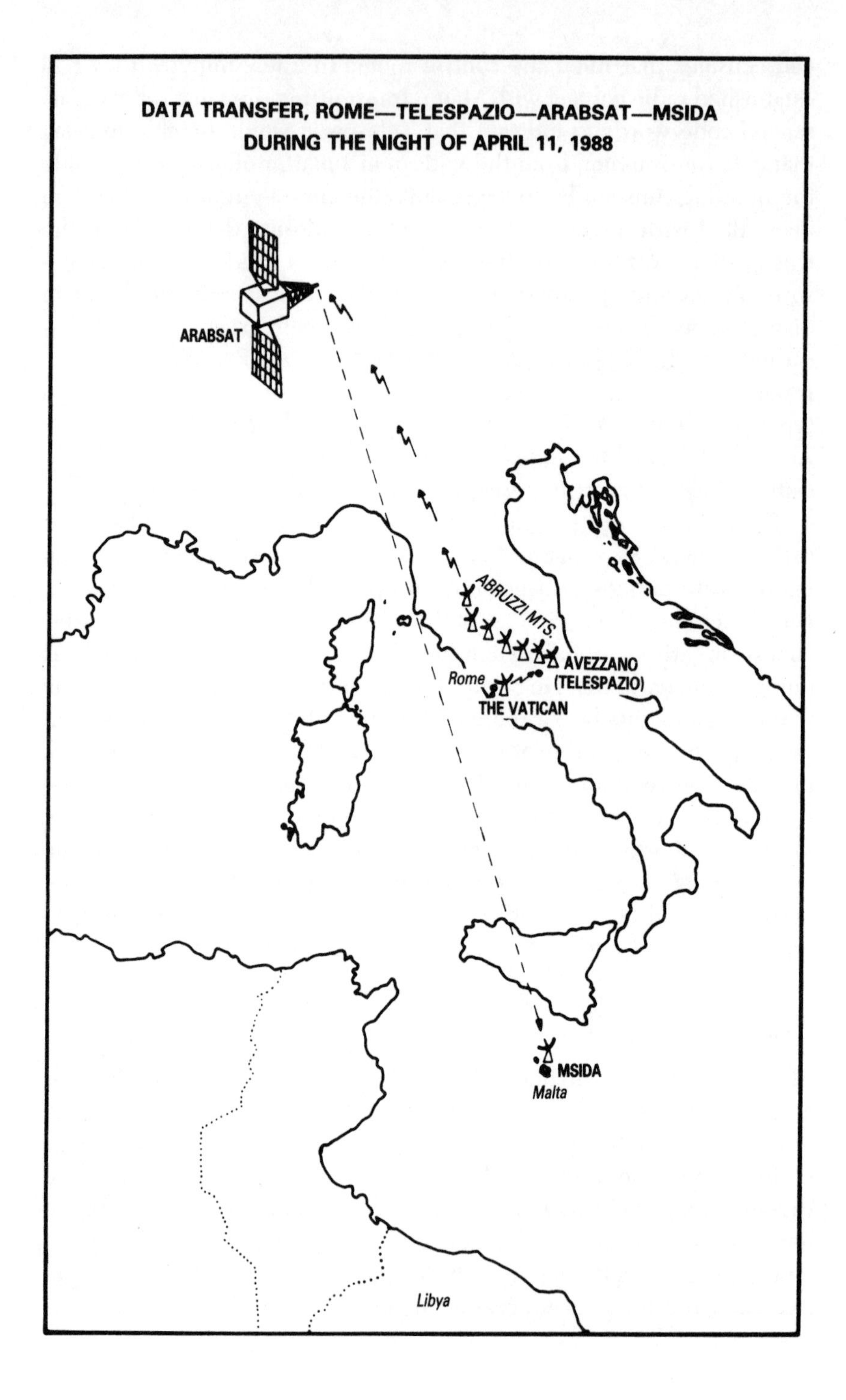
DATA TRANSFER, ROME—TELESPAZIO—ARABSAT—MSIDA
DURING THE NIGHT OF APRIL 11, 1988
ARABSAT
ABRUZZI MTS.
AVEZZANO
(TELESPAZIO)
Rome
THE VATICAN
MSIDA
Malta
Libya

the machine was carrying out this rather eccentric set of instructions, Wendy erased the screen and glanced over at Nicholas. He seemed completely absorbed in his contemplation of the *go-ban*. She decided it was safe enough to take a few more minutes and typed *NC22* followed by *BB34* on the keyboard. The first lines of Michael's journal began to appear on the screen.

Monday, November 30

The Japanese engineering team that's installing the PSI have decided to stay on an extra week. This makes 10 days now that I've been trying to figure out how the bugger works, often in bemused consultation with them or my new bedmate (a 100 lb. assemblage of mixed documentation that, if nec'y., can be arranged into a nostalgic approximation of a female human form). Yesterday, for ex., I spent a long time pacing off the limits of a large section of memory posted with numerous NO TRESPASSING signs--"Address not currently accessible to user" is the way it's put.

When I asked my Japanese mentors about this, I felt a little like one of Bluebeard's wives in the fairy tale pestering for a look at his secret closet. About all they'd say on the subject, even after considerable prompting, was "That section of memory is inaccessible because it is the heart of the machine, and you cannot penetrate the heart of the machine." Very Eastern to be sure. When I asked where this forbidden realm was actually, physically situated, they obliged with a few local addresses, but not in a way that was meant to be helpful (since I couldn't call them up). Acc'dg. to this manual, there are in fact *several thousand* points of intersection on the grid beyond which it's theoretically impossible to venture--a rather substantial NO GO zone, to adopt the terminology of dear ould Belfast.

Not daunted by all this, I wrote up a program that would test each of these points of intersection on the grid to find out if there might be one that would let me into the NO GO zone. I let it run for 2 successive nights, and I've just discovered the one little door in the wall, which, as you know perfectly well yourself, is NC22. Further investigation confirms that there are a number of totally virgin memory boards in the PSI here on Malta, perhaps to expedite some future modification or expansion of the machine's capabilities, though what these could possibly involve I can't imagine. The available applications, especially to my own little realm of biophysics, seem quite enough for a couple of lifetimes as it is. Refer to this address for subsq. developments.

Wendy decided she would have to content herself with just one installment, closed the file, and went back into the next room. Nicholas had taken advantage of her absence to revise his plan of campaign and, apparently, to launch a fresh offensive. This time, she felt she had lost her attacking edge and had even reverted to that old, unpleasant feeling of transparency, that she could not hide anything from him, either the maneuvers she was preparing on the board or the various furtive activities she was carrying out in the next room.

He put out his hand to remove a few captured black stones from the board; the new position was not very promising, not very promising at all. She remembered the old man at the tournament, the one she had imagined as the master of go, nodding and smiling with pleasure or widening his eyes in disbelief. She smiled. As if he really had been some sort of demigod, just the thought of him had given her an idea, one that would not necessarily turn the tide but would at least keep her from going under for a little bit longer. Nicholas was looking at her in an amused, puzzled way.

"You seem very pleased to be losing your men like that. Have I stepped into another one of your traps, or is it just that you weren't especially fond of them?"

"I think I'll have to give you another few minutes to think that one out for yourself."

"What, you're off again? Already?"

"Well, I did warn you, you know."

"That you wouldn't be able to give me your undivided attention? Yes, you did. I suppose I should be grateful that you couldn't spare me any more. . . . And I mustn't interfere with the good of the project. That would be tantamount to sabotage, wouldn't it?"

He could hardly put it any more clearly than that! she thought. *But if he knows all about it, then why does he just keep sitting there? Why doesn't he get up and do something about it?* She still found it hard to imagine him creeping up behind her and stunning her with a blow from a ten-pound programmer's manual or pinioning both arms and calling out, "Guards! Take this person away!"

"Actually," she said, a little crisply, as she stepped toward the door, "I could have been there and back by now."

The data transfer was still proceeding according to plan, which meant that the memory contents of the PSI were pouring out at the rate of several million basic instructions per second. She read quickly through the next several entries in Michael's diary, hoping to hear more of his daring forays into the NO GO zone (this was the name that had been given in the early 1970s to the section of the Roman Catholic ghetto in Belfast that was patrolled by Catholic militants and into which the police and special constables could only venture at their peril; she hoped that the comparison was apt). The next several days, however, he appeared to have spent musing and exclaiming over the PSI's ability to create new and ever more elaborate simulations of neuronal pathways, ion-exchange boundaries, transmitters and inhibitors, and other biophysical phenomena. This was very instructive, but not something she really had time for at the moment. She skipped ahead to the entry for Wednesday, December 9:

I've made a v. interesting though totally fortuitous discovery, one that actually concerns neurology, though of a somewhat different species than our own. *The machine dreams.* I've been starting my daily stint at the center at around midnight, so as not to be underfoot when my Japanese friends are around. Last night I drove over from the clinic at 3 A.M., even later than usual. I've also got into the habit of running a random check on the processors, just to see what they're up to at various times. Last night they shouldn't have been up to anything much. Hardly anyone else is using the machine as yet, and nothing was left running from earlier that day. My terminal was absolutely the only one switched on, and yet the machine was already in a state of intense, not to say furious, activity.

I know you've already heard quite enough about dreams and REMs and such, but I swear that last night the machine was dreaming. Actually, it's like what we call paradoxical sleep, where the EEG shows a pattern of intense activity whilst by all other neurological criteria the subject is in a state of complete repose. The PSI was running all sorts of programs, even though no one had asked it to. Whether the operations performed bore the same relationship to ordinary computations as dream logic does to ordinary waking logic is not something I'm privileged to tell you yet.

Wendy glanced away from the screen for a moment. Nicholas was standing by the doorway with a quizzical look on his face. When he saw that she was still sitting at the console, he turned and walked slowly back into the other room with a sort of ostentatious furtiveness, like a waiter or a hotel chambermaid. As if, she thought, he wanted to make it absolutely clear that he had no intention of infringing on her privacy or interfering with her work. She hesitated for a moment, but she still hadn't finished the entry for December 9.

Every analogy has its limits, of course. As to whether the PSI ever has nightmares or wakes up in a cold sweat, I'd have to say, Too early to tell. Naturally, it's occurred to me that this apparently self-starting, self-motivating activity might all be taking place inside the NO GO zone. Since I've already identified the particular processor that permits information to be exchanged across this barrier, I assumed it would be simple enough to verify this conjecture.

Not so. I ran the same program as before (see entry for Nov. 30) for an entire hour and a half whilst regaling my own much-abused brain with fantasies of a computer that was sufficiently like a human brain that you wouldn't even have to know what the answer was in advance in order to be able to phrase the question properly in the first place. . . . When I awoke from this dream of peace, it was almost 6 A.M., the hour at which the "support team" of Soviet technicians was scheduled to arrive. My program was still running and had nothing much to tell me. I shut it down and shuffled off into the cool gray dawn; they'll have to wait to hear my official speech of welcome. Meanwhile, I expect I'll try to get back into the NO GO zone again tonight.

Wendy pressed the ERASE key and hurried back into the other room. As soon as she looked at the board she saw why Nicholas had been so impatient a few minutes earlier, and tried very hard not to smile. He had done very well; he almost certainly had a won game, in fact, and that was always worth showing off. But the game, after all, was only a diversion, a distraction from the more important of her tasks in the machine room; she was just about to put down a stone at random when she remembered that the data transfer was not complete yet and there still might be a great many lines in Michael's journal. An ordinary player, certainly a gentlemanly player like Nicholas, would have resigned, but she could not afford the luxury of defeat at this point. She felt that she had to finish reading the journal, which made it that many times more likely that she would be interrupted by the auditors if Nicholas was not there to protect her.

And then something very strange happened. They had both seen it at once, Wendy could have sworn it, and it was not all that difficult to see. There was a clear-cut sequence of moves that would certainly win the game for him and in very short order. Still, he seemed reluctant to acknowledge this, holding the white stone in the hollow of his hand like a precious bird's egg. When he did set it down, it was somewhere very different; he had made the kind of blunder that even a beginner could hardly make deliberately.

Wendy felt herself blushing. It seemed that he was also playing for time, or rather that he was willing to give her all the time she needed. *Why?* To test her, to see how far she dared to go? More likely to confront her with her options and her responsibilities, like an officer in disgrace left alone with his loaded revolver. She was being given a chance to redeem herself by taking the honorable way out. This was infuriating. At least he did not seem at all surprised when she got up from the board without a word and went back into the machine room; he seemed to be looking after her with a kind of sadness in his face, as if he had reached out his hand to her and she had refused to take it. On Malta, she saw that two more days had gone by.

Friday, December 11

Partial success. First, accd'g. to all external indicators, mine was the only terminal connected, but there was clearly a great deal going on inside. At least my program was able to lead to the source of all the activity--a brand-new vantage point from which I've been able to survey a great deal of what goes on inside this allegedly virgin territory. Unfortunately, like Moses on the mountaintop, I've been permitted to take a peek but not actually set foot. . . . The gist of it seems to be that the "unused" memory boards that basically comprise the NO GO zone have this one very special peculiarity. They enable anyone who has access to this particular point to monitor *every-*

thing that's been written by the machine during the course of the previous day. A most remarkable feature, you'll agree (and one certainly not mentioned in the sales literature that I've seen).

The way it works is simple enough. The machine automatically makes a copy of every file that's written in and stores it here, in the NO GO zone, for at least a couple of hours. So you see, the so-called heart of the machine turns out to be a lot more like the unconscious mind, taking it all in during the day, reprocessing and re-editing and running it back in the form of (dare I say it?) *dreams* at night. This fits in very nicely with one of my own pet theories, namely that during paradoxical sleep, the brain is not just a kind of tape recorder, replaying the events of the day that's just gone by, perhaps splicing in an occasional interesting bit from long-term memory, but an independent organism with a life of its own.

However, as usual, I digress. A far likelier hypothesis is that there's someone in there, or rather out there, reading everything that's written by the machine, possibly including everything that passes between the two of us as well. Thus, this is no longer a matter of strictly academic interest. The next question is how it's possible for an outside user (there aren't even supposed to be any outside users, at least not yet) not only to get into the machine on a routine basis but also to get into a part of the machine that's meant to be totally inaccessible.

Is this some sort of ultra-paranoid security system installed at the behest of the Libyans or Col. A? If so, it's a bit more sophisticated than the traditional microphone in the fruit basket or the overhead lighting fixtures. In any case, I'll have to run a more elaborate test program to interrogate (!) every bloody one of the processors in order to find out where the leak is. This should take another couple of nights, but may very well permit us to identify the villainous Svengali (or perhaps the loony Dr. Caligari) who's been forcing both of us, me and the PSI, to lead this somnambulistic double life. *(to be cont.)*

After she had returned to the *go-ban,* Wendy realized that, what with the competing attractions of Nicholas and Michael, it had been a good twenty minutes since she had checked to see that the data transfer to Telespazio was still proceeding smoothly. She felt quite incapable of turning around and walking back into the machine room now. She was surprised by how little this upset her. For a long time—it seemed almost as long as she could remember—she had thought of the contest between the organizers of Project Arcade and her Libyan comrades (among others) as an important "world historical event," as Abdul would say, and thus thought that a great many things would be different if the battle turned out one way or the other.

Now she felt convinced that she would only know who had won or lost, and what the stakes had been, as Michael's journal appeared in shining letters on the console screen. A victory, of sorts, for innocence over experience. And as far as Abdul was concerned, if something happened that she needed to know about, she was sure he would find some way of bringing it to her attention.

Avezzano
April 12

At ten minutes after midnight, Mohammed Khomsi heard a voice call out from behind him in the control room. "We're all finished! Their accursed machine's been drained to the dregs. They must have it all on Malta by now."

"You'd better check on that."

The Iranian who had been monitoring the transmission from the Vatican tapped on his keyboard and waited for several seconds until this message appeared:

```
Transfer completed. Break contact at will.
```

The two other Iranians in the control room (the fourth was still looking after the hostages upstairs) were waiting at the control panel to return the giant reflector to its original position. It was unlikely that anyone in the crowd outside would notice that one of the antennas had rotated just a few degrees on its stalk, but it was still possible. Khomsi decided it would be best to minimize the chances of this by presenting them with a diversion. He pushed open the steel door of the control block, which had been badly warped by the explosion of the truck, and stepped out into the glare of the floodlights with his bullhorn raised to his lips.

A half hour earlier, he had been informed by the station commander that the Italian government would not consider the release of Mehmet Ali Agca under any circumstances. He looked out at the distant rampart of sandbags and beyond that at a clutter of military vehicles, jeeps and troop carriers, even a small armored car. As the great silver bowl rotated slowly on its pedestal, Khomsi began to speak once again of Allah and the imam, but this time there was no more talk of Mehmet Ali Agca. They had carried out their instructions, and now it was time for them to think about saving their skins.

"Listen!" he called out through the bullhorn. A volley of rifle shots could be heard inside the control block. "The first of the hostages has been executed. . . . This is just as we have told you it would be, and this is the way it will continue to be until we have left this place. However, now it should be quite easy for you to save the lives of your men! We renounce all our former demands! All we ask is for safe passage, and a helicopter and pilot that can carry us out of this country—without any refueling stops—to a friendly territory. You will have one hour in which to consider our proposal. If you want more time than that, it will cost you the life of another one of your men."

Rome

The game had been going on for long enough that the shapes and patterns on the board had become almost incomprehensibly complex, but Wendy was perfectly well aware that her position was steadily eroding, and she knew herself well enough to be convinced that no further flights of invention were to be expected. She was reduced to such obvious time-wasting ploys as letting the sand run out on even the simplest forced moves. Then she tried to distract Nicholas by getting him to talk about anything she could think of. He was a little unresponsive at first, but it was not really in his nature to withhold his own observations on any subject.

This was the first opportunity he had had to discuss his personal life—his childhood in a little village in Piedmont, the long philosophical detour that had led to the priesthood by way of the labyrinthine bypaths of computational logic and computer engineering. The game was almost forgotten, but Wendy was afraid to step away from the board again, even though she could hardly concentrate on what Nicholas was saying and could think of nothing but reading the rest of the message that Michael had left for her and wondering how many of her questions would be answered there.

"I can't help but get the feeling you've lost interest in the game," said Nicholas finally. "Do you think it's time for an adjournment?"

"Oh, no."

"And you seem to have forgotten all about your other duties as well—your compilation for example."

Wendy raised her eyebrows and gave him a look in return that was both grateful and incomprehending. "You're right. Perhaps it's time I went in and had a look at it." Why was he making it so easy for her? He had just finished explaining to her that Project Arcade represented the culmination of all his worldly ambitions and spiritual strivings. She did not like to think of the reasons that he could possibly have for helping her to destroy it. . . . In the machine she called up Michael's journal and rapidly scrolled ahead.

Sunday, December 13

Now I have proof that at least one of the processors in this treacherous machine has been penetrated from the outside. The other terminal is most certainly not on the premises (because there's no indicator reading corresponding to the machine's episodes of paradoxical sleep, as noted), probably not in Msida or even on Malta. Clearly, the pirate should not be able to copy and transmit programs via regular telephone link without leaving some trace of his activity (or even gain access to the NO GO zone in the first place). This suggests that the systems program of the PSI has been tampered with, or--since "tampered with" implies subsq., illicit modification of a bona fide original--that the pirate was actually present at its creation, that this particular feature of the PSI was *designed* to meet his specifications. The rest of my inquiries will have to be conducted elsewhere, in the Real World, and may not be all that conclusive. Lucky you, all you have to do is scroll on, whereas I fear I'm in for a couple of days of tedious and potentially hazardous real-time activity. . . .

Wednesday, December 16

Being able to trade on my father's name (plus that of an influential but not really very respectable local character called

Henry Zubbieq) has made things a whole lot easier than I'd dared to hope. Our minister of posts and telecommunications is (or was) well acquainted with both, and, being a seasoned gov't. official on Malta, may even be used to receiving eccentric and slightly furtive requests for info of this kind. I imagine that word has been out for some time now that I'm doing some kind of secret job for the gov't; so in return for a few stumbling and ill-chosen words on my part about "securing the university computer complex from unauthorized penetration," I received many linear feet of printout, listing all overseas calls routed through the Valletta exchange between the hours of 3 and 5 A.M. for the last 3 weeks.

Someone has been calling somebody in or around Valletta every night and talking (perhaps just listening) for about an hour and 40 minutes--and running up a whopper of a phone bill to be sure. All the printout can tell me is total elapsed time for each call and the base rate used in computing total charges. Base rate in question is applicable to a number of distant places on the other side of the globe, Japan among them. Does that surprise you? Did you think the Micronesians or the New Zealanders were behind it all along? Nor me. To get more conclusive data (phone nos., e.g.) I would have to request the personal intervention of Mr. H. Zubbieq, or someone like him, and/or make further inquiries at the other end of the line, both of which I am obviously loath to do. I think we have enough for a working hypothesis as it is, don't you? (*to be cont.*)

Wendy pressed the ERASE key and hurried back into the other room. To say that it all came together for her at once—or even to say that she felt like a perfected multiprocessor or a true master of go—would have been a slight exaggeration, but two big things and a great many small ones did seem very clear at once. She sat down at the board, pushed her chair forward, and suddenly scraped it back. She *knew* that she would be able to find the one right spot where she should put her stone, but it was hard for her to concentrate just then, since her head was too full of ideas and pictures—the wood box turned upside down and a folded piece of newsprint on the rug in the cabin at Compiègne, the old man at the tournament and the four men at the restaurant in Tokyo, the absurd and now not-so-absurd idea that the Japanese were everywhere, from the Piazza di Spagna to the innermost recesses of the PSI-100. One in Malta and one in Rome, like two chess knights stationed in the center of the board—in the heart of the Western logical continent, as Nicholas and d'Anglebert liked to put it . . .

She set her stone down with a click, and Nicholas looked at her as if she had performed some feat of magic, like turning it into a sparrow or a toad before his eyes. She did not have time to think what it meant in terms of the game; she knew it was up to him to worry about that. She was thinking about this other business now, though in her mind the two things were of equal and alternately consuming importance. She had always imagined the Japanese to be the *objective allies* of the Vatican, the Americans, and all the rest, therefore the *objective enemies* of the Libyans and the other Islamic states as well as the Soviets. The latest bulletin from Malta (though now stale news, almost five months old) suggested otherwise—in the great battle that was taking place for the mastery of space and the possession of the most advanced information media, the Japanese had decided to secure their own position by building not one but two enormous Trojan horses and wheeling them right up to the gates, not just of their enemies but of their friends as well. . . .

"And I thought you were getting tired," said Nicholas, not taking his eyes off the board.

"I was, I am. . . . I just had a sort of lucky breakthrough, I expect."

"A breakthrough, in any case. How about a cup of tea, by the way? I could certainly use a little stimulation at this point."

Wendy had to restrain herself to keep from leaping out of her chair.

"I'm going to try to make myself useful by checking to see that all the terminals are shut down properly," Nicholas added, "except for yours, of course."

"Thanks," she said. "And I'd love a cup of tea."

Friday, December 18

A PSI on Malta, another in Rome. Needless duplication because it turns out we're all working for the Japanese, and that includes you and me and Abdul and Father R and Col. A. (That normally means lifetime job security and a whopping pension, but I wouldn't count on it in a case like this.) At first, it just seemed like they were interested in keeping an eye on things, in collecting information, even in this monumentally unobtrusive way. I can't say I completely understand what it's all about, but it really seems there's a lot more to it than that.

I expect it might have started out as a simple case of industrial--or rather, postindustrial--espionage. The Japanese have pulled way out in front as far as computer research is concerned, but even having come up with a machine like the PSI, they're still having trouble developing the software to support some of their more astounding technical innovations. Presumably, by producing a deluxe export model with this built-in capacity for clandestine retrieval of all the programs devised by their foreign customers, they've already taken a giant step toward solving the problem.

Another big problem they have to face is the rivalry between East and West, which has this way of threatening to destroy the world--a very big market for the Japanese, the world. But who was it who said, "Pray for peace, prepare for war?" Maybe they can't compete so well in certain areas--blackmailing other countries by withholding basic resources, stockpiling nuclear weapons--and they certainly lack what your friend Father Nick would call the ideological magnetism of the Chinese and Islamic models (I've been reading up on his stuff, I'm afraid).

On the other hand, they appear to have a very strong lead in developing unconventional weapons (like this one), and unlike most sophisticated and expensive weapons systems, it's one that the other people pay *you* for using on *them*. Full marks also for tact and diplomacy, since, unlike the last time, they've been able to mount a brilliant surprise attack without the painful necessity of notifying the enemy that they've been surrounded, so to speak, from within. Perhaps I'm giving them too much credit here; perhaps, as I said before, they merely intended to keep a close watch, to keep things from getting out of hand, and then couldn't resist the urge to step in and take over. (I know I couldn't; I'm hoping you won't be able to either.)

Perhaps this is the way that war is going to be waged in the future. From where I sit, it's even beginning to look like there are such things as these "logical states" so beloved of Col. A and Father R, and if there can be a logical state, why not a logical invasion? (Of which the simultaneous infiltration of the command HQs of both pro- and anti-Arcade forces will serve as the classic textbook example.) This sort of thing may be all the rage in a couple of years. While the struggle between East and West, between North and South, intensifies, the Japanese will be busy behind the lines, and while they appear to have gotten in ahead of everyone else in this respect, no doubt others will follow. No worries, though, this is actually a Good Thing.

These days it seems you can hardly open a newspaper or turn on the telly without hearing somebody mooing about Things fall apart, the center cannot hold (one of your Irishmen said that, I believe). I think the problem is going to be that, on the contrary, the center is going to be trying its damnedest to hold on and for all it's worth. I think that every society, to the extent that it's affected by these bizarre technological developments, will soon start to unravel into a progressively larger and more varied assortment of little tribal and cultural tangles. And then such great political, economic, and of course religious power centers as remain are going to be vying for the allegiances of all these little entities and trying to round them up and stick them back together, probably in the form of brand-new extra-large-size logical empires.

Perhaps that's not a bad description of this business we've gotten ourselves involved in. I won't say it makes no difference how it turns out, but it doesn't seem to me that any of the probable outcomes bodes very well for the future of the planet. I believe that we're only morally obliged to defend the individual, the family, the free association of individuals, or collective, and then the world. Speaking as the offspring of a bastard nation and a poor excuse for a country, I suggest we forget all about the other categories, especially the ones--countries, religions, and so on--that try to crowd in between the collectives and the world.

I don't think I can stay in the game for much longer. I know you'll do what you have to, but if you've agreed with what I've said so far, please consider: I think this knowledge makes us a lot stronger, and gives us a few more choices, than we could possibly have imagined up to now. We may not be able to push the pawns (we are the pawns, needless to say), or put the king in check, or pick up any stones (I'll never understand that bloody game) BUT WE CAN KNOCK OVER THE FUCKING BOARD ANY TIME WE WANT. . . . You'll notice I say "we," because I can't do it without your help. I'll tell you how when the time comes, probably quite soon. . . .

Wendy had to steady her hand against the console before she could give the key command to advance the text. She was terribly afraid that nothing else was going to come up. In fact, this was the last of his "day-to-day observations," but there was one final message, written just a few hours ago:

Monday, April 11

The last message I'll be able to leave for you here. In a few minutes, I'll be driving over to Msida to take care of the data transfer. I had a telephone call just now from the office of the papal nuncio. "His Excellency" wants to discuss something very important with me tomorrow morning. The fellow said I'd know what it was all about. I guess the coppers (and their ilk) always pretend they know all about it when they only suspect. Anyway, by tomorrow morning, when Col. A no longer has any particular reason to retain my services, I expect I'll feel safer in the company of the papal nuncio.

That's true, said Wendy to herself, remembering her conversation with Akhmedov in Suzanne's little apartment. The Russians had suspected for several weeks that the Japanese were playing their own game, that they had followed her from Tokyo, and this had been some time before Michael had made his remarkable discovery. *And Nicholas—what had he discovered? And why was it taking him such a very long time to brew up two cups of tea?*

I've just found out something that's considerably clarified my thinking on this subject. I came across a draft of a letter in my father's study that he intended to send to one of his old cronies in the gov't. Contrary to what I'd been told, he was going to advise *against* acquiring the PSI-100. He had no objection to taking money from the Russians, or anyone else foolish enough to offer it to us, but he was convinced the Japanese would never have agreed to such a scheme in the first place unless they were planning on sabotaging the entire operation or they had some sort of long-term counterintelligence objectives of their own (in collusion with the West perhaps), neither of which could be of any conceivable benefit to Malta.

That means of course that if he'd lived, the clinic never would have been involved with any of this business. Looking at it another way, I've also become convinced that if he hadn't put it about that he opposed the "purchase" of the PSI, then there would have been absolutely no need for him to have had a fatal heart attack. Ever since I've been back here, people have been constantly urging me to live up to his memory, to do things the way he would have wanted them done. I think I've finally figured out a way of doing precisely that.

I've written a program--or rather, in all modesty, it's really a modification of the routine that permits all new file entries to be surreptitiously copied down in the NO GO zone for later examination by our faraway friends. The difference is that my program will instruct all the other processors in the PSI to simultaneously *erase*, rather than copy, the entire memory contents not just of the NO GO zone but of the whole machine, files, programs, the lot. Eventually--in several tenths of a second, i.e.--the plague virus will spread as far as the systems program itself, and the PSI will suffer total and instantaneous brain death, what we callous neurologists refer to as *flatlining*. If, after you've thought it all over, you decide you'd like to do me this little favor, just access NC22, then enter [here followed four lines of coded instructions broken up into blocks of four or five characters each].

I'm hoping that once the data transfer has been taken care of, the Russians will give me a few hours to myself. I won't be able to go back home, of course, but I still have a number of friends on the island who have no connection with the government, and, as I say, it shouldn't take me more than a couple of hours to make my escape. It may be awhile before it will be safe for me to turn up again, however, possibly even years. Shall we say two years, if only for the sake of symmetry? And it may very well be that at the end of those two years I'll be turning up in your life again, just the way you did in mine almost a year ago. And I think I'll love you just as much as I do now.

If you hear a bomb ticking, don't be alarmed, it's your finger that's on the button (does a time bomb have a button?) In

```
any case, it won't go off unless you tell it to. I'm really not
sure what you're going to make of all this, but somehow I'm quite
convinced that, as I say, you'll do this favor for me. For one
thing, it seems very likely that if you don't, we'll never see
each other again. And that hardly seems possible, does it? log
out M
```

When she looked up from the console, Nicholas was standing on the other side of the glass partition with a mug of tea in each hand; it was possible that he had been standing there for some time. Before she went in to join him, she remembered to check her message file. The signal *All OK* had been entered thirty-eight minutes earlier. The data transfer was complete, the great brain of the PSI was in repose once more, and the Soviet technicians on Malta were safely in possession of every program and every data file that composed the earthly body of Project Arcade.

She walked slowly over to the board, taking small, precise steps, her mind trying to imagine Michael as she hoped he would be in another hour or so, climbing over the rail of the fishing boat with patched and tattered sails or—more likely, knowing him—settling down on the comfortable cushions of somebody's private jet. *Not too far away, please, Michael. I want to be sure I'll still be getting you back one day.*

"Your tea's getting cold," said Nicholas.

She sat down heavily in her chair. "I'm afraid I've made rather a mess of it this time, haven't I?"

"I'd say the position's difficult but far from hopeless."

Tears were flowing down her cheeks. "I know, Nicholas. First it's one way, then the other. But this time I can see quite clearly that you've won, and that's the end of it." She started to laugh, and she felt that it had been months since she had been able to laugh like that.

Epilogue

Rome

At 2:30 P.M. on April 15, a life-sized image of the pope appeared before Catholics gathered in churches in forty countries around the world, and, as in the days of the Apostles, hundreds of millions heard him pronounce the first words of his address in the language of their own country. The synthesized voice-overs in fifteen languages generated by the PSI-100 perfectly mimicked the pitch, tone, timbre, and inflection of the original recordings of John Paul's voice. To the simpler members of these far-flung congregations, it seemed that the Holy Ghost had returned to earth once more, to the more sophisticated, that the Holy Ghost was speaking with a slight Polish accent.

"Today, my beloved brothers and sisters, begins a new era in the history of our Church and of our civilization, an era that will surely be known as the Age of Communication. . . ."

In the telecommunications control room beneath the Vatican gardens, the face of the Holy Father filled sixteen different screens, occupying an entire wall, and since the Italian channel was the only one that was open, one would have thought that his address was being broadcast exclusively in that language.

On the other side of the Mediterranean, Abdul, who had returned to Tripoli several days earlier so he could experience the crowning phase of the operation at the side of Colonel Qaddafi, was listening to the pope's address in Arabic. He was very curious to hear how this miracle would be accomplished, how the giant computer and the program provided by Wendy and considerably expanded and refined by the Soviet experts on Malta would manage to adapt the pope's courtly expressions of gratitude toward his Euro-American sponsors into a bold critique of their imperialist designs, their attempts to corrupt the message of true religion with bribery and coercion . . . everything short of an out-and-out endorsement of the Islamic revolution and a recital of the latest communiqué from the Sword of Saladin.

Not too many miles away, Colonel Akhmedov, dressed a little incongruously in a florid sportsshirt and charcoal-gray slacks, was sitting in the basement computer room of the university medical school at Msida, listening to the pope's address in English, with one eye on the gleaming metal panels and limpid display screens of the PSI-100, alert for the slightest sign of trouble (though what visible form this trouble might actually be expected to take he would have been a little hard pressed to explain).

Mohammed Khomsi, along with his four companions and two of their hostages, had been flown by an Italian military helicopter to a spot very close to Tiranë, Albania. They would not be able to hear the pope's address in any language; the Albanian government had briefly amazed the world by agreeing to provide sanctuary to the commandos of the Sword of Saladin, but had amazed no one by refusing to air the pope's broadcast on their single national television channel.

The precise whereabouts of Dr. Michael de Bonno were still unknown. He had disappeared from the Msida computer center early on the morning of April 12, shortly after the data transfer was concluded. A rapid reconnaissance of the university grounds by Leilah, a more systematic search carried out by Soviet technicians, and subsequent inquiries by the Maltese authorities (who were not notified until many hours later) failed to yield any conclusive results. He was not at home to receive a phone call from the office of the papal nuncio at 8:45 that morning. Perhaps the only one who might have been able to assist the Maltese authorities with their investigation, Father Michel d'Anglebert, had already left the island.

Wendy was thinking about all these people, Michael in particular, as the pope began his address in slow, serene cadences, alternately drawing apart and bringing together his broad white sleeves. She began to feel a kind of panic mounting inside her. She knew that Nicholas was watching her, his face full of confidence and approval. Was he going to congratulate her the way that Abdul had after she had returned to her apartment the other night? She tried very hard to think about Michael, and nothing else.

Nicholas was standing at the control board, turning up the potentiometers that controlled the levels on each of the sixteen separate audio channels, one by one. The room began to fill with a chanting choir of voices, the words quiet, rhythmic, insistent, yet devoid of meaning, like a choral work by some modernist composer. It took some time to realize that each of the voices was the same, in Italian, English, Spanish, French, Portuguese, Tagalog, German, Dutch, Lingala, Flemish, Arabic, Cantonese, Malagasy, Tamil, Xhosa, Malay . . . though not, or not yet, in Polish, Czech, Hungarian, Slovak, Byelorussian, or Romanian. On each of the screens the pope's lips were forming the same sounds, and it was, quite unmistakably, his voice that was speaking. Nicholas was smiling.

Wendy was thinking of Abdul in Tripoli and Akhmedov on Malta, no doubt frantic with impatience since they had relinquished all control of their great world-shaking enterprise to their wonderful machine. It was not supposed to be very long before the PSI on Malta would be injecting its own impertinent commentary into the broadcast, taking advantage of the glacial pace of the human voice and mind to transform the pope's stately paean of praise for this new era of global social communication into perhaps (Abdul and the colonel had not taken her into their confidence on this point) a stern reminder of the dangers of becoming overly dependent on the technological achievements of a small handful of nations, of the dangers of allowing the purity of the Gospel to be tainted by the corruptions of superpower politics. In human terms, the computer would have the equivalent of two or three *weeks* between each word to plan its next step, to convert, by a series of linguistically plausible and politically advantageous little detours, the pope's first real sermon to the world Catholic congregation into a paranoid diatribe worthy of Mohammed Khomsi or Father David Kingsley.

This was one version of the future, the course that had been traced out for it in Tripoli and Moscow. There was the other version that had been planned by Michael. She was surprised to find herself smiling as she imagined how that future would be in its first few moments if she entered those four lines of code dictated by Michael into the heart of the machine. She imagined the scene on Malta—the startled faces of the technicians, red warning lights on the console, perhaps a wailing Klaxon of distress, and finally, the bland, uncomprehending face of

Colonel Akhmedov, his little rat's eyes blinking behind his bottle glasses. On the console screens would appear nothing but those four lines of code, as if the machine had managed to sputter out a few last words of gibberish before it died, and then nothing at all.

She imagined the scene in Tripoli, perhaps Abdul and the Colonel and a portable television set on one of those low tables in the Colonel's tent. She pictured them drinking their scented tea and waiting impatiently, like two crazed alchemists, for the success of their experiment, for the transformation that was not going to occur. She imagined the three of them, Akhmedov, Abdul, and Qaddafi, brought together, as she had seen them on one occasion, in time to realize that something had Gone Wrong, that, in spite of all their shrewd and cynical precautions, the pope was not going to be transformed into Mohammed Khomsi, or even Father Kingsley. She thought, with the impulse of the true creative artist, that having taken the trouble to imagine such a thing, she could hardly deprive herself of the still greater pleasure of making it a reality.

She thought of Michael and how much she really owed to him. How could she refuse to do the little favor he had asked of her? And Nicholas—who had trusted her all along and had left her in total freedom, up to this very moment, to make all these decisions for herself. Now he was standing a few feet away from her, his eyes fixed on the television monitor screens, his breathing a little labored. He knew, but he was not about to say a word. She felt for the terminal keyboard and began to type. *NC22* . . . The four lines of code had circled around in her mind for so many hours that she had ended up knowing them by heart.

On the other side of the Mediterranean, these four lines appeared for a moment on the console screens in the computer room at Msida and just as quickly disappeared. The entire contents of the PSI-100, all the programs and all the memory files, had disappeared as well, just as surely as if someone had passed a single computer microdisk through the field of a powerful magnet or exposed a roll of film to the light of the sun.

Wendy pressed ERASE and then sat quietly for what seemed like a very long time, listening to the strangely soothing babble of the audio channels, staring at her own blank display screen rather than the TV monitors. Then the pope's address was finished, and there was a loud volley of applause, which did not come from the speakers overhead but from the technicians in the control room behind her. Phones were ringing, and excited men were embracing and shouting into the telephones and at one another, also in a babble of many different languages. It was a scene she had witnessed many times in films and on television but never thought she would be expected to take part in—the control room after the successful missile launch, the locker room of the World Cup winners.

This time Nicholas was not content with a furtive scraping of cheeks; he opened his arms wide and embraced her and held her tight. He kissed her on the cheek, near the corner of her eye, where he could taste the salt of her tears.

"Thank you so much, Wendy."

"My God, Nicholas, what's to become of me? . . . And Michael. I don't even know—" She choked back a sob and could not say any more. Nicholas was still holding on to her, and she was a little ashamed to realize that she was trembling uncontrollably.

"I knew that we could trust you," he said softly, like someone trying to soothe a frightened child. "I never doubted for a moment. . . . And as for what's to become of you, we've even thought about that, you know."

"How do you mean?"

"I suppose it comes under the heading of the Church looking after its own. And you'll also be reassured to hear that Father Michel d'Anglebert has recently been on Malta; he was able to make inquiries and he's come away convinced that Michael de Bonno left the island a free man and entirely of his own accord. More than that I'm afraid I can't tell you at the moment. And as for yourself . . ." He paused for a moment and smiled. "There've been inquiries made about you as well. Only this morning I was talking on the phone with Mother Marie-Bernadette. It seems she's been quite concerned about you—I'm sure she's convinced that this playing about with satellites and computers can only come to no good. She also mentioned that a novice has just left the abbey. That means of course that there's an empty cell, a fairly large one that gets quite a bit of sun in the morning. It also comes equipped with a table, I should imagine about the size of a *go-ban* as she described it.

"And yes, I should also mention that the young woman who takes up residence in this cell—she will not be required to take any formal vows—will be going under the name of Catherine Levasseur. I think it might be a good idea if Miss Wendy Keenes could contrive to erase all memory of herself for a little while, don't you agree? I think that the Church can guarantee your protection, and we want to make sure you're still in fine form when Dr. de Bonno turns up again."

"Yes, I think I'd prefer that too."

Nicholas smiled and took her by the arm. "I see they have quite a few bottles of champagne over there. Perhaps you'd like to come and have some with me and we can put off talking about this other business till a little bit later on."

Champagne corks were rebounding from the monitor screens and consoles and shielded cables; technicians were ceremoniously toasting one another, cautiously tapping champagne-filled paper cups. Someone was running the videotapes of the papal broadcast, with the audio turned up to maximum volume on all sixteen channels, drowning out the soft persistent humming of the machines all around them.